Collected memories of a bygone era

Treasured Tales
of the Countryside

David & Charles

A DAVID & CHARLES BOOK

First published in the UK in 2003

Copyright © John Humphreys, Tom Quinn, Brian P. Martin, Euan Corrie, Jennifer Davies, Jean Stone, Louise Brodie, Valerie Porter 2003

Distributed in North America
by F&W Publications, Inc.
4700 E. Galbraith Rd., Cincinnati, OH 45236
1-800-289-0963

A catalogue record for this book is available from the British Library.

ISBN 0 7153 1645 1

Commissioning Editor: Jane Trollope
Art Editor: Sue Cleave
Desk Editor: Sandra Pruski
Production Controller: Jennifer Campbell

Printed in Singapore by KHL Printing Co Pte Ltd
for David & Charles
Brunel House Newton Abbot Devon

CONTENTS

INTRODUCTION

Many people feel they are more at home in the country than in a city. There is a constant yearning to return to rural roots, reflected in television programmes, magazines and books. Yet should they return, the average person will almost certainly find that today's country life is far removed from the rural idyll of memory — now there are 4 x 4s speeding round the lanes, the noise of farm machinery, and the smell of diesel lingering in the air.

Memories of a rural childhood, of visits or of holidays spent on a farm might fade, but they will be brought vividly back to life by this collection of sometimes comic, sometimes moving, but always evocative reminiscences of the day before yesterday. Here are tales of poachers and gamekeepers, huntsmen and horses, farmers and the men and women who lived and worked on the big country estates between the two World Wars. They were self-reliant, close-knit communities, whose expectations perhaps were smaller than they would be today, but honest for all that. Hardy countrymen and women with a philosophical turn of mind born of living close to nature and its many whims.

Some of the books that these tales are taken from were published more than ten years ago. Many of the people within its pages, who were interviewed and who gave their reminiscences so freely and eloquently for those original books, are no longer alive. But they live on in these, their own stories, which will bring pleasure to another generation of country-lovers. This evocative compilation of anecdotes reflects country life as it was more than half a century ago, when the main power on a farm was still horse power, when a network of branch railway lines still criss-crossed the countryside — and before poaching became big business.

Long-distance Boating

Violet Mould: Grand Union Canal

LONG-DISTANCE BOATING

Fellows Morton & Clayton Ltd was one of the largest general carriers to operate on the narrow canals. James Fellows established the forerunner of this business at West Bromwich in 1837. His principal trade was southwards from the Birmingham canals, along what later became the Grand Union system towards London. In 1876 his son Joshua, with partners including Frederick Morton, took over many of the boats and much trade from the Grand Junction Canal Company's carrying establishment. Their company expanded, absorbing the London & Midland Counties Carrying Company in 1887. In 1889 Fellows Morton & Clayton Ltd (FMC) was incorporated, bringing in craft owned by William Clayton of Saltley.

The latter also operated special tank-craft for the carriage of liquids, which were transferred to a separate concern (Thomas Clayton Ltd, based at Oldbury, just north-west of Birmingham).

By the beginning of the twentieth century FMC was operating throughout the canal system from Ellesmere Port and Manchester to Birmingham, and along the Grand Junction Canal to the Thames. Their services also covered the Trent & Mersey Canal between the Bridgewater Canal and the river Trent extending

as far as Nottingham, and the Leicester line of canals between there and the Grand Junction.

Many families worked for the company through several generations, with the younger menfolk finding profitable employment on the flyboats which worked non-stop to regular schedules. By the end of the 1880s many of these services were operated by steam-powered narrow boats, the last of which were not replaced by semi-diesel engines until the 1920s. Violet Mould was born against this background at the beginning of the twentieth century. Most of those who have kindly agreed to tell their stories in these pages have had to endure my intrusion into their homes, but Violet was keen for a change of scene and jumped at the chance to sit on my boat and look out at the occasional autumn pleasure boat passing whilst we talked.

Violet was a Griffiths before she married, her great-great-great-grandfather being a brother to John Griffiths, the carrier from Bedworth. But he didn't have anything to do with his family's boat dock at Charity as he wasn't the eldest: that went to the first son, another John.

'I weren't born on a boat, no. Me dad had got a steamer when we was young; going night and day, he was. Me mum and dad had a house at

Braunston, on the Grand Union Canal, near Rugby, that is. I think the First War was starting and it caused quite a lot of people to come onto the boats. The young men was going off to the army, so we started to go night and day. My mum and dad kept the house at Braunston because sometimes when we were passing we used to tie up at the bottom of the garden and go up to the house. It was all right empty like that, but I expect they sold it after a bit, I don't know.

'Me dad had the Sultan new, and she was a steamer.'

Sultan had been built for Fellows Morton & Clayton, with an iron-sided, wooden-bottomed hull at their Saltley boat dock in Birmingham in June 1899. She was fitted with a Haines-type single-cylinder steam engine that may also have been built at the boatyard. When this was replaced with a Bolinder semi-diesel engine in May 1924, her cabins were rebuilt to increase the capacity of the cargo hold, using the space vacated by the bunkers and boiler of the steam plant.

Violet Mould's father, William Griffiths, steers Fellows Morton & Clayton steamer Sultan up from lock 11 to lock 10 at Long Buckby on the Grand Junction Canal, which was later amalgamated into the Grand Union's London to Birmingham main line. Note the length of boiler room and cabin which reduced the cargo capacity of these boats, and the crew of four to tend the steam plant and work the locks. They worked continuously in shifts whilst the boats were on the move and would be assisted by up to three further hands on the butty when towing

'Me dad had the Vanguard, later; that was a steamer, too. Then the Admiral. Then he went into Spain and Glascote, which were horse boats. He used to wear white cords and a black velvet waistcoat on the steamers – every day he used to wear them; me mum had two pair, like, to keep washing one. He sometimes wore a drab-coloured cardigan. But the men used to look ever so nice on there.'

The steamers were the prestige expresses of the canals. Their crews not only drew the best pay,

Steamer Sultan and its butty Kegworth at Fellows Morton & Clayton's Nottingham Wharf after a trip from the City Road Basin in London

but were appropriately proud of their charges.

'There was four children besides me, and Mum and Dad: Lucy, Lizzie, Florrie and then me – I was a twin with William, but he died as a baby. Eli was the last one. We worked the locks and so on more or less straightaway, just as early as I can remember, really. But mostly we was at Braunston, going to school we was, while me dad had the steamer.'

Two of Violet's sisters married steamboat captains, so there was her father as well as two brothers-in-law on steamers.

'Dad had a motor after the First War, Seal, and we did the same runs with that. He said we should have to have another boat to get everybody in – we had a butty all the while then, the Exe. We had Seal and Exe from new: Seal was a wooden motor built at Uxbridge by Fellows Morton themselves; she was launched in June 1920. [Exe followed about twelve months later from the same builder.]

'We've been through up here [the river Soar] night and day, no stopping. We come through from City Road Basin in London, and we used to empty half at Leicester and the other half at Nottingham. Then if there was any goods at Nottingham to go back we'd load that and straight through to the City Road again. If there weren't no loading we'd go up to Shipley for coal and take that, but we didn't take coal every time; that mostly went back to Uxbridge. We've carried everything, everything you can think of. We've had spelter [an alloy used in casting and galvanising], in drums, and timber, and we used to bring tea up from the City Road. We used to get 50 ton on with the butty behind the steamer as well when it was a load like coal or spelter. That was in big drums which went to Fazeley Street, in Birmingham.

'They'd send you all ways from City Road; so you could go to Birmingham or Preston Brook as well. We sometimes emptied at Birmingham and then went off to Ellesmere Port — they didn't always send you back to London. It was the same after I was with my husband, Ralph. My mum and dad was dead by then.'

Fellows Morton & Clayton were not known as coal carriers, or indeed bulk carriers of any material. I went over this point more than once with Violet, but she has clear memories of these cargoes. It is possible that the return loads of coal were consumed at the company's own boatyard and on their craft rather than being delivered to independent merchants. This trade, and much of the coal carried to canal-side factories along the lower part of the Grand Union Canal, was in the hands of a few factors and a large fleet of independent owner-boatmen until the later 1930s. These proud independents were gradually forced into the service of the big carriers, particularly by the Grand Union Canal Carrying Co, which, with its large fleet of new motor-driven craft, was able to undercut their rates. At the same time, this rapidly expanding company was desperate for the services of experienced boat crews and so was prepared to guarantee the former

'That's me and me sisters on our motor, *Seal*, at Brentford; the tallest is me mother and there's Eli, on the left. Jack Creswell and his Mrs [Alice] are on the butty *Amesbury* on the path behind. It's taken below Brentford Lock and round the corner a bit. We've got 25 ton of sugar on there. That's the school in the background. The boats are facing ready for going up the river Brent to get into the Grand Union Canal. There was a very high tide in the night and it lifted the boats on there and left 'em up there when the tide went out again. Dad hadn't got time to get her off. She floated off all right with the next high tide, she didn't leak. Dad wouldn't keep shoving at her because of hurting her bottom so he just left her until she floated. There was several boats got on that day because it was such a high tide in the early morning, before it was light.'

*Routes from the
south to
Nottinghamshire
and Derbyshire
frequented by
Violet Mould*

owner-boatmen employment should they sell their older craft. Thus the coal trade gradually passed to the GUCC Co rather than to FMC.

'We liked the lock keepers at Red Hill, where you come out of the Soar into the Trent. We used to take the tonnage ticket in the office here every time. We've been down here when the water was right up – I've steered down here when there's been water all over these fields because they was wanting the goods at Nottingham. You had to mind how you went on round here because you've got the weir on the Trent at this corner and it could fetch you astern over the weir. Me dad used to be on the motor and we'd all be on the butty. We'd just be on a short strap, say, 20ft, and he'd say, "Now have that lock ready". So me and Florrie, he used to make us get off at Ratcliffe and run down here to get Red Hill Lock

*Ferrying horses
across the Trent
near the entrance
to the Erewash
Canal*

ready. He wanted it ready when he arrived because it was running water, and it would pull you over into the weir at the top of the lock. The water could be on the towpath when you went into the Trent to get to Cranfleet Cut. There were gates at the top of that cut which might be closed if the water was too high, and you'd have to tie up. But we used to have to get down because they wanted the loads, you see.'

There was a little ferry between the towpath from the river Soar and the Trent path near the junction with the Erewash Canal. 'It was like a punt, that boat, and we used to have to get the horse in it and get him across. Me dad used to work the boat, like. He just shoved the boat across with the pole – it didn't have any line onto the land or anything. Then one of us girls used to have to hold the horse's head while we went across. He could be a bit frightened. You see, we used to put the boat over first and then take the punt and fetch the horse. You had to go a bit upstream before crossing, and then push across. At least Ralph and I never had a horse to cross here because the Seal had a Bolinder in it.'

Ralph's father was in iron moulding, but he used to have trouble keeping in work because it tended to be seasonal; so then he would help out at Leicester Wharf with the loading and unloading, and in this way came to work a boat locally: Leicester, Nottingham and up the Erewash Canal to load coal for the electricity companies. Eventually this became his full-time employment, with Ralph as mate. When Ralph was old enough he took a boat of his own; he went to Fellows Morton & Clayton when he was seventeen. To start with he was given a single motor, but as he gained experience they found him a mate, and they were entrusted with a pair of boats.

Violet has described the necessity to boat down the river Soar and cross the Trent to the Erewash Canal, or to continue down the larger river to Fellows Morton & Clayton's depot at Nottingham whatever the weather and in almost any prevailing river conditions. Because stillwater canal boatmen were not used to the currents and changing channels of the rivers, FMC used to retain the services of an experienced local boatman; in the 1930s and 1940s the position of river pilot was filled by Bill Roberts. A postcard or telegram from the owners would advise him where and when to expect to meet craft requiring his assistance. Ralph's sister, Carrie, married Bill Roberts, and they went to live at Sawley.

'Ralph was on the motors with Fellows Morton – we was always on Fellows Morton's. We used to meet passing or at loading places. The steamers would be all finished before Ralph and me was married. I was married to Ralph in 1938. We was married in the church at Deritend, in Birmingham; my parents were married at Warwick.

'Of my own children there was only Jill and Glenys was born on the boat, the second one and the last. Wendy was born at Brentford and Elaine at Braunston. Ralph and I never had a house, just the boats. We had various different ones.

'They would start on the cargo as soon as we arrived at City Road, or the other wharves. We've met some boats the other side of Leicester and they've said, "They're waiting for you at Leicester to unload". We used to like coming to Leicester. It was better than going to Birmingham – it was all work, was Birmingham! There was such a lot of little locks, they was little locks all the way from Braunston. In the end, they made 'em bigger, and then it was better because you'd get both boats in.'

Violet was referring to a government-sponsored, job creation scheme of the early 1930s when the fifty-two locks from Braunston to the outskirts of Birmingham were rebuilt into fifty-one large enough to take two narrowboats side by side. Many bridges were also reconstructed, and miles of bank protection carried out. But the

scheme was never carried through to the extent that had been planned, which would have seen the introduction of bigger, wide-beam motor barges to replace the pairs of narrowboats.

'We used to load tubes at Coombeswood and take them to Brentford, and there they put them in a lighter and took them down the river. They used to come in bundles, and they'd tip your boat right over as each one landed. We could get 22 ton on the butty with them, and 20 ton on the motor. Then we'd go Camp Hill way back. We've took sacks of buttons from City Road to Birmingham,

This pair of horse-drawn craft were not so fortunate as Violet's family in making the crossing from the river Soar to the Erewash Canal. It appears that a horse towing line broke and the Trent current pushed them down to Thrumpton Weir. Except in time of high flood there is insufficient depth of water to float such boats over the weir cill. Nowadays the approach is in any case guarded by a substantial boom

and bedsteads and timber, sawn deals. I helped to load them, off a barge. We used to take 50 ton of sugar from Brentford to Bournville; then they'd load chocolate, there, back to London. We'd load that crumb [part-processed chocolate] as well to Knighton, on the Shropshire Union, and that went to make the chocolate. We'd load back, I've forgot what it would be, I suppose it was dried milk. Some people used to like to get a bag of crumb from there, but we never bothered. The men that worked there used to bring a bit out to us from time to time. We did Guinness in barrels

Work under way to replace the twenty-one narrow locks at Hatton with chambers wide enough to take a pair of narrowboats together. When Violet first went boating the route from Braunston to Birmingham seemed to be all work, although it includes level pounds of eight and ten miles between locks, and she preferred the Nottingham run

from Park Royal, as well. Ralph used to always keep one watercan empty when we arrived, and they'd fill it up for us!

'We went down to the ships in Regent's Dock sometimes, perhaps for copper sheet and that sort of thing. It was all right, but you had to mind what you did with those big barges about. I didn't like those cow-mouthed barges, as they call them – you see, they would come right over the top of your cabin. Ralph used to have to keep an eye on them, but the dockers used to put it in for you. They'd gauge you at Commercial Road, and after that each lock keeper would check your ticket up

to Cowley where they'd gauge you again. Then Cowroast [above Berkhamsted, the summit of the climb out of the Thames basin] and the top lock of Bugby [Long Buckby, near Daventry]; then stop at the ticket office at Braunston, and then top of Wigrams [Calcutt Locks, near Southam] and to the top of Camp Hill, in Birmingham. Then down to Warwick Wharf.

'I've lots of relations at Braunston; it's a nice little place, Braunston. City Road was good for shopping, though. You wouldn't be more than two days in the basin there, but there was a nice little shopping centre on the top of the tunnel and you'd got time to go shopping whilst they was emptying you and reloading. The children would play in the warehouses there. They got playing in the top warehouse once and Elaine, she fell down a hole in the middle of all the bales of rags – they went to the paper mill with them. The men had to dig her out, but there was no

harm done. Me uncle Ned was boating regular on the paper mill job, but we only did it very occasionally. They never had much sleep, they didn't, it was non-stop. [Fellows Morton & Clayton had craft on long-term charter to paper-makers John Dickinson whose Apsley, Nash and Croxley mills were alongside the Grand Union Canal. Some of the craft were painted in Dickinson's own livery and operated almost non-stop on short-haul work between the various mills and wharves.] We used to tie up of a night, but we might start very early.

'You could get some nice materials and that sort of thing at the shops near City Road; we used to make our own clothes, and Mum used to make the old-fashioned bonnets, printed material they was, then put lace over them, too. When she was doing them she'd say, "Don't touch that bonnet!" You hadn't got to touch anything. We'd got a little hand machine, a

A pair of Fellows Morton boats loading overside from a ship in Regent's Canal Dock. Amongst those waiting astern is the motorised steamer Baron whose steerer can just be seen trying to push the boat safely out from beneath the overhanging lighter. Violet was not keen on taking her home in amongst these heavy and roughly handled, outsized craft

Singer it was. Glenys has got it now. I didn't wear a bonnet, but me aunt Ethel used to, and me uncle Jack Griffiths' wife. Folk used to get me mother to make them; they were usually white or cream with little flowers on, especially before they was married.

'If we had a nice day I'd do the wash because I had a little bath which I could put on the bank. When I was young, Granny was at Braunston and she used to do the washing for Mother. We used to leave all the dirty clothes on the way through, and pick up all the clean ones from her when we came back, all starched and ironed.

'He could ease the motor and the butty would catch up ... so I could pass his plate over.'

'Then when we was going I did all the cooking on the butty, and walked along to the fore end with it for Ralph. He could ease up the motor and the butty would catch up to the motor as the line went slack so I could pass his plate over. Otherwise you had to time it right so it was ready when you came in a lock with the boats together.

'Ralph kept a gun, and sometimes we'd get a rabbit or a hare and then we'd to hold the butty in and jump off and run to pick it up. The gun was kept on the motor, and there was a fishing net, too, because you could get eggs with that – swan's eggs were good. You could also get mushrooms and watercress, and raspberries or blackberries.

'We used to stand a jar of flowers against the watercan, some we'd picked along the way; when the brass bands were done on the chimney and that it used to look all right. We had three brass rims, not too much, and we'd a rod along over the range. The ticket drawer had a brass knob and some crochet work round the bottom. We used to call it "needle-bobbing" that: I used to put the tiller under my arm or against my hip, and me dad used to shout back from the motor, "Keep the boat straight – you ain't needle-bobbing again, are you?" We didn't have as much as some of them do now; it's overdone, now, some-

times. I had a lot of them hanging-up plates. I used to have a nice brass lamp with a glass globe on it and a bow of red ribbon round. Then there was a row of plates down the back of the range. We didn't make any more dust from the range than we could help, so it didn't take you too long to keep it nice.

'When you went on a new boat at the dock, you see, there'd be iron knobs and everything, but you had to bring all your brass with you from the other boat. You had your own range. There was always a stove in, you see, but it was a straight up one, like a bottle stove, you know, and you couldn't cook on that. So you took that back to the dock and put your own cooking range in. We used to have a Larbert range – it was a nice range. It was as big as would fit in the space, like. You brought all your own things onto the change boat if your'n was going on the dock. It used to take less than half a day to change over. But we was always pleased to get our own boat back.

'At Uxbridge they used to do all the painting inside, and castles on the doors. They were nice painted at Uxbridge. You used to do one round trip whilst it was being docked, about a fortnight, and it would be ready when you got back. Some people used to like the change boat because it would be all cleaned out and nice, but really you never knew who had had them before, and sometimes you'd get one which had had a family in who hadn't kept it clean. Then you'd to clean it all out before you could take over. It would be about every two years that they docked the boats.

'Ralph always had everything in place on the boats: it was all neat, and you knowed where to get on and off, and where everything was when you was working. He used to scrub all the ropework and that, to keep 'em white, and the back fender on the motor; he used to get the boat brush and scrub them and give them a good doshing. But he didn't have any of those strings at the cabin side, he didn't like them. We just had the one to tie the watercan in case it got knocked.

'You'd get the inspector on sometimes, like

at Birmingham where there was a lot of boats. He'd get on them all and check them all up. They didn't bother so much at Nottingham or Leicester. We never had any bother with them; they just stepped on the side and looked in, and said, "Oh, it's no good going in there, it's all right". They could see it was clean, you know. But some boats, they had big families on and the inspector didn't like that.

'Mac Anderson was the boss [the southern fleet superintendent for Fellows Morton & Clayton] and he used to like to come to us, he did. We used to generally give him a cup of tea. He was the head man. I don't think he had a cup of tea off anybody else. If he had somebody as wanted a trip on a boat, he used to send 'em with us. He used to talk to my dad ever so nice. We took a schoolteacher once.'

Ralph and Violet had a good reputation for looking after the company's visitors like that:

'We kept that Seal and Exe till we came off the boats. We always got on all right on the rivers because we seen that everything was done right, all the lines in good order and everything.'

Ralph and Violet gave up working the carrying boats in about 1953; Ralph then worked for a number of years for British Waterways on maintenance on the Soar. At first, he and Violet lived in a converted narrowboat at Thurmaston: Evelyn, one of George Garside's former sand-carrying boats from Leighton Buzzard. Ralph and Violet bought it, the then British Waterways carpenter converted it for residential use, and they lived aboard with their four daughters for a number of years. Three went regularly to school, though the eldest was already too old. Then they bought a Victorian houseboat, which is still at Thurmaston, and lived in that until about three years ago.

'Me and Ralph put all new bottom in that houseboat when we got it – that might be forty years ago, now. Ralph didn't want to go in one of those lock houses. He did tug driving and moving the maintenance boats, and he also steered pleasure boats and trip boats from Thurmaston.

They were a harbour-launch type of thing, mostly tripping in Abbey Park, at Leicester.

'We decided to have a pleasure boat later on. We bought the hull, and Ralph built all the cabin on it. We went different places with the pleasure boat, that we hadn't been with Fellows Morton's. We've been to Macclesfield and Llangollen.'

Following Ralph's death, Violet found it impossible to continue to maintain the houseboat on a river Soar backwater, her home for forty years, and she was persuaded to move into a small flat in the village centre a few hundred yards from the river. This was the first time that she had lived

Once they had settled into their houseboat and the children were grown Ralph and Violet made extensive trips with

'on the land' since the beginning of World War I. It is significant, however, that whilst we sat on my boat and talked, she had smiled and sparkled as she harked back sixty and seventy years to the boats and her unceasing travels on the water; yet she visibly wilted whenever the flat was mentioned. 'I don't like it in here, it isn't like my houseboat,' she said in parting at her door. Friends around her were struggling to persuade her not to give up – but after a mere twenty years working on boats and waterways in between my writing, I can understand the bond with the water and just how she felt, even if I find it hard to explain in modern terms.

NOTE: I am very sorry to have to record that Violet Mould died in December 1996.

their pleasure boat. Here Violet is steering Les and Freda Hales boat whilst towing their own through some thick surface weed which was causing them engine problems

The Stud Groom

Brian Higham: Badminton, Gloucestershire

THE STUD GROOM

The last time they met, Brian Higham recalls that H M the Queen told him: 'Every time I see you Brian, you personify Badminton'. And he does, because in his capacity of stud groom Brian rules over the 11th Duke of Beaufort's stable yard. His charges include thirty horses looked after by eight girl grooms, and every day Brian himself will be seen somewhere on Badminton estate exercising the Duke's horses or in the stable yard overseeing their welfare. Hunting evenings in particular involve checking over each animal thoroughly for cuts and bruises sustained whilst out with the famous 'Blue and Buffs', the alternative name for the Beaufort Hunt and taken from the colours of the hunt livery.

Opposite: Brian Higham telling one of his infamous jokes

Below: Badminton village with the Estate Office in the background

Brian's weathered face is serious, and he betrays a feeling of nostalgia as he looks around the stable yard: 'I often think this is probably the last place where things are run on traditional lines. In the past all big houses had stable yards like this, but over the years the cost of keeping them running has proved too much. I'm glad this place is being written about, because it can't go on for ever.'

A native of Snainton in the Vale of Pickering in Yorkshire, Brian came to Badminton in 1959. He is from a long line of men whose professions have lain with country estates. One of his ancestors was a gamekeeper, Matthew Pateman, who worked at Ebberston Hall for Squire George Osbaldeston, a gentleman famous for being the 'hunting squire of England'. A century later, and Matthew's kin, Bert Pateman, was carrying on the tradition of working for a hunting man, but further south: Bert was employed by the 10th Duke of Beaufort on the beautiful Badminton estate a few miles from Tetbury in Gloucestershire. In his thirty years of service to the Duke he worked as whipper-in; then kennel huntsman and finally huntsman. And when, during that time, an extra hand was needed in the stable yard at Badminton, Bert spoke up for his sister's boy, Brian Higham.

Brian was living in Yorkshire at the time, and recalls being interviewed for the job by the Duke himself when he was judging at the Great Yorkshire Show. And thus it was that he came to Badminton as second horseman and second man. Uncle Bert is now dead and Brian is in his thirty-eighth season. 'A season starts from the first of May,' he explains, adding 'I've been stud groom since 1966. This means I am in charge of the stables and the grooms, and that it is my responsibility to produce fit horses for the Masters and Hunt staff and guests for the whole season.'

Brian is married, and he met his pretty

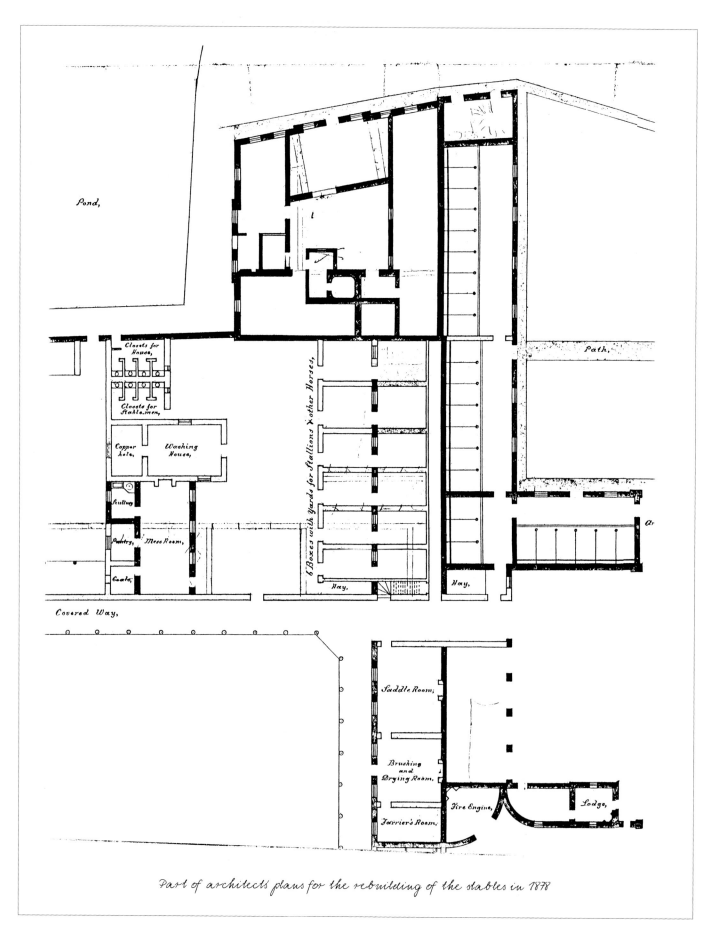

Pond,

Path,

Closets for Horses,

Closets for Stablemen,

Copper hole,

Washing House,

6 Boxes with yards for Stallions & other Horses,

Scullery,

Pantry,

Mess Room,

Coals,

Hay,

Hay,

Covered Way,

Saddle Room,

Brushing and Drying Room,

Farrier's Room,

Fire Engine,

Lodge,

Part of architect's plans for the rebuilding of the stables in 1878

American wife, Sherry, when she had sought his advice whilst on a horse-buying trip from the States; they live in a spacious cottage a stone's throw from the stable yard. Its entrance bedecked by flower baskets, the cottage is entirely in keeping with the picture-postcard beauty of Badminton village. The single village street is flanked by houses built of mellow Bath stone, their woodwork painted yellow-buff, the estate colour. The street's timeless appearance is a fitting introduction to the old-fashioned stable yard beyond. Even so, Brian hasn't forgotten his Yorkshire humour: 'Musn't forget my cap, there's woodpeckers about,' he is wont to say, setting that accessory firmly on his head en route from cottage to stable-yard door.

The handle set into the yard's huge door is fashioned in the shape of a stirrup, and like the rest of the estate woodwork, the door itself is painted buff to match the buff of the Duke's hunt livery. It opens onto a vast square yard with buildings on all four sides. There is a wooden tower on the north side, on its roof a weather vane in the shape of a fox stretching its iron forepaws perpetually in the direction of the wind. The yard was built in 1887 and the weather vane also dates from that time: thus a glance at this very same vane would have shown a Victorian stud groom the way the wind was blowing, and helped him to work out how to keep an even pressure of air within the stables. He did this by opening and closing the windows according to the horses' comings and goings – because heaven forbid that his equine charges be subjected to draughts! Brian no longer practises such niceties, but is full of admiration for the way the stables are built:

'Years ago they knew all about animals requiring good ventilation. The stables here are very warm and airy in the winter, and cool and airy in the summer. They're high, 14ft to the eves, and this gives plenty of room so that the dust can get above the horses. A lot of stables today have low ceilings, and horses will develop respiratory problems from that sort of housing

because the dust from the hay and straw, and probably the sprays and fertilisers used on them, can't get out.'

Each doorway from the yard leads into a line of looseboxes. Outside each box is a polished brass hook for hanging a headcollar, and the latch on each door is also brass; and every Sunday all the brass throughout the stables is cleaned. Brian admits with pride that there is not a stable in the country still run on such traditional lines. An iron saddle horse is fitted to each loosebox post; when not in use these fold away so there is no risk of the horses knocking against them.

Halfway up the stable wall nearest the yard, iron racks hold brushes and forks: stored safely in this way, they pose no risk of injury should a horse get out in the night. With equal care for safety, the water taps in this same wall are set in

The weather vane with a hunting theme

ornate Victorian iron alcoves. Brian also points out the doorways, which are all built wide so that horses don't knock their hip bones as they are led in and out.

As well as the stables, the yard is extremely well appointed as regards rooms where all the different tasks concomitant with running a high class yard can be accomplished. Thus the tack man works in a 'cleaning room' complete with a copper and a sink. There is a glass case lined with baize which holds clean spurs and bits, and polished oak stands where saddles can be racked up to air. When the tack is clean it is stored in the 'best tack room'. The one at Badminton is panelled in wood to the full height of its 20ft [6m] high walls, with saddle trees, complete with saddles, set one above the other from head height to ceiling; the higher ones are reached by a long wooden ladder. Other saddles are stored over old wooden 'Toblerone'-shaped rests, polished bright by use. The room is heated by rows of nineteenth-century, 4in iron hot-water pipes.

Within the rich gloom Brian says 'The "best tack room" can be the holiest, even now, and in times past no one would have been allowed in here except the tack man. He would always have been immensely proud of his work, and would have kept everything in immaculate order. Pride was an essential ingredient in every sort of job then — and there was nothing wrong with being proud, that's where it's a changing world today.'

He picks up some of the tack: 'Leather today is tanned differently to how it was years ago; it's not as good, and it doesn't last as long. And you never saw numnahs, the saddle-shaped piece of sheepskin or fabric that people put beneath their saddle nowadays. That's because in the old days a saddle was made to fit the horse for which it was intended, and it had a linen lining with a bit at the back blancoed white. Today the linings are leather. At one time when this place was in full swing there was a saddler's shop at Badminton — of course in those days there was also the carriage harness to see to, and all that worn by the farm horses.'

On the north side of the yard is the feed store. A bit like the quality leather, there have been changes in this department too. Brian explains: 'In the last thirty-five to forty years feed merchants' policy has been increasingly to compound feedstuffs into nut or cube form. Before that feed was mainly provided as chaff and oats, or chaff, beans, oats and different types of clover. They used to pour molasses over the feed, too, whereas now molasses comes in the compounds. However, I would say that in general, horses look better today than they did years ago.

'As regards feeding, a big yard would have a yard man, and some still do. He'd make the mash with a hand-turned chaff cutter, in the days before there was an electric machine to do it. We have an old mash house here, with metal coppers which would be warmed by lighting fires underneath them.'

Brian's office is at the far end of the east side of the yard. One of the doorways from it is in direct line with a doorway leading to a row of looseboxes running down the south side, and with both doors open there is a clear view down the whole row. Brian says that you do have to walk along the boxes to check them properly, but there is no doubt that both now, as in years gone by, from this doorway vantage point a stud groom can keep a fairly close eye on stable lads and lasses.

The office has a black chest-high Victorian desk, and rows of old books. These include diaries from the mid-nineteenth century which record carriage runs between Bath and Bristol, and also various wage-books. Brian opens one dated 1908: 'There were forty men here then, so there'd 've been over a hundred horses. The stud groom received 27s and there was even a woman paid to do the mess-room.'

Various old veterinary aids hang on the office wall and Brian lifts a few down. 'This is a drenching horn — years ago one reason for drenching was to alleviate colic. You'd put the prongs of a pitchfork through the horse's head-collar and, standing on a bin, use the horn to

Opposite:
The tack room at Badminton. It has features that the ordinary horse owner can only envy, such as the heated racks to dry tack

*Far right:
A picturesque
corner of the
Badminton estate*

pour a mixture down his throat. Another old remedy was nutmeg and horse-hair to get rid of parasitical worms; horses can't be sick like humans, so the idea was to purge them. Those who knew how would make up balls of medicine, and a skilled man could put a ball down with his hand or use one of these balling guns — this bar goes on the back of the tongue and is then pressed down.' Brian then proceeds to describe the yard and the running of it, both as it used to be, and as it is now:

Brian with a 'baller'; one of the old tools kept at Badminton. It was used to open a horse's mouth so a draught or pill could be inserted

'There's a wash-box in the yard. Not that we always wash horses, but we might want to wash one that's injured. There is also a room known as the "pharmacy". It's never been in use in my time, but it still contains old blue poison bottles and apothecary scales, and there used to be a hand-written book of horse cures in it, many of which we still use. For example in a wet season a constant problem is mud fever, basically an inflammation of the skin because of mud getting into the pores; a horse's legs may swell, and bad cases can't hunt. To treat it we mix up copper sulphate, meths, vinegar and water and apply it for three or four days, and this works better than a lot of the modern treatments. And an old way of drying the mud and wet quickly from a horse's heels is to apply sawdust or bran — bran is thought to be best because there's a soothing quality in flour.

A healthfull drink for a horse.

Boyl half a dozen cloves of Garlick for some time
in 3 pints of Ale, being straind, add half an ounce
of Elicampane, y^e like quantity of Bay-berries, w^th
Diapente, & Turmorick, wch wth an ounce of Venice
Treacle, & 2 spoonfulls of honey, make into a drink

                              Probatum est.

For ye Scratches.

Cut away ye hair, rub off ye scabs, & wash ye horses legs w^th
old urine, Alome, & salt, mixt together, & heated, as hot as
ye horse can endure it, y^n take ye tops & buds of Elder, & ye greē
berries of bryers, boyld in a pottle of Stale worte, to wch add
a good quantity of Alome, & wth this, wash ye part griev̄
twice or thrice a day.   Probatum.

                    Or.

Let ye horse blood in ye Fetlock vein, suffring him to blee
pretty freely; ye next day wash & clean ye part wth warm
water then cliping away ye hair anoint it wth this oyntm^nt.
Take Verdigrease, & green Copperas of each 2 Ounces, & 4 of
Honey well pounded & mixt together.

Some wonderful remedies for horses from the Badminton archives

'I still boil up the herb comfrey and bandage it around swollen knees. In fact you can use any sort of brassica for this, because they all have great drawing qualities.

'There's an old saying, "If a horse has got a headache, check his feet", and it's remarkable how true this is. If a horse is "footy" I may use cow dung to ease the pain – and pig dung is useful too, but for another reason: if a horse is biting his rug, smear some on the spot, and he'll soon stop!

'As regards the general care and management of horses, there used to be men in these sorts of yards with job titles you never hear today. For example a "nagsman" was someone who would "make" the young horses – he would "nag" 'em about, ride 'em hunting and make them at home before they went hunting properly with their owners or their guests.

'Then there were "strappers"; today we call this sort of person a 'groom' though part of the strapper's job was to "wisp" or "strap" a horse, and this is rarely done nowadays. He would make a "wisp" out of hay or straw, depending on the quality of the forage, by twisting it round until it was quite substantial, and then he would slap or "bang" the horse with it over its neck, quarters and loins. It didn't hurt the horse but it was said to help build up his muscles. Old-fashioned people still do it, but it's all about time and labour, and today a girl groom probably looks after four horses so she hasn't got time to do it.

'Strappers also used to have certain ways of doing things: for instance it was tradition to put an odd number of plaits on a lady's horse; and the length of a hunter's tail was also important – the correct length was one inch above the chestnuts when the horse was stood square. Now you see all lengths, and nobody would care if it was touching the ground or not; but years ago grooms were immensely proud of the horses from their yard, and they'd be watching others very carefully, too.

'There was also much more emphasis on "spit and polish" and finishing touches. Strappers would take the trouble to weave straw round a pitch-fork handle and lay it across the doorway so that the stall looked tidy. Another trick was to outline the estate crest in sawdust at the box entrance. Actually I've never seen that done, but I've heard old chaps talk of it.

'Jockey Matthews, who's sadly passed on, could remember all the old ways – he was a proper little strapper fellow. He used to ride second horse to the 10th Duke; before that, Jockey used to take the 9th Duke out in a donkey cart when the Duke couldn't ride because he had gout and weighed twenty stone.

'There's a blacksmith's shop in this yard, and I've heard it said that there was once a tailor's premises, probably in the estate yard – there was so much livery in those days. The second horsemen used to wear green coats: before horseboxes it was their job to hack the horses to a meet, and also to take fresh – or "second" – horses to a pre-arranged spot partway through the day, for the Duke and each of his party.

'Big yards like this would also have one man solely responsible for clipping and trimming, probably someone very experienced who didn't ride any more. He would do this in a clipping box, and would be hugely proud of his skill. Nowadays, well, you could go to a meet today and think some of the horses had been clipped with a knife and fork – but nobody takes any notice because so many people just don't know the difference.'

Brian chuckles. Needless to say, Badminton horses keep up the traditionally high standard in their clipped appearance. The final touch for a really smart job is to singe off the longer 'cats-hairs', particularly in the spring, and sure enough, there is an old brass singeing-lamp amongst Brian's tools. He explains how the handle of the lamp is filled with meths, and how, lit by a match, a wick within the lamp feeds a flame. The flame then fans out in the shape of the bristle end of a paintbrush. Deftly and quickly Brian demonstrates, running the flame over one of the horse's coats, burning off any stray long hairs.

Overleaf:
An extract from the House, Park and Farm accounts, Badminton archives

1901					£	s	d		£	s	d
	Stables continued	Brought Forward £			2313	5	7		3147	17	6
12 Jany	Geo Williams & Son V S°	examining horse at Tattersals			1	1	-				
12 Jany 11-6-9 11 July 12-4-6	A. Turpin	Chemist			23	11	3				
21 Jany	J & G. Lock	Livery hats & hunting caps for second horsemen			19	13	-				
4 July 36-13-6 19 Dec 32-11-6	W. E. Cross	Livery for coach establishment £69 - 5 - 0									
4 July 13-2-0 19 Dec 153-1-6	do	do hunting do	166 - 3 - 6		235	8	6				
21 Jany	Bartley & Sons	top boots for coachmen and second horsemen			33	13	9				
21 Jany	Thos Callow & Son	horse thongs, crops &c			19	6	6				
22 "	The reps of the late E. H. Baker	saddlery ½ year to Christmas 1900	255-5-6								
16 April 55-5-5 5 July 17-6-8 29 " -19-0 8 Oct 137-17-0	Shattock Hunter & Co	saddlery	211-7-10		466	13	4				
9 Feby	G. Dallimore	Shoeing horses at Semington			2	10	-				
9 May 32-13-6 12 July 12-18-0 27 Aug 6-9-6 3 Sep 6-14-10	Peat Moss Litter Co	Moss litter			58	15	10				
16 May 2-2-0 12 Dec 2-8-0	Exec" of late E. Sharp	standing and feed for hound van horses	4-10-0								
16 May 1-16-0 30 Nov -18-0 12 Dec 1-16-0	R. Careless	do	4-10-0								
16 May -12-0 12 Dec 1-4-0	T. Blackman	do	1-16-0		10	16	-				
31 Oct	Hood & Moore	forage for London carriage horses			47	15	6				
3 July	A. Thompson	vetches	4-14-0								
" "	H. Butler	do	23-4-0		27	18	-				
12 "	Musgrave & Co Ld	mangers			6	18	6				
12 Sep	Gillett & Johnston	a new turret clock	105-0-0								
12 Oct	J. Long	winding up do one year to 29 Sep	1-6-0		106	6	-				
13 Sept	J. Slade	carriage of goods			-	4	-				
31 Oct	Cotterell Bros	wall paper			-	5	10				
26 "	W. E. Spencer	hunter			63	-	-				
					3437	5	7				
	License Duties										
19 Jany	Collector of Inland Revenue	for 45 male servants	33-15-0								
		Carried Forward £	33-15-0		3437	5	7		3147	17	6

Account

			£ s d	£ s d	£ s d
		Brought Forward £	33 15 -	3437 5 7	3147 17 6

Stables cont.ᵈ
Licenses

Date					
14 Jany	Collector of Inland Revenue	9 - 4 wheel - 2 horse carriages	18 18 -		
		1 - 4 wheel 1 horse - do -	1 1 -		
"		3 - 2 wheel 1 horse - do -	2 5 -		
"		Armorial, bearings	2 2 -	58 1 -	

Repairs

Date					
fortnightly from 18 Jany	C. E. Lewis	tradesmens work, and for shoeing, one year to the 28ᵗ Dec.ʳ 1901	177 8 1		
13 July 1-6-0 27 " 1-10-7	A. Perks	Whitewashing	2 16 7		
6 Sep	Ino Turnor	painter	30 - -		
9 Nov.ʳ	J. Clark & Sons	cow hair	6 2 6		
14 Dec	E. Russell	smith	- 17 9		
16 "	May & Hassell	timber	15 15 -		
18 "	Thos Reynolds &a	Ironmongery	15 1 -		
21 "	W.ᵐ D. Patterson	- do -	8 10 6		
	S. & J. Cole	Carpenters	12 16 -	269 7 5	3764 14 -
					6912 11 6
					3147 17 6
					3764 14 -

Kennels

Date					
	W.ᵐ Dale Huntsman, one year's salary to Christmas 1901		200 - -		
	- do.	Miscellaneous Xpenses	76 - 11 - 8		
30 July	- do.	Xpenses to Peterboro' Show	13 - 12 - 2	90 3 10	
	J. Maloney, 1ˢᵗ whip one year's wages to Xmas 1901		80 - 0 - 0		
5 Oct	- do.	expenses	1 - 6 - 5	81 6 5	
	T. Newman 2ⁿᵈ whip one year's wages to Xmas 1901		60 - 0 - 0		
5 Oct	- do.	expenses	- 7 - 0	60 7 -	
	W.ᵐ Chiles Kennelman one year's wages to Xmas 1901		52 - 0 - 0		
	- do.	293 hides at 9ᵈ	13 - 13 - 0	65 13 -	
fortnightly &c Jany	W.ᵐ Dale	under kennelmens wages one year to 28 December 1901		101 7 -	
		Carried Forward £		598 17 3	6912 11 6

The 10th Duke of Beaufort

'There won't be many people singe today, I would imagine,' he observes. 'But it's very practical in the spring when you stop clipping, because as the horses' summer coats come through they also grow these cats-hairs down the back of the legs and under the jaw in particular, but all over the coat, too. Singeing these off makes them look much neater, and they love having it done because it's warm. I've never had a horse you couldn't do, once it realises the lamp's not actually going to burn it.'

Brian also prefers the traditional methods for breaking in young horses, and at certain times of the year he can be seen in the lanes around Badminton walking behind a young horse which he is controlling with long reins. 'You have to handle them well from birth, and again, it's all about time – some people are inclined to try and break a horse too quickly. Of course, you can always try the old horseman's remedy to make a horse obey you: that is to get a foal's "false tongue", a piece which is present in the afterbirth, once a foal's been born. Some old chaps used to dry this out and carry it in their pocket, and this was supposed to make any horse respect the man carrying it.'

Brian considers the question of what makes a good hunter:

'Everybody has his or her own ideas. I like the Irish Draught/Thoroughbred cross, which has a bit of limb and a good temperament. And for people that can ride them, Thoroughbreds – they wear well because often they've got enough bone, and plenty of spirit – an ounce of blood is worth an inch of bone, as the saying goes! I was fortunate enough to be given the 10th Duke's horse, Jupiter; and the one I have now, a grey called Lord, was given to me by the 11th, the present Duke. In fact it's not part of my job to go hunting, and if I do go out it's a perk.

'Our routine is to bring in a few horses from grass in June, early July, ready for autumn hunting, and these are in use by the end of August. They need seven to eight weeks to get reasonably fit. Nowadays these could be any horses, though years ago you probably kept a few horses that weren't sound enough to go the whole season and used them just to September or October. All the horses are up before the end of July. Hunting proper starts in November, but most of the horses won't be really fit until mid-December.

'Years ago they didn't turn the horses out in the summer at all; they had enough labour to keep them ticking over in the stable. They used to bring them vetches and grasses from the fields, and kept them on very light work, so they were never allowed to go right down, to become really unfit. Of course, in those days the season was longer – they used to catch a May fox here, the season finished at the end of that month, and autumn hunting started at the end of August; so it didn't pay to put the horses out fit and well, and then they would be really gross and soft by the time they were brought back in.

'I am no chauvinist when it comes to looking to the future: a stud groom was always a very respected position, still is. Most big hunts have probably got a man stud groom still, but they are becoming fewer because hunts have cut down the number of horses – it's all down to costs, again. I think eventually a good lady could do the same job, and often does in some cases. In fact, I think in general girls do a very good job and work equally as many hours today as men did in stables years ago.'

When he's not to be found in the stable

The first vet's inspection takes place in front of the house at Badminton, before the Trials start

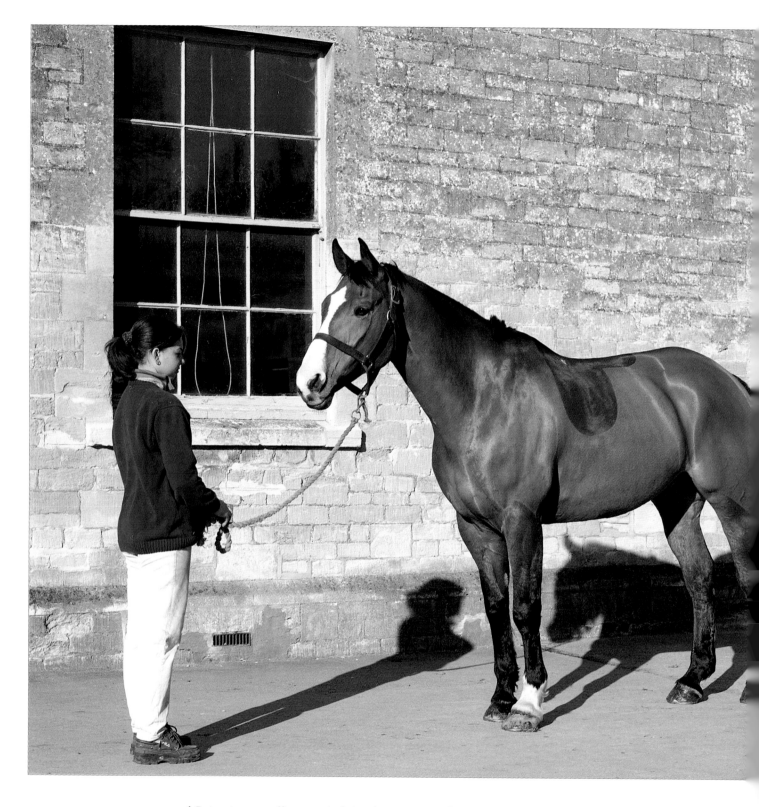

yard Brian is generally away judging horses at shows in different parts of the country. Or he could be buying horses in Ireland, and meeting his old friend Mick O'Connor there. Mick is a breeder and dealer of some repute, whose customers include the British army. Sefton, who the nation grew to love in the early 1980s following his injuries from an IRA nail bomb at a London barracks, was originally one of Mick's horses.

Brian's own judgement when it comes to choosing a horse for purchase is highly respected,

sensible, secure headwear in windy spring weather. He also wears his bowler when he mingles amongst the crowds keeping an eye on things during the four days of the famous Badminton Horse Trials.

The horse trials take place at the beginning of May and are, of course, a major event in his calendar. During the weeks leading up to them, he arranges for all the stables to be thoroughly washed out, disinfected and put ready for the international influx of competitors' horses which will inhabit them. Even an individual horse's preference for straw, paper or shavings as bedding is taken into account

Riders appreciate this care, and also Brian's presence. Karen Dixon says: 'Brian Higham is one in a lifetime. To the riders that have the pleasure of returning to Badminton later in the year after the horse trials, to train as part of the British team, he is an intricate part of the place. Not only his knowledge of horses, his local knowledge is enormous too – as is his character and his heart. And he is always one for a new joke, particularly if it's rude; he never fails to make you laugh.

She adds: 'Over the last fifteen years he has been of enormous support to me, and become a good friend. Long may he remain fit, healthy, and one of the cornerstones of Badminton.'

Mary King (née Thomson) has been competing at Badminton Horse Trials since 1985. She, too, admits that arrival time at the stable yard is laced with joke-swapping: 'Brian generally has a new crop to tell.'

Like Karen, she also meets Brian when she is part of the British team training at Badminton. Mary remembers that on the last such occasion, which was prior to the Olympics, Brian and Sherry, in a typically kind gesture, invited all the girl grooms round to their house. Indeed, during Trials week itself, the Higham household is swelled by visiting Masters, farriers, friends from Ireland and any number of people connected with horses. Such happy, chaotic interludes are part of life at Badminton.

Brian is, of course, an excellent judge of horseflesh. Here he gives one of the hunt horses a thorough check

Below: Brian in one of the stable blocks lined with beautiful old looseboxes

so much so that he was entrusted with negotiating the purchase of a pony for Princess Beatrice, a gift from her grandmother, the Queen.

When the occasion demands it, Brian is a smartly dressed man. For a day at Cheltenham races he wears a bowler hat, and considers it

Three Men, One Estate

*Bob Beattie, Arnold Mallinson
& Jack Stephenson: Cumbria*

THREE MEN, ONE ESTATE

With the daggers of taxation and recession constantly stabbing at their hearts, Britain's great estates needed long ownership by families with strong custodial spirit to survive the turmoil of the twentieth century. But they also owe much to the skills and loyalty of their long-serving labourers, men whose honest toil has provided sound bedrock through both war and peace. Few have contributed more than Jack Stephenson, Arnold Mallinson and Bob Beattie, whose remarkable combined service of some 150 years on Cumbria's Brackenburgh estate has helped four generations of the Harris family to remain at the forefront of estate management.

ROBERT BEATTIE

Although these three men have always lived in the same region of Cumbria and have such an impressive record on the Calthwaite estate, midway between Penrith and Carlisle, in earlier years they also served many other employers. Robert Beattie was actually born at Brackenburgh, on 21

November 1914; his father William worked on the estate for an impressive sixty years! And despite living through times even tougher than those Bob endured, William soldiered on to the then exceptional age of eighty-six.

With nine children to feed, there were few luxuries in the Beattie cottage.

'Mother made a lot of meals of sheep's head,

Right: Bob's father, William, wearing his long-service medal outside the house where Bob was born

Far right: Bob's mother Hannah with her 'Christmas' geese

mostly soup, and we ate a lot of rabbits given to us by the gamekeepers. We also had crow [rook] pie – using only the breasts – when the keepers shot the young birds in spring. Lots of people had these pies then. And sometimes the fishermen used to come round with a cart or motorbike and sidecar, shouting 'Fresh herring', which were thirteen for a shilling.

'Nearly all our clothes and clogs were handed down. Father spent all his spare time putting caulkers [metal reinforcements] on the clogs, maybe three or four a night. He got the nails from the blacksmith's shop. All farmers and workers and their families had clogs then. You'd hear the pitter-patter of the children's feet on the road as they went to school.'

Being the second oldest, Bob had to supplement the meagre family income as soon as possible. At the age of only ten he began working on the home farm:

'I scaled [scattered] manure in the stitches [ridges of soil thrown up by a plough] and milked by hand. For six evenings working from about four to six, or as late as ten o'clock in midsummer, I got half-a-crown [12½p]; and I worked right through the month's school holiday as well.

'One evening when I was twelve or thirteen I was sent to look for sheep in a field. But there was this big stag there with the horns [antlers] on, and I didn't know what to do because it didn't even move for my dog. So I went to the keeper and he told Mr Joe [Harris], who got his rifle and shot it. The flesh was divided up among the workers, and they still have the horns hanging in the big house.'

On leaving school at fourteen Bob worked as a full-time labourer on the home farm. 'In those days the estate was more or less self-sufficient, with its own masons and carpenters, and there were lots of us on the land. When we went out in

the morning we took bread and jam, and tea in a tin bottle with a cork in the top. This was called "ten o'clocks", even though we had it at nine. We went back home for dinner [lunch], and in the afternoon went out with our "three o'clocks" and "six o'clocks". And when milking was finished they'd bring out a big bucket of milk and we'd all help ourselves.'

At the age of sixteen Bob moved to another farm, just one mile away. But although he had been brought up on a farm and could do most things as well as any man, he was still paid only 'a boy's wage': for his first six-month contract he received just eighteen 'punds' [pounds]. So he moved around in an attempt to better himself.

One spell of eighteen months was spent in the gardens at Brackenburgh. 'There had been twelve gardeners there, but then it was down to four; the men lived in a bothy in the garden, where they saw to themselves. I left when they were cutting down on labour – the usual case of last in, first out.'

During the seventeen years he was at Middle Yard Farm Bob sold his first horse, in the 1930s. 'I walked the twenty-two miles each way to Wigton sales. But it was worth it, because I bought that horse as a foal for just twenty-something pounds at Penrith auction and sold it at two years, broken in, for £35. That was the start of my bank account!'

But there was one occasion when an animal got the better of Bob: 'I was catchin' this bull. But someone put a sneck [bolt] through a latch, and the bull's head pushed it straight through my hand. I had seventeen stitches. Apart from that the only other time I was in danger was when I turned a tractor over while pulling a big stone out the ground. But I got away with it.'

Bob also drove a tractor during the latter part of the seventeen years full-time and fifteen years part-time (three days a week after the age of sixty-five) he worked in the Brackenburgh forestry department. But during that long period he never found anything interesting in the woods, 'only bloody hard work!'

Bob's wife, Eileen, came from Edinburgh in 1947 'to work with horses, but she ended up doing everything', and the two met while she was a maid at Brackenburgh.

JACK STEPHENSON

Jack Stephenson's greater service of fifty-three years earned him an estate cottage for his retirement. When I visited him and his wife Betty, the hens were pecking around the garden, bees were humming soothingly about his old hives and rural relics were scattered about. It is hard to believe that the M6 is so close. But Jack admits that he can 'smell and hear the motorway when the wind is in the wrong direction. It cut the estate in two, and as a result some of the farms were no longer viable. The "amputated" land was either attached to other tenanted farms, or taken in hand by the Harris family.'

Jack was born at the Lessonhall estate, Wigton, on 3 March 1912. Christened John, and one of six children, he never expected to do any more than follow the furrow set by his farm-labouring father and grandfather. 'Father earned only twelve shillings a week, but they were happier days then when we didn't have any money. You didn't need to lock your door, and neighbours would always help you out. There were many more birds then, and I always liked the spring of the year best. My favourite was the peewit, a great bird for keeping the crows away. We always used to take care to move its nest when the corn was coming through and we rolled the field with a horse.'

Typical of the generation, the school Jack attended, Waverbridge, was very strict. He describes those times:

'We often had the stick over the desk, but we had lots of nature walks. And we were more than happy playing hoops, skipping and corner-to-corner [rounders]. There were lots of trout and other fish to catch in the River Waver, with fly and worm. One time the water dried right up, and a great many fish, including big eels, were left stranded in the pools, easy to catch. I also helped Father with the snares and ferrets – I put the nets on – to catch rabbits, which we sold.

'I never had much more than a bone and a couple of sandwiches to take to school. Our drink was the usual bottle of tea with a stocking on, and we all put them round the pot-bellied stove to warm up. If they got too near, the corks popped off.

'Breakfast was mainly porridge, maybe a bit of bacon of a Sunday morning, and there was a joint of beef or mutton at the weekend. The Sunday tea treat was two jellies and a big tin of fruit, and there was always a bit of good farm butter.'

Like most countrymen, Jack's father always kept a pig or two for fattening. 'They were just like pets, always rubbing up against you, and we used to scratch their ears. Mother kept hens, too, and we grew all our own veg. But lots of the old folk in Wigton were very poor, and some houses still had sandstone floors. Doorsteps were always coloured red with the rud fetched up from the beck. One old lady who came round selling it was known as Ruddy Mary.'

Jack's parents also lived at 'The Moat', Longtown. There, Jack and the other children had to attend Sunday school at Netherby, cross-

'My favourite was the peewit…'

ing the River Esk on a swing bridge to get there. When Jack left school at fourteen, he and his father went to work at Dockray Hall. He recollects the start of his working life:

'Like everyone else then, I was hired for six months at a time. At Whitsuntide and Martinmas the lads used to congregate in Wigton for the term hirings, and when the farmers came along they'd say: 'What can'st thou do?' The two hiring fairs were the highlight of the year, and the only time you had a holiday. If you got taken on, the farmer would give you a shilling to seal the contract. For my first six months I got £10 at the end, less any subs. But you lived in at the Hall and ate with the farmer, which was considered part of your pay.

'The money just wasn't there in them days, even for the poor old farmer. If you really

worked for him he'd look after you. But if you didn't like it, at the end of that term you moved on. I stayed at Dockray for eighteen months, and during that time managed to save up thirty shillings to buy my first bicycle, a secondhand Raleigh.

Jack then spent two years at Tarn Rigg Moor, Wigton, before moving to Anthorn, Wigton, 'at the tip of the Solway. A fellow up the village had a flat boat [punt] and a big gun which he'd take after the geese. And I used to fish in the Solway for flounders; I got them with the gripe [four-pronged fork] at low tide, and managed a living out of them. At that time I used to take a horse and cart with four bags of grain to the mill at nearby Kirkbride. While they crushed the grain into oats for porridge and cattle food I took the horse to be shod, at about 7s 6d for a set of shoes.'

After thirty months at Anthorn, Jack worked for two years for George Dixon at Easton, Wigton. By then he was very experienced in laying hedges and drains, making and thatching stacks, and ploughing. 'Draining was all spadework then, and every wet spot had to be investigated. Tree roots, especially chestnut, were devils for blocking up along the green lane. And in the open fields we were forever replacing

POCKET MONEY

*While still at school, Jack earned a little pocket money
thinning turnips by hand for only 3d a hundred yards,
but that rose to 6d by the time we came here. The farmer
was always pleased to see you. I also used to help Father at
Lessonhall with the milking, feeding the horses and
ploughing. And the cowman had a three-wheeler pushbike
which we used to go shepherdin' on, and which we had some
great fun falling off.'*

the tiles – in heavy ground they don't want to be too deep, and so they were always breaking because of the weight of the new machinery. It was OK while we had the horses.'

The best pay he'd ever had – '£30 a half-year' – attracted Jack to Winder Hall, Penrith, for the next thirty months. Then followed five years at Abbot Lodge, Clifton, near Penrith, where Jack married Betty, a maid in the house. There Jack earned thirty-six shillings a week, and rented a nearby cottage for four shillings a week; he had an AJS 500 motorbike, bought in 1935 for £10, to go back and forth.

Next came two years at Kirkby Thore, near Appleby, before the Stephensons settled into their present house at Brackenburgh, in 1941:

'It was long hours, hard work and very little pay – just thirty-four shillings a week – and we had two children to feed; but we were allowed a quart of milk a day and some potatoes. We were paid in cash once a fortnight. The old man, farm bailiff Faulder, used to go to Penrith to get the money and handed it out through a window if the weather was all right.

'There was a big staff then. The person who used to live in this lodge got £2 a year for opening and closing the gate. And when the grandparents of Mr Joe [the head of the Harris family] used to walk down past here, followed by the staff in crocodile fashion on the way to Plumpton church, someone even had to clean all the horse muck off the drive first. The boss then was also called Mr Joe, as each generation is called Joseph or John alternately.'

Jack started as under-horseman in a team of three, but he was not restricted simply to working with horses. One of his duties was to help clip the flock of Oxford Down sheep, 'and woe betide anyone who cut one, especially the tups [rams]. The first Sunday in September was known as Tup Sunday, when other farmers came to see the tups prior to them being taken to the ram sales at Kelso in Scotland. This was a huge effort for the shepherd, who had to take enough food for the sheep to last three days.'

PLOUGHING

At haytime we could yoke sixteen horses and carts up. As well as generally caring for the horses and breaking them in, my duties included binding and stooking, and making stitches for potatoes and turnips. The manure in the bottom of each stitch [ridge] was put out by hand from a horse and cart. Then the spuds were dropped in by hand, and I split the stitches with a plough, covering two rows at once.

Most ploughing was done in the spring, so there were always lots of stubble fields, which were grand for the pheasants and partridges to pick over. But with the war we had to plough a lot more out. I always used to whistle and sing while I was ploughing, as the horses liked it. One I had was so obedient you could just tap his knee and he'd get down on the ground. Some of the quiet ones were sent to work in the estate woods and sawmill.

Our working clothes was always heavy cords and kittul [a sort of dark-grey denim] jackets. And in wet weather we tied brats [hessian sacks] round our waists and over our shoulders to keep dry. Our clogs had laced leather uppers and wooden soles, most with caulkers bought from the local smithy. Some had a duck neb [beak] front, but rounded ones were more popular.

Mr Faulder was lame and getting on a bit, but he missed nothing and was always very particular. Everything had to come up to Mr Joe senior's standards. Faulder had a pony and trap and on Tuesday morning, which was market day at Penrith, during the years petrol was rationed, someone had to harness the pony to the trap and drive the bailiff to Plumpton station. He had to be collected again at tea-time.

One Tuesday when petrol was allowed, Faulder was driven to Penrith by his grandson. On their return he wanted to see how one of my workmates was getting on stitching a field. He took one look and blew his top, as the poor man had a dog-leg [a bad bend] in the stitches. Being a roadside field this had to be altered right away, as anyone could see these dog-legs. So I was ordered to rub the stitches down and re-stitch the field, but I wasn't very happy about this and felt sorry for my mate.

Mr Joe senior was a man who expected things to be done properly. It was nothing fresh to see him wandering in the fields with a thing that looked like a walking stick with a blade and hook on the end to dig up thistles and nettles with.

Previous pages:
Farm labourers
gathered in Carlisle
for the biannual
hiring fair

Another of Jack's tasks was hedge trimming. 'All the beech hedges were dressed by hand, between haytime and harvest, and all the farm men took part. Two went with sickles to clean the bottoms of the hedges, others followed and clipped the sides with shears, and I did the tops. Then a horse and cart came and picked up the clippings. In later years I was provided with a hedge clipper run off the tractor, but it still took me three weeks to cut all the hedges, a job I took great pride in. I did this for three years after I retired from full-time work.'

Being in a reserved occupation, Jack was exempt from war service, but he joined the Home Guard. He describes the duties expected of them:

WEATHER WATCH

As a ploughman, Jack always kept a close eye on the weather, and was a firm believer in country lore:

'If you saw Noah's Ark – a boat-shaped cloud formation, pointed at one end, with streaks feathering out – you knew it would be wet the following day. A big weather change would always be on the quarter full [moon]. If there was a storm brewin', the cattle and sheep would always look for shelter and the rooks would fly round in rings and go wild. Wet weather caused a lot of extra work with all the turning of the corn stooks.'

'I can still get into that uniform below the stairs, but I haven't got the boots now. We used to guard the railway, the airfield and the A6, where there was a hut, with three of us inside and three out. Any vehicle which didn't stop you gave them a ping. You had to unload when you came back into the hut, but one fellow, who was supposed to be in charge, forgot and accidentally fired a round through the roof! They were tiring days as we still had to do our own work after.'

Land work was especially difficult during and after the severe winter of 1946–7:

'We couldn't start ploughing until 8 April, and even then the frost was still in some edges. It took us nine weeks, working from 7am to 9pm Sunday to Saturday. In 1962–3 there was not so much snow, but everything was at absolute starvation and the road surfaces lifted with frost.

'But there was always plenty of fuel on the estate as Mr Joe was a coalpit owner. Every time he had coal or coke sent down, six horses and a cart were required to collect it from the station, no matter what was going on. The greenhouses used a lot and the main house had sixty ton for the winter. When the coal, all big lumps, was neatly stacked in the open shed, the front layer was whitewashed so that nobody could pull a lump out without it being spotted.

'Old Mr Joe was very against the introduction of the tractor, but changed his mind when he saw what it could do. I can't tell you what happened to all the horses – mainly Clydesdales – after they went to the auctions at Carlisle. Before pneumatic tyres came in, the spade-lug tractors had to have wooden bands made of beech wood put on them to go on the road, to stop them tearing the surface up.

Mrs Stephenson still remembers when Jack helped with the thrashing, 'when he came in smelling of rats and mice, and was so dirty you could only see the whites of his eyes. He still works five mornings a week, plucking and cleaning gamebirds (though he now has an electric machine to help), taking logs into the house, mucking out, keeping Mrs Joe's rose garden, all sorts of different jobs. He's her blue-eyed boy, and she even keeps a pair of slippers up there for him!' In 1990 Jack won a ploughing prize (for best Ins and Outs at the Carlisle and District Vintage Society match), and in his eighties was still showing flowers and vegetables, and hardly missed a shoot, usually standing as 'stop'.

When Jack was sixty-five, his loyal service was rewarded with the customary gold watch and pension, but the Harris family have valued his long friendship and wisdom too. When he received his long service medal at the Royal Show he talked to Princess Anne about their shared love of horses; but I think he was more proud of the fact that Mr Joe, director of the show for five years, 'laid on a coach, which was full up, to take us all there. And we've been to all the Harris children's weddings around the country, all expenses paid.' One of those children, John, is the fourth generation of the Harris family to be chief steward of the sheep section at the Royal Show. He still wears the silver RASE badge – the only one to survive – worn by his great grandfather, Joe, when he became a council member in 1905.

ARNOLD MALLINSON

The third great stalwart of Brackenburgh is Arnold Mallinson, who came to work in the woods in 1938 and still lives with his wife Amy in one of the estate cottages. Christened Thomas Arnold, the son of a farmer and sole survivor of three brothers, he was born at Newbiggin Dacre, near Penrith, on 1 October 1915. Arnold's earliest memories are from Raughton Head, a few miles to the north, where he lived from the age of three or four until he was eleven or twelve.

'I can still mind [remember] all them days of cutting grass for hay with the old machines, when two small farms would often join together. I helped Dad take the corn to mill to get ground into oatmeal for our own consumption and into rough maize for the farm stock. Then there were many more skylarks, and lots of corncrakes – I

found their nests in our grass fields, and even a few black grouse on Lazonby Fell.

'We went four miles to Dalston Station, near Carlisle, with horse and cart to get the coal. Lighting was by paraffin lamp and water came from a garden well. We cured our own bacon and made black pudding, brawn and a good sausage. There was lots of rabbit catchin' with snares and ferrets for a bit of pocket money. We sold some in Penrith, where there were more barefoot children than out in the country.

'Near our school an old chap would sit by the roadside with a heap of stones twice the size of this room. At a certain time of year the farmers took them from their fields to prevent damage to machinery and this man broke them up with ordinary hammers so that they could be used to fill in road potholes.

'Each Saturday Mother went to Carlisle, where she left her trap at Dalton's Mart and then took her own butter and eggs in baskets to sell in the market. She did that for years, until Dad started to sell his milk, when we moved to Sceugh Dyke, where there was lots of fruit. He sold much of it, especially damsons. One year we had so many that half a ton went to a jam factory, and it was all hand-picked.

Jack eating lunch beside his 1942 Fordson tractor at Spittals Farm, Kirkby Thore, in 1970

'If a cow had a sore udder you just rubbed it with your own concoction'.

'There were lots of tramps doing their rounds then, and sometimes droves of horses and dozens of caravans came through with gypsies on their way to Appleby Fair. They just used to let their horses into our fields, at about midnight. This lasted about a fortnight as they went through, and then they all came back again. It was a time the gamekeepers were up day and night.'

On leaving school at fourteen, Arnold helped his father on the farm:

'At first we had mostly British shorthorn cattle, about twenty to twenty-five, but then we gradually got into the better milking strains with, for example, Friesians. If a cow had a sore udder you just rubbed it with your own concoction, as there was no bother with the vet'nary then.

'Our eighty to a hundred sheep were Suffolk cross; they were treated with Jeyes fluid or dipped if struck with the maggot. In any case, all were dipped twice a year, and each time you had to go to the local policeman to get the dipping papers to fill in. Usually he came out to see it was done properly – and that bobby went everywhere on his bike.

'Then, in 1938, we came to live in a rented house just south of Calthwaite, at Firwood, and I went into the forestry at Brackenburgh. There were more than a dozen of us and I earned 33 shillings a week. After having no proper wage with Father it was like a fortune for a while!

'We sowed our own seed and had our own nursery wood on Lazonby Fell, with Norway spruce, larches and hybrids. Woods were planted out in March and April and every section had to be rabbit-fenced. Deer were a problem, too – mostly roe, but you rarely saw a stag. Another pest was pine weevils, which used to bark round the bottom of a tree and make it die. Then there were lots more red squirrels and birds of prey, especially owls. But we still see an occasional pine marten.

'Much later on, most of the sycamores got black blotches and died, and then Dutch elm disease took hold. And sometimes we'd fell a whole plantation if it was badly blown. The war made a big difference, as a lot of timber was felled before its proper time because felling was compulsory. It mostly went for pit props and packing cases. But our old manager fought tooth and nail to keep the old trees.'

As in many other large forests, starling roosts occasionally caused considerable damage, especially through the chemical action of their droppings. Arnold recalls how the men used to stand around at dusk in an effort to keep the birds out: 'It was always in the early spring, just before they dispersed to breed. One year it was terrible, and night after night we had men out in each wood, rattling tins and firing guns. But the best thing was to put a lot of wet stuff on a good fire to get a bit of smoke going.'

During the war Arnold often saw prisoners-of-war walking around as they worked on local farms. He remembers those times:

'I was in the Home Guard and it was pretty tiring on nights, but that was only about once a fortnight as we were in groups of about half-a-dozen from the different villages.

'Rabbits fetched a good price in the war, but we couldn't do much rabbitin' on the forestry. The estate had three gamekeepers and a rabbit catcher. There was always a little bit of friction between the head forester and the head keeper when we wanted to work in certain areas. In the old days the keeper always came first, because estate owners had more money to spend on sport, but now there's only one keeper here and the area of forestry has increased slightly, being about a thousand acres.

'In 1937 almost all the forestry on Lazonby Fell was wiped out by fire, which went right through from the Plumpton road to the Lazonby road. In those days there was no help from the fire brigade, and it was left to the workers to try to beat it out. It swept through heather with flames six feet high, and they had to fight it night and day for a week because it got into the peat

and kept breaking out again. Sometimes you could hear it roaring a mile away. It was such a waste, though some of the blackened stumps were OK for railway sleepers and pit props.'

Arnold married in 1942 and was given a little estate cottage.

'In those days the village practically relied on the estate for work. We were a very close community, and after the war held a big village welcome-home party for the troops. I was secretary of the fund and every man away, as well as the Land Army, was given some of the money we raised through sports days, concerts and whist drives.

*Overleaf:
The farmer's
daughter helps out
by collecting
fleeces on a
Cumberland farm*

*Haytiming for
Arnold*

Arnold's mother and sister minding the horses while the men were eating before they went off to cut corn

GULGAITH CUMBERLAND Nº 17

'All estate employees were expected to beat on the shoot if required, yet those who came in specially got ten shillings each. I've done it practically every year since 1938. But we always got a hot meal for lunch. During the war there was only the odd shoot as no real rearing was allowed.'

At first, Arnold worked mostly with Clydesdale horses in the woods:

'All the timber used to be shifted by horse and wagon after being felled by axe and crosscut saw. The horses took it out to the road, and if they couldn't pull it, they rolled it. At the roadside we had a 'three-legs', about fifteen to twenty feet high, to hoist the logs onto the wagon. But sometimes we put a ramp up the wagon and the horses pulled the logs up from the other side. Occasionally when you went to anchor a horse up it was gone. And you couldn't go home with just one, as you need two to pull the weight. So you had to tie one horse up while you went in search of the other.'

Arnold's duties were very varied and included fencing as well as sawmill work, but he always preferred being outdoors.

'Mind you, getting about used to be difficult in the more remote parts, as we only had a horse or a bike for transport. Some of the old chaps used to take enough food for themselves and their horses for two or three days when the work was too distant to make it worth going home at night. There used to be a special stable up on the fell.

'I was sorry to see the horses go, but towards the end, when the old horseman retired, we had to feed and muck them out ourselves, at week-ends as well. Up to 1955 we had nothing but two horses, two carts and the wood wagon. Then we got the Fordson Major tractor.

'Another noted machine in the area was the steam Fodden wagon, which transported stone from the Lazonby Fell quarries, some going to Calthwaite and Plumpton railway stations and then abroad. The quarries were worked by the estate, and the various colours of stone went to build local houses, the white sandstone being used for Brackenburgh mansion. The stone was loaded onto the Fodden by hand or by hand-crane. The wagon came off the road in about 1939.'

When Arnold became head forester he had a team of eight men, which had fallen to four by the time he retired from full-time work at the age of sixty-five.

Arnold (left) receives his Royal Agricultural Society 40-year long-service medal from Princess Alice, the Duke of Gloucester's mother, in 1979; he is watched by his boss, Joe Harris

The Hurdle-maker

George May: Hampshire

THE HURDLE-MAKER

The Old Sarum Road from Winchester westwards is a long, narrow lane where cars must pull to the verge when they meet. For much of the way it follows the course of the old Roman road to Salisbury and passes through some delightful countryside of downs and woodland, punctuated by ancient tumuli and other earthworks. A few miles beyond Winchester the original Roman route passes close to the old village of King's Somborne, the largest of the Sombornes that form the heart of one of the few areas of Hampshire hazel that are still actively coppiced.

*Opposite:
George May with
one of his six-foot
hurdles*

In a place of great peace and solitude, reached from a dwindling farm lane by a muddy, winding track George May is weaving hazel hurdles. He takes an immense pride in 'his' woodland and knows every inch of it; after all, he has been working his way in rotation through this and a nearby wood for most of his seventy or more years, and his father worked the same rotation before him. When a man knows that he will be returning to a patch several times in his own lifetime, he takes great care in maintaining its health and vigour. Methodically he works through, taking a crop here one year to work up into hurdles and moving on to another section, completing the cycle eight or nine years later when the poles thrown up by the stools he had trimmed will be of just the right size for cutting again. 'Hazel goes on forever but what keeps it alive, you might say, is to keep it cut in rotation. Once it gets over twenty, maybe twenty-five, years old it begins to play out. Yeah.'

This particular wood is an extensive area of hazel, the shrubby layer dotted with standard oaks well spaced out, and the size of the harvested patch feels comfortably human in its scale. It is surrounded by patches at different stages in the cycle: each is more or less uniform overall, but older or younger than its neighbour. George looks around proudly. 'Up here it's all nice young woods been cut behind. This is where my father worked, and this is the exact same spot where I learned as well, same spot exactly.' It is quite beautifully quiet here and the modern world seems an age away.

George can remember the days when there were more than twenty of them working the hazel locally. Today there are but two of them in the village of King's Somborne. In the old days, George explains, hurdles were '*the* fencing', the ordinary, everyday fencing used not only by shepherds but also to surround cottage gardens and other areas. Today, the situation is reversed: larchlap and other types of fencing have replaced

Roe deer

it and now George's hurdles are bought 'as a specialty, you might say, or novelty, if you like to put it, and there's a certain class of people that will have nothing different because it's the old English craft. Oh yes.' Long gone are the days when great cartloads of hurdles would be taken down to the local railway station for dispatch all over the country.

There is still plenty of hazel for the harvesting round abouts. The Little Somborne estate, where he is working now, has three hundred acres of the crop, and there is also the Sandydown estate three or four miles away, with a fine setting from which the views stretch to Stockbridge Down in one direction and to a tower on the distant southern horizon in the other.

George was born just after World War I in the same village of King's Somborne where he lives now, though not in the same house. His father's name was, oddly, Holland May. 'Because his father — that's my grandfather — emigrated to Canada for two or three years and the boat they came back on was called the Holland, and he was born after they got back so they named him Holland. Things had been pretty poor in this country back in the 1870s, 1880s, and you could emigrate out there for next to nothing — and they promised all this, that and the other, but when they got there they found it was just the opposite so they came back again. Back to his old job here.'

He well remembers the time when JHB from Astolat first came across Holland May working in a wood alongside the road and began to buy his hurdles — and May hurdles have been bought by the Betteridges ever since. 'They wouldn't get them from anybody else!' he says emphatically. He prefers to sell wholesale in this way rather than retail the hurdles himself. 'Well, you'd need a truck — you have to go and deliver. It's best for me to sell loads like I do to Astolat: they pick them up and that finishes it. It's no trouble.' George finds no shortage of demand and he makes nothing but hurdles, though others make thatching spars as well. 'And there used to be crate rods, for up the Midlands — go round tubs

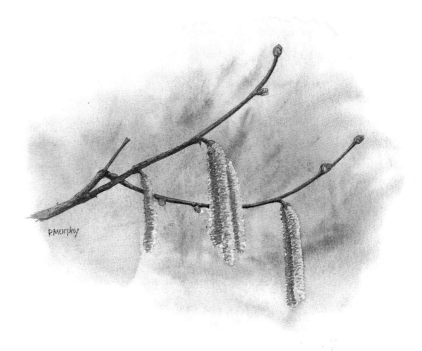

and that sort of thing. Well, that's no longer needed now. But one or two still make spars round here.'

He did not have much choice in the matter when he first became a hurdle-maker: the only work available was either on the farms or in the woods, and it was natural to follow the family tradition. As a schoolboy, he used to join his father in the woods on Saturdays and gradually picked up the craft from him that way, starting with many blisters on his hands. He worked with him on a full-time basis when he left school at fourteen and stayed with him for another five years. 'I didn't quite have the wrist for it when I was young. You got to grow into it, see. Now my muscles are just trained to the job, of course. See, with those six-foot panels there, they weigh perhaps half a hundredweight — yeah, they would do. Well, I can pick one of those up and throw 'em on the lorry. But I couldn't go and pick up half a hundredweight of potatoes, you see — same weights, but the balance is different.' George, incidentally, is barely five feet tall.

In the days when he helped his father, the system was based on auctions. 'They had auction sales here for the wood and you used to buy so

Hazel catkins

Opposite:
A farmer using
hurdles to create
pens for his sheep

Billhook

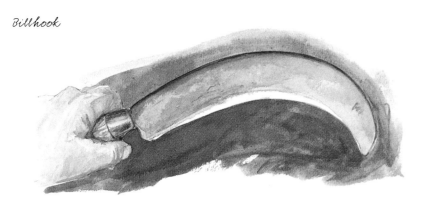

much for the twelvemonth, every year. Of course, that's discontinued here now. They'd have it just here, at Little Somborne, give us bread and cheese. The auctioneer used to provide plenty of beer, you see – gave them a good drink before a sale and then of course they had too much and got lolled about and the auctioneer talked up the bid, then they used to run up the bidder – heh! Yeah. Well, father and me, we could see what the game was and we never had a drink, keep away from that.' (George is a deeply religious man.) 'But the others – yeah, they'd buy what they didn't mean to and for too much.'

Today George gets all the standing wood he wants – landowners are only too happy to see the hazel put to good use. He does not need to travel further than four miles, a journey he used to do on a pushbike, then a motorbike, but now in the van. His skills are rare enough for him to pick and choose.

'Oh, its no fool's game, no, it isn't. It might look easy doing it but it's no fool's game. Splitting it, that's an art. Use a billhook for that, still do. I've had one of them for years and years – I've got one now over a hundred years old, with a crook on it. One's a family one, one I had given me twenty years ago, a small one. But I've been using a chainsaw for twenty years now for sawing down – we used to use an axe or a big bill-hook but we do it the easy way now. The May, Way, they call it! And they said in the beginning the chainsaw would hurt the stools, but see for yourself – if you do it right with the chainsaw it's probably less harmful than a cackhanded man with an axe or billhook.'

At nineteen, he went off on his own down to Bishop's Waltham. The war came along and he was exempt from military service, as his hurdles were in great demand for the war effort. In the early part of the war, it was always expected that the Germans would invade southern England and thousands of men laboured to dig out anti-tank trenches. The sides of the trenches were shored up with hurdles and George used to make truckloads of them down at Wickham. 'I worked all night some nights, because the army

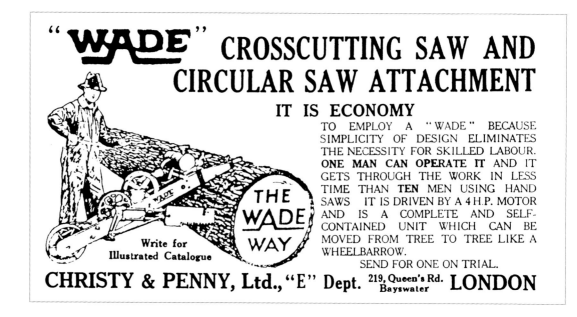

wanted them in a hurry to get a certain job done. Up in the woods with a lantern covered with a sheet of galvanised. Oh yeah. I could tell a few stories. Jerries used to be overhead, bombs dropping across there. One day when it was cloudy they come down low and machine-gunned right through the woods where I was. Oh yeah. They knew there was a lot of ammunition dumps in there, you see. So I just stood behind a tree until they'd gone.'

He stayed down in the Bishop's Waltham area from 1940 until 1964, mostly cutting the hazel before it was cleared for other timber crops. 'They planted up with fir and one thing and another. The hazel — well, for the owner there was nothing in it. Couldn't get anything for it — they used to *give* it to me to cut, you see. It's changed again now: they are not allowed to push any more hazel out like that now.'

The war years had made a big difference to the hazel industry. Gradually, as the older men died, the younger ones no longer came forward: other industries had developed. 'After the war there was the building, the motor trade and all that, and they went into easier things, the younger ones, as they grew up.' But George just kept at it. The work itself did not change very much, except for the size of hurdle. 'In my grandfather's day there wasn't the big hurdles made. There's all sheep hurdles, see, about three feet high for the sheep. But then after the *first* World War they made the bigger ones, up to six feet high and six feet square. I still make them — I've got some now, ready to go away next week. I don't know why they started making the big ones then. Started making four feet, five feet, six feet high. Six feet is the most popular now, for gardens, windbreaks and that. Still make the sheep hurdle *size* but they're not used for sheep now, they're just fencing.'

He cuts during most months of the year except from mid-April to mid-June. 'Well, the

sap is coming up then and the hurdles wouldn't last very long. It's best to work when the wood's cut and *dried* – oh yes, it makes a far better hurdle, so up until then I get enough cut down to last me to middle of June.'

His production rate is high and he makes a very tidy hurdle. He proudly shows some photographs taken for Hampshire County Council and others, including a museum, a few years ago: in one, he is wearing a dashing red beret, but that was only for the occasion, a bit of a joke – it's not his customary wear. He does always wear strong knee-pads, though: he uses his knee to push down the rods as he weaves them, rarely resorting to any knocking-down tool.

The hurdle is set up with the help of a heavy timber block, which he calls a frame or mould, drilled with holes to take the uprights, or sails, while the work is in progress. The line of holes is deliberately but slightly curved, which seems to help the hurdle keep its shape later. 'If I make

them straight, they'd probably go inside out,' he explains, 'but if I make them curved they gradually straighten out. Then of course they tightens up a bit as well. They've always been made on a slight curve.'

There are nine uprights for the standard length of six feet, though it would be possible to make a wider hurdle by adding more sails. The lower courses of the weaving are made good and tight by using round or 'brown' small wood – entire rods complete with bark – and so are the final rods, which are given a double twist to keep them in place. The rest of the hurdle is normally filled with split rods, with all the split faces to the same side, so that the finished hurdle is white on one side and brown on the other. It is exactly like weaving a basket except for the wrist-breaking art of twisting the rods to break the fibres at the end of the row before doubling back to weave in the opposite direction.

During the 1950s and early 1960s, when

George was working through fifty acres at Sladford Wood, Rowhay, Lower Upham – not far from Marwell Zoo – he often slept in his caravan nearby rather than return home to King's Somborne. His father was alive then and still making a few hurdles himself. Some of the hurdles were used as sheep pens for early lambing even in the 1960s and he was still kept busy all year round by the demand for his products.

Unlike many other woodland craftsmen, he does not usually bother with demonstrating at shows now. 'It's no advantage. Waste of time, really,' he says. He would much rather be working quietly in his local woods, churning out the hurdles and building up good stacks of them for collecting by Astolat.

Over tea at home (and a good slice of his birthday cake: he was seventy-four at the beginning of May 1993) he talks about the village of King's Somborne, which has changed a lot in recent years. 'Well, your original villagers have died off and there's been a bit of building, and a

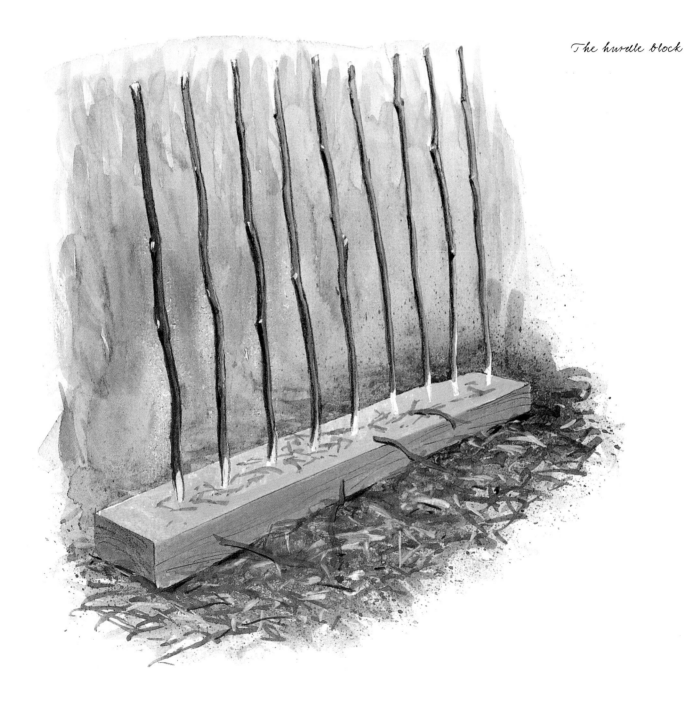

The hurdle block

Opposite:
A thatcher using
hazel rods to
secure the straw

lot of fresh people come in. It isn't so rough as it was. It was known as a rough village. I remember up the other end of the village, used to get a punch-up every Saturday night. Don't get that now, it's just the opposite now. Used to fight with other villages, you see. If you wanted to go the next place up, you had to fight your way in!

George admits that he is 'getting on a bit' now and does not know how much longer he will keep on with it. 'The young don't want hard work today, you know. Some would like to, perhaps, if there were a pound or two to be made, but they don't want hard work. And it *is* hard work. I only do four or five days a week now – it was six when I started. But I don't work in the wet – I work in the open, see. The work keeps you fit – sure does. It's not good to retire – I how too many who stop working and rust away and die.'

As we finally part, I shake his hand. It is as hard and smooth as polished wood.

HAMPSHIRE HAZEL FACTS

Number of hazel coppice workers, southern counties, 1950s (Source: Forestry Commission, *Utilisation of Hazel Coppice, 1956*)

Hampshire & Isle of Wight	77
Dorset	52
Wiltshire	16
Surrey	20
Sussex	48
Total throughout the country	300

In Sussex hazel coppice working appears to have died out except on one estate and in Surrey it is found on only two estates. Outside the central southern counties (Hampshire, Wiltshire and Dorset)...no county had more than three full-time workers. In 1990 there were 70 full-time and part-time underwood workers operating in Hampshire and the Isle of Wight with at least 45 of them resident and the others coming in from Dorset and Wiltshire. Today the industry is in the middle of a revival, mainly on the back of a buoyant thatching industry with its prodigious demand for spars (15 to 20 million a year) and a renewed interest in hurdles for garden fences. Many new entrants have appeared in the last few years.

Hampshire County Council, *Hazel Coppice, past, present and future*.
The Hampshire Experience, 1991

In cycle-Hazel Coppice in Hampshire:

1895	95,000 acres (probably an overestimate)
1947	3,800 acres (including [plus?] derelict: 32,312)
1986	1,235 acres (overestimate)
1990	670 acres

Memories of Grease Corner

Bill Sidwell, Railwayman

MEMORIES OF GREASE CORNER

Bill Sidwell started work on the railway in 1927 aged sixteen. Born in 1911 in Lincoln, he moved with his parents to Derby, then at the heart of the railway industry in Britain, when he was two. His immediate family had no connection with the railways (although an uncle had been a signalman) but transport, in the form of early motor lorries, provided employment for his father. 'Dad was one of the last people, in fact, to drive a lorry with solid rubber tyres and no windscreen. Lorries were an unusual sight at that time, as most road transport was still by horse-drawn wagon. My dad had started work as a chauffeur at about the turn of the century when cars were also a novelty on the road.'

Living in Derby, then one of the biggest railway centres in Britain, it was almost a foregone conclusion that Bill should go into railway work; he'd always been interested in the practical side of things, so when he left school, he chose to start as an apprentice engineer at the Derby locomotive works. Day one saw him in the machine shop, in grease corner, as it was known: 'I was set to work putting threads on nuts – that's what everyone started on in those days. Everything seemed to be done in vast quantities of oil; at the end of the first week I was absolutely covered in the stuff.' Bill laughs loudly at the memory, a reaction typical of his tolerant and amused view of life.

After that grubby introduction he moved around through the various departments and workshops: machine shop, boiler shop, erecting shop, foundry. This was where the practical work was done, the work that kept the railway functioning. His next move was to what was then known as the progress office: 'This is where the work was all planned, and it's from here that the instructions and orders for work emanated. What struck me most about it was how meticulous and thorough everything seemed to be.'

After a few months he saw a sign on a notice-board inviting people to apply for what was called a 'privileged apprenticeship'. Having only recently left grammar school he thought he might have a chance. He applied, was accepted, and to this day chuckles at what the job involved. 'Well, it was ridiculous really, because all the privilege part of it meant was that you spent two and a half days each week at technical college and got absolutely no pay for it!'

During the 1920s and 1930s there was no set pattern of progress toward the goal of fully qualified fitter or engineer; it all depended on vacancies and seniority. It was only much later that a proper training course was instituted. But for now, Bill was happy in his new role: 'Our chief engineer was Sir Henry Fowler, and I remember he got all us privileged apprentices together one day and said he'd agreed a big concession for us: instead of disappearing for two and a half days each week – unpaid, if you recall – we would now be sent off to technical college one day a week. And the really good news was that we still wouldn't be paid for it!'

In Derby the atmosphere of the trains was everywhere – 'they absolutely dominated the town,' says Bill – and once you'd started work in the industry it would have been highly unusual

to have opted out and tried something else, as Bill explains: 'Well, a lot of it had to do with the Depression in the 1930s. You were so lucky to have a job of any sort that you counted your lucky stars and never even thought about changing. Apart from anything else, in Derby there wasn't much else to do anyway. When I started, the other problem was that the country was still on the road to recovery from the Great War, and when you did get a job there was no career structure or career planning involved as there is today; no one thought about such things.

'My father first spoke to a local builder about getting me a job. At that time most boys left school at fourteen, but I'd won a scholarship to the local grammar school so I got another two years. The builder I might have gone to work for had a relative who worked on the railway, and he suggested I apply for the apprenticeship. I remember being asked at the interview what I eventually wanted. I said I wanted to be a draughtsman, but the man interviewing me put "fitter" on the paper. I don't think he liked the idea of my getting a bit above myself.'

Bill was apprenticed for five years, and he knew that to improve his chances of future promotion he would need to get a technical qualification: 'You had to pass at a number of things,' he recalls. 'For example, technical drawing was a major part of the apprenticeship—I remember it took up about half our time, as well as three evenings a week. At the end of the five years I

A 4F 0-6-0 locomotive under construction at Derby locomotive works in 1926

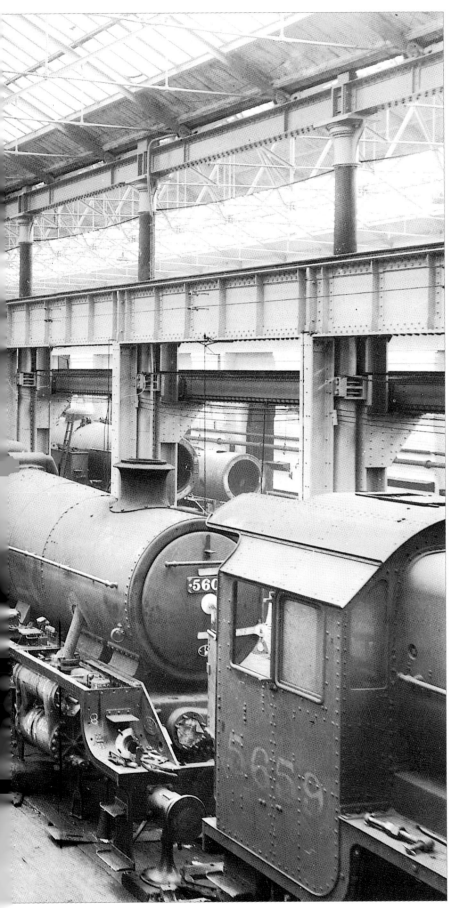

got what I suppose would be the equivalent of a BSc today. It was a pretty thorough course: we dealt with the mechanics of fluids, higher maths, the structure of metals — the whole lot. I got my college diploma and then joined the Institute of Mechanical Engineers, and ultimately I qualified as a fellow of the institute; that was a proud moment.'

Bill's engineering skills, although certainly comparable to those needed for general construction, were actually directed at fulfilling the needs of the industry that dominated the town in which he'd been brought up. It's difficult to imagine, now that so much heavy industry has closed down, that Derby was almost entirely taken up with the railway in the early part of the twentieth century, and that by the 1930s some six thousand people worked in the carriage works, and another six thousand in the railways proper. But despite the demand for qualified people, jobs were still scarce. 'A lot of apprentices were simply discharged at the end of their five years,' explains Bill. 'You had no guarantee of a job at the end. Some of those who weren't required went to Rolls Royce who were just starting up in Derby. I remember we all used to go into town on the trams which ran in from all directions. We lived in a village called Challaston a few miles outside Derby, and I saw the tram lines laid to my village and I lived to see them all dug up again. Challaston was on a branch line which closed in 1929, so for my first two years I went by train, thereafter on the tram. I was pleased about the tram coming really, because the train station was quite a way from my home — a lot of village stations tended to be quite a distance from the centre of the village. There were buses, too, and I think it was the buses that really killed the local railway.

The erecting shop at Derby locomotive works in 1938

*Previous page:
The 'Crabbs' were
the first mixed
traffic Moguls for
the LMS, and
could be seen all
over the Derby area
from the late 1920s;
the example seen
here is hauling a
passenger train at
Ambergate, north
of Derby*

'I was one of the lucky ones, and when I'd finished my training I was asked if I wanted to go in what was called the Motive Power Department. I was accepted here and went to London immediately for eighteen months.'

In London, Bill continued his training. He was based in Camden, to the north of the City, and the next year and a half was spent doing three-month stints in different departments: three months with the fitters, whose job it was to examine and repair the locomotives; three months with the shed staff cleaning boilers; three months with the running foreman, the man who told the drivers where they were going; and finally three months on the footplate on shunters, local passenger trains and passenger expresses out of Euston.

'I remember there was no difference in status between drivers of expresses and drivers of local trains,' he recalls. 'If an express driver pulled up alongside a shunting engine at Euston and the driver shouted over to the shunting engine driver, "What price your little loco?" the little loco driver would always shout back, "Same as yours – ninety bob a week!" I enjoyed those eighteen months enormously; I met some wonderful old Cockney characters and had some marvellous experiences on the footplate. The pay was rotten, of course – in fact it was barely enough to pay for my digs in Chalk Farm. If I remember rightly my digs were about thirty bob a week and my pay sixty-five bob.

After his eighteen months in London, Bill set off back to Derby to the old headquarters of the

ON THE FOOTPLATE

'Footplate work was undoubtedly the most interesting aspect of the work, but it was uncomfortable. I don't think people realise how uncomfortable it was, and they certainly don't if they never travelled on it themselves. You were more or less open to the elements, it was noisy and dirty, and it could also be very bumpy. But I remember how impressed I was when I saw the way a loco picked up water in a scoop while moving – although it didn't always go as smoothly as it did the first time I saw it. One day for instance I was on the footplate heading towards London when the locomotive failed and we had to change it at Derby. We got going again on a London North Western Prince of Wales, only to find that we were soon short of steam. We put the water scoop down and then found we couldn't get it up again, with the result that we got half a ton of water over us – the whole footplate was absolutely soaked.

' On another occasion we were going to what was then known as London Road Manchester (it's now Manchester Piccadilly) on a Royal Scot-type loco called Girl Guide – I remember it was No 6169 – and we'd just stopped at the buffers at London Road Manchester. We were watching the passengers leave the station when a little old lady noticed the name of the loco and smiled up at us. 'How nice,' she said, 'I used to be a girl guide.' I remember the old driver mumbled after she'd left, 'God help any girl guide whose as rough as this old girl!' What he meant was that the Royal Scot was a good engine but it was bloody uncomfortable to ride in. A lot of London Midland engines were very rough riding. Great Western engines were definitely better; they had a few shortcomings but no Great Western man would ever admit it or tell you what they were.'

LMS for a period in what was called the shopping bureau. This was where the engines were repaired and where essential maintenance work was carried out, including major overhauls. The thing that struck Bill most was the skill of the men in the workshops: 'I spent a few months here, and then went back to Euston doing the same work, more or less. Seeing how those men kept the engines going was a lesson; they knew them inside out and would make light work of what, to a newcomer, looked impossibly difficult.'

Next stop for Bill was Rugby: 'They moved everyone a lot in those days, from the highest to the lowest. It would have been about 1935 when I got back to my home town, and there I came across a man in the works who was doing what was called a work study. Basically he was a sort of time-and-motion man, looking at how we did things, and assessing whether they could be done more efficiently. I was made part of the study and I had to time the fitters at their various tasks – and that didn't go down well, I can tell you. I did nine months of that. It was interesting, though nothing compared to being on the footplate.'

Eventually Bill was put in charge of a depot at Widnes, Lancashire, as a running shed foreman, a job that was later re-christened shed master. Nine months later he did the same job at Llandudno Junction, where he was assistant supervisor: 'I remember one Christmas Eve I'd got permission to go home on the two o'clock train once the afternoon foreman had relieved me. He turned up at two o'clock prompt and I went off to catch my train – only to discover that there was no locomotive to be found. This was particularly funny as I was supposed to be in charge of making sure that all the engines were where they should be at the appropriate time. I rang the controller, and more by luck than judgement, managed to get a freight train that was at Rhyll. We brought it down, turned it round and I was at home for Christmas – but only just.

'Just before I left Llandudno Junction a chap rang from Crewe to tell me I'd been given a post elsewhere. For some reason which escapes me now he couldn't tell me exactly where, but he explained that I would receive the details in a

*Fortunately
accidents, like this
one at Oakley
Viaduct in 1949,
were rare*

letter. The letter duly arrived and off I went to Mirfield in Yorkshire. I was to be shift foreman: my first proper staff appointment. All the others had been in the way of gaining experience and training. There were three shifts here, from midnight to 8am, 8am to 4pm, and 4pm to midnight, but luckily the running shed foreman did the midnight to 8am shift. I worked six days a week, but not Sundays.'

Bill found that he'd been thrown in at the deep end: he spent every minute rushing around making sure all the locomotives were being properly serviced, and making sure the right drivers and firemen turned up at the right time, and all this had to be done to time. Mirfield had local passenger work to Leeds, Huddersfield and Holmfirth, and of course there were specials and excursion trains to organise:

'I was there in 1937, the coronation year of George VI. The coronation was on the Thursday before Whit Sunday and it was a national holiday so we ran specials to Blackpool. On Whit Sunday morning I got a call to say we'd been asked to

supply fifty specials for Blackpool on the Monday. "How many can you do?" I was asked. I finished by being able to offer about thirteen, but we had to use six double-home drivers – that is, drivers who lodged away from home. Also, from Mirfield there are twenty-seven variations of the route to Blackpool, if you can believe it, so I had to make sure that each driver knew the particular route he was going to take. It was a bit of a nightmare, but we got there in the end.'

This was the sort of pressure on which Bill thrived, but in addition to problems caused by timetabling and organisation, there was the sheer graft of engineering work that had to go on twenty-four hours a day if the trains were to be able to do their job.

On the London Midland steam raisers were not employed, and the firemen were expected to fire the engines themselves. This was also known as fire-dropping. It was a very dirty job, and it is one of the reasons why Bill, like so many steam railwaymen, considers that the men welcomed diesel when it came in. Whatever the pleasures of driving steam trains there is no doubt that one or two jobs, like fire-dropping and boiler washing, really didn't have anything to recommend them; indeed by the 1950s it had become increasingly difficult to get people to do this sort of work at all. In the 1930s when jobs were in short supply it didn't matter how dirty the job was – you could always get someone to do it.

'Boiler washing was a filthy job,' says Bill, 'but loco boilers were still always cleaned once a week or once a fortnight. On the Western Region we didn't go in for water softening which some areas had. Where you used soft water it meant a loco boiler only had to be washed perhaps once a month. This was a big saving because it can take twelve hours to wash a boiler properly.'

After Mirfield, Bill was given a shed at Oldham in Lancashire: 'More moving round the country,' he says with a grin. 'It never seemed to stop, and they'd almost expect you to go anywhere. At Oldham I looked after twenty-three locomotives. It's difficult to say exactly how many loco sheds there were nationally at this time, but there would have been eighty or ninety districts, each with five or six sheds, so that gives you some idea. Most towns had their own locomotive depot.'

From Oldham, Bill went to Manchester as a locomotive inspector; he was there from 1938 until 1944. During the war the railways really came into their own because there was no petrol for private cars: 'Everyone relied on us, which is why, like many railwaymen, I couldn't be released for war service because ours was a reserved occupation. Mind you, judging by the way railways were targeted by the Germans I don't think we got off that lightly; the Manchester office got blitzed and an awful lot of depots were damaged in the war. Many were never rebuilt.

'When we knew war was inevitable I was given the job of supplying every depot with what we called anti-glare sheets. These were blackout sheets, made out of canvas that had been treated with waterproofing; each one had to have fittings for the various classes of engine, and I had to make sure it all went smoothly. On the railways, as pretty much in every walk of life, the war created a great feeling of camaraderie.'

Towards the end of the war Bill went as an assistant district locomotive superintendent to Gloucester; the job involved freight traffic to the ports, and he was there from 1944 to 1949 looking after seventy engines as well as several subdepots. 'I was at Gloucester in 1948 when nationalisation came and I can honestly say it made absolutely no difference to me; but on the dot of midnight on the day it happened, all the trains in the area blew their whistles. I remember my phone ringing at around this time, about a train that had been derailed on the Great Western. We were the London and Midland, but we had a crane that would be suitable for this particular derailment. When the person on the other end

STEAM RAISERS

'From an engineering point of view a steam engine presents interesting problems,' says Bill. 'From cold, it takes eight hours to get an engine ready to go. The reason is, that you've got two to three thousand gallons of water to be heated before anything can happen, and that water has to reach boiling point under pressure before you can move anything. We had men called steam raisers to get the locomotives going from cold. The steam raiser was told what time the engine was needed, and it was then left to him to start work at a time that would ensure the train would go out on time. He'd start the fire by putting a bit of wood and a few rags in – it really was as simple a starting point as that, just like starting a coal fire at home. With a steam engine, of course, he'd keep adding coal until he had a hell of a blaze going and the water had reached the required temperature.

'Once the water was boiling you could put on the blower to improve the draught; that made more heat, but burnt more coal. One trick on the midnight shift when you were firing engines for 6am was to put your hand on the ash pan – if that was warm you knew all would be well for the morning. At Mirfield we had sixty locomotives and one steam raiser per shift, but a good man could do a lot on his own.'

1952: the funeral train of King George VI leaving Paddington station

of the line asked for the crane he said he wanted it for the British Railways Board, and this sounded so strange because it was the first time I'd heard the name.'

Bill thinks nationalisation was a good thing in many ways; for instance, it helped speed up the exchange of information and ideas between different areas. Financially, however, it made little initial difference. 'When nationalisation took effect the railways were very run down, largely because of the war and the lack of funds that resulted from it. Before that the government had always taken the profits the railways had made, but they never put anything back; to some extent that situation continued when nationalisation came, too, and the move from steam to diesel was all done on a shoestring.

Some railways even toyed with the idea of running buses – they had quite a fleet for taking stuff from various depots. To my mind, rail never went sufficiently in search of business because for so long, and particularly during the war, they'd had a virtual monopoly on transport.'

Nationalisation also meant that, at last, standard locomotives began to be built, and they were still being built as diesel trains began to come in. After various jobs in different parts of the country Bill ended up back in London; and then in 1963, a decision was taken to cease classifying footplate staff as engineers. Instead they were placed under the control of operations, a recognition, it seems, of the difference between being a steam-train driver and a diesel or electric driver.

'People were excited about the new diesel

trains because of the novelty, but they created as many problems as they solved. Apart from anything else, there were so many different kinds of diesel engine, and there was no attempt to be consistent when it came to buying them. The last of our steam engines – I'd inherited some five hundred at Old Oak Common in West London in 1959 – ran from Oxford to Birmingham. In many respects I was sad at the end.'

The most memorable event in Bill's forty-five years' service came on the day that Winston Churchill was buried in 1965. 'That was an extraordinary day in every respect: so much meticulous planning went into it, but we only narrowly avoided a very embarrassing incident. I had the responsibility of making sure the funeral train stopped at precisely the right spot so that the bearer party could get the coffin out and down the ramp. The train stopped just right as it turned out, but when the guardsmen in the train tried to open the doors from the inside, their combined weight – they were all standing on the side of the train by the doors – tipped the coach over so far

that the door wouldn't open. Nothing happened for a few seconds, then the Duke of Norfolk marched up and asked what was going on. I'd hidden six platelayers nearby in case there was trouble, so they rushed up and moved the wooden ramp which had been jamming the doors. Once the doors were open, the ramp went back and the ceremony could continue. With the television cameras there and people watching all over the world, it was a tense moment, I can tell you.

'Another incident I remember well involved the royal train. It used to come through regularly, but on this particular occasion the present Queen and Prince Philip were on a three-day visit to the Worcester area. They were sleeping on the train and we had to stable it on a branch line just the other side of Worcester itself; it was about midnight, and we were at the branch line waiting for the train to arrive. It came into view, and then at that very minute we heard three shots. Immediately all hell broke loose – the train stopped and everyone seemed to panic. The three shots were to signify danger: we knew

3440 City of Truro at Old Oak Common in 1957; this locomotive achieved a speed of 102mph on the descent of Wellington Bank, Somerset, in May 1905

they weren't gunshots, they were detonators, but that might mean another train was on a collision course.

'Anyway we discovered that a platelayer had put the shots down because a horse had jumped on the line. So we got a tow-rope and set off after the horse which, luckily, we found quite quickly. But heaven knows what the royal party must have thought when they heard those bangs.

'Each region had its own royal train in those days, but I think Prince Charles is the member of the royal family who still uses the one remaining royal train.

'The other royal train I remember particularly was the King George VI which carried the body of the King from Paddington in 1952. I remember the men lining up along the trackside and all along the platform with their caps off. Mind you, that train wasn't the King George VI at all – the real King George VI was being repaired at the time, so we took the name-plate off it and put it on another train. I don't think that's ever been revealed before. We nearly had a problem, too, because that engine had to be kept ready to go for a long time, with plenty of steam and so on – but it was also important that it didn't make too much noise; and as the delay lengthened, we thought we might have to let her get rid of some steam, and that would have made a terrible racket. Anyway, we got the band to play again (and loudly) and we put more water in, and that just about did the trick until we were ready to go.'

Bill has nothing but praise for the men he worked with over the years – 'the drivers were a great bunch, to a man,' he insists – and whether a problem arose with a royal train or a humble freight wagon, someone could always be found to sort the situation out. But as in all walks of life, the railway organ-isation was subject to human error: 'Most accidents that I can recall – and there were regular freight derailments – were due to human error. The worst I remember happened on Sharnbrook Viaduct near Bedford, when the signalman let a one-hundred-wagon coal train through and it ran into another coal train. The loco and tender and thirty wagons swept over the side of the viaduct, and the driver and fireman were killed; it was a terrible mess. However, when you think that the whole system in the steam days was run using only men and mechanical aids, it is a tribute to their skill that so few accidents actually did occur.'

Workmen on the LMS cleaning engines in preparation for Easter

Survivor of the Trenches

Ned Turvey: Staffordshire

SURVIVOR OF THE TRENCHES

When 19-year-old gamekeeper Ned Turvey volunteered for the army in World War I he was completely unaware of the carnage which lay ahead of him. Aged ninety-eight when he was interviewed, he remained a firm believer in discipline and reflected on the sad decline of the old-fashioned virtues which helped him survive both the terror of the trenches and a lifetime in keepering.

Five-year-old Ned Turvey (extreme right) at a shoot in 1900. His father is far left, holding a gun

One of seven children, Edward Victor Randolph Turvey (always known as Ned) was born on 20 September 1895, at Hilton Park, near Wolverhampton, where his father was head-keeper for A L Vernon for twelve years. His paternal grandfather had been an estate labourer.

At the age of three-and-a-half, Ned went to Essington School – 'all galvanised sheeting, just like the church. We used to walk through the woods to get there. I had a good, firm master. People used to say, "Mr Walker's a very good man – he goes to church on Sunday and prays to the Lord to give him strength to wallop the kids on Monday". Parents don't bother with their children now. It's all too easy.

'Owing to ill health in the family, the doctor advised my parents to leave the house, so in 1900 we moved to Lord Hatherton's estate, between Cannock and Penkridge, where father was head keeper. Then I went to Cannock National School.

'Father was a good provider and we was a happy family. We always went to church and Sunday school and was taught things properly. There was always a rabbit or pigeon to eat and you always had a good garden. Mother was a tiptop cook too – been in gentlemen's service. We 'ad a lot of good soup then and plenty of good bacon. All meat was no price: hip-bone steak just 10d (4p) a pound and sausages 4d a pound – none of these fancy prices now. Meat was much tastier too, with a little bit of fat – that's what you want. Mother always knew what to buy – she 'ad to as there was nine of us in the house with a keeper lodgin'.

'Our lighting was all oil lamps of course, but things improved later on when the Tilley lamp came in. We always burned coal and logs. Even

Philip Murphy

Underkeeper Ned Turvey,
aged 17, in 1912

Volunteer for the
Great War, aged 19

when I got married to Alice in 1921 coal was still only 14/6d a ton, and half a crown to draw it with horse and cart. Now only last week I paid £150 for a ton and a half – and that was supposed to be a special price. No – it's all twisted now. When I was a lad, ordinary whisky was only four bob a bottle, but Black Label was twelve shillings.

'Years ago a lad used to bring out the Guns' lunches from Paterson's at Birmingham – everythin' you could want. Then my wife took over, and everybody loved mother's damson jam. Before the first war father used to get Flower's best bitter delivered from Penkridge for 10d a gallon. Even the very best bitter was only shilling a gallon. It came on the train, then the local grocer brought it out.

'Then there was plenty of wildlife of every description, including corncrakes, nightjars and quails. 'Course the vermin was kept down and that made the difference. There it is – the law of the land. And the woods was magnificent with bluebells and daffodils. I remember years later, when they cut all the trees down, I've never seen such a pretty sight as all the foxgloves.'

Because Ned had to walk three miles to school he became very familiar with all the birds and flowers which were still very common. But the daily exercise was never any excuse for slacking. Indeed, when Ned came out of school he often had to help dad on the rearing field. 'I suppose it was education as far as me father was concerned.'

Ned never had any secret ambition while still in education and it was no surprise when he left school, at the age of thirteen years and four months in 1908, to work with his father. 'Everythin' was dead against you then, and in the keeperin' world at least you very soon learned that a still tongue was a wise tongue.'

Without motorised transport in relatively isolated rural communities, Ned and his generation rapidly learned to become self-sufficient. And as the doctor had to be paid for his services, many folk had their own remedies for various ailments. Ned has certainly stuck by his. Indeed,

After two years of marriage it appeared that Alice ruled the Turvey roost!

as we spoke he noticed that I was looking distinctly uncomfortable because my long car journey had aggravated a back complaint. 'I reckon you've got a touch of lumbago there', he said. 'I've got a good cure for that – always carry a lump of nutmeg about in your pocket. I've got a little bit on me now.' And with that he reached deep into his trousers pocket to produce a little cloth bag, the drawstring of which he unravelled with some difficulty to reveal a piece of nutmeg worn smooth with the years. 'I can guarantee that if ever I forget it I get twinges. 'Course me father had it very bad.'

I asked how his dad had travelled around. 'Oh, he 'ad a bicycle. It'd be a strong one of course – an Ideal – because he was a big chap – eighteen stone. We all 'ad bikes in them days, soon as we could afford 'em. Mind you, the train service was good then, with lots more stations, and they was always on time.'

Ned's starting pay was seven shillings a week and he was general dogsbody for dad and two other keepers. 'I did all the odd jobs such as cleaning and feeding the dogs – retrievers and spaniels – and lookin' after the ferrets. We really kept the rabbits down then. After the main shooting was over I had to get two gallons of paraffin from a shop in the village, soak pieces of sacking, light them and drop 'em down the holes to stink the rabbits out. 'Course you 'ad a lighted piece with you all the time as there was no matches. This took me about a week, then the Guns had a day's shooting and killed about 150 rabbits.

'The keepers always had a nice tweed suit and a cap. We used to go to the best tailor in Wolverhampton – Burslem's, it's gone now. For four guineas you had big, skin leather leggings made in Germany, as well as the suit.

'Shooting was a real pleasure then – everybody was happy. I remember one time a Gun's hat blew off and 'e said "Don't worry, my dog will fetch it". Instead of that the dog buried it and we all had a jolly good laugh. It were the sort of thing that made a day. No one was bothered about these huge bags then. If they killed a hundred or more they was really pleased. 'Course, there was plenty of keepers then – everywhere. And there was always plenty of partridges for 1 September.

'In my young days all the shooting was walkin' the fields with the Guns in line through the roots. Partridges were everywhere and there were lots of hares. But it could be dangerous and if you got your dog lost that was the end of it till 'e was found. But I like duck shooting best of all, at night on a fed pond.

'When I was sixteen I took a chap's beat and became underkeeper, with full responsibility for a 140-acre of wood at Penkridge. Altogether we reared about 2,500 pheasants and there were traps all over the place then. The hedgehog was the worst vermin on a partridge beat. We 'ad to 'ave pole traps for the brown owl – they was very destructive, but I did protect the white owl.

'We bought some eggs, but plenty was picked up along the roadsides. Then the roads was just rough stones rolled in and when a car went by you saw the dust for hell of a while after.'

In January 1915 Ned joined the 8th South Staffordshire Regiment, 17th Division. 'We went to Lichfield Barracks for five days, then they put sixty of us on the trains and sent us down to Bovington Camp in Dorset. There we 'ad lots of bayonet practice and route marchin' round Tolpuddle and all about. But I took it all in me stride – we went to serve king and country and thought it'd be all over by Christmas. I met some very decent people, *very* decent, and in England the food was good.'

After two months Ned was sent to Lulworth Cove, where the men were under canvas. 'In April they ordered us to bathe in the sea, but it was too damn cold and we very soon put our clothes on. A month later we marched to Winchester, to Flower Down Camp, to fire our course over the range.' There certainly wasn't

much regard for human dignity in the Army then, as Ned bitterly recalls. 'Outside Winchester we all had to line up naked for a medical along the roadside. Anybody could 'ave come along and seen us.

'By golly there were mugs with rifles there, but we got by. After a short time we got on the train at Basingstoke and went to Dover, then crossed to Boulogne. They took us up in cattle trucks to St Omer and then we had to march the rest of the way, to a place called St Eloi. We were there seventeen days – went in spick and span and came out lousy as the Devil – just holdin' the line. We had a very good officer for our platoon, S R Edwards from Sussex, a grand chap who had the men's interest at heart. He wanted me to be a

sniper, which I didn't want. Anyway, he didn't last ten days in the trenches as a shell killed him by my side – 'ad his head half cut right off.

'Then I took up stretcher-bearing and as a Lance-Corporal I 'ad eight men under me. This lasted for two and a half years until the regiment was broken up with losses. I was then transferred to the 7th South Staffordshire Regiment, 11th Division. We travelled most parts of the line. It was all bad and dangerous and we got down ready for the Somme advance.

'In July 1916 we started at a place called Fricourt village, where we were rushed after another regiment had been in and got cut up badly. We hadn't been in the trenches long when I heard a shout for help, in no man's land. It was a German officer with a fractured femur, but he was not bleeding. I got some more stretcher-bearers across and we took him to the doctors' dug-out. We always treated everybody the same. Then he pulled his platinum ring off and gave it to me. Since then I have passed the ring on to my granddaughter.

'We then went to Delville Wood to hold on to it after the South Africans had been carved up. I was told there was a man in front wounded, so I crawled forward in the daylight to help him. I was about fifty yards out in no man's land and calling as quietly as I could when I felt a crack on my back. It was a sniper cut my webbing belt off with a bullet. Anyway I couldn't find the man, so I crawled back into the trenches.

'Next day I had another lucky escape when a shell killed two men in the trench within three yards of me. But everyone had that risk. We wrapped 'em up in oil cloth and took 'em down to the road for collection, but they were still just layin' there a week after when we came away. Your groundsheet was your coffin then.

'I spent my 21st birthday on the Somme, at Hebetune. Mother sent me a chicken and a plum puddin' and four of us ate it all that night. By golly that were a good change. All we had to drink was the water brought up in petrol cans, but the food helped us forget the thousands of rats, which 'ad many a carcass there.

'When I finished stretcher-bearing I was made the sergeant of a platoon, towards the end of the war. And when the big push came it was all over. I happened to be home on leave when armistice was declared. My sister got married at exactly the same time – 11am on 11 November 1918 – at Penkridge church, and I was best man. Then I was transferred back to France and eventually returned to England and Hatherton Hall in February 1919. Then I really 'ad to start work.'

While Ned had been away his father had suffered two serious illnesses, 'So the place was run-down, well poached with ferrets and whippets and overrun with vermin. But I soon got busy and gave the poachers and pest a tannin', which is not done today. For each case proved I 'ad 3/6d off the magistrates' clerk – it all came out of costs, so the poachers paid. And if one man had a gun they 'ad the others for aidin' and abettin'. 'Course, the police were different then – great big chaps too.

'I always 'ad a damn good staff [stick] and most of the time the poachers 'ad only got to see it. But sometimes I 'ad a battle royal. Some gypsies came in once – they'd been drinkin'. I sent my son to tell 'em to go, but they didn't so I went up. There were three vans of 'em. I said, "Come on, off you go". Then one struck at me and I 'it 'im with me truncheon on the head and the blood really fled. But I was sorry for him. Then another came on, but I 'ad 'im too and then they cleared off.

'There were a tremendous amount of gypsies about in them days. You were supposed to get the police in to move 'em on. As well as game they took wood for pegs and even ferns to sell. To help catch the poachers we used to set a stuffed cock pheasant by the road and watch for them to come for it.'

In 1931 two of the shooting syndicate died and Ned's father retired. Ned took over as head-keeper for a new syndicate. 'Me pay went up from about 35 bob to £2 a week, rent and rates were free and I had a ton of coal and a suit of clothes a year. The Guns liked about 1,000 pheasants reared each season and there was a good supply of partridges about.'

When World War II came along Ned was exempt from service as he was in charge of a small acreage and required to keep the vermin down and grow crops. 'In any case there was no way I was goin' in that bloody lot again. Feeding the birds was not allowed then but sometimes I 'ad the puggins [tail-end corn] to keep the pheasants together.'

The winter of 1940–41 was very hard. 'The snow blocked us in for six weeks. That's what we're short of now – there's never any snow water to fill the passages up. We only 'ad a small skitterin' this last time [winter 1991–92]. Not like 1947 – that were a damn bad 'un. In the April we went down to Ilfracombe for a while so that

Alice could rest after a serious illness, and there was sheep lyin' dead all over the place.'

Family holidays were always by train as Ned never owned a car. 'One of the gents was goin' to give me one once, but 'e died. It were tough for the toffs too when taxation got in and then they weren't so liberal. In the old days you always 'ad yer £5 Christmas box on Boxing Day and that were somethin' then. Sometimes people did 'ave a golden sovereign, but never once did I 'ave a £5 tip, not like today when a tenner is looked down on.'

After 1940 no rearing was done, the woods were cut down and Ned worked for various shooting tenants on his own up to retirement in 1962, by which time he had served the 3,500-acre estate for fifty-four years — his entire working life apart from war service. By coincidence, he was headkeeper for exactly the same length of time as his father - thirty-one seasons, 'though I did help out for another month or so until they found someone else to replace me.' But sadly, Ned does not have the CLA long-service award for which he is more than qualified. 'I could 'ave gone up to Scotland and 'ad the silver medal *and* a bar, but it were too costly. Anyway, I've got three medals from the first war.'

Having enjoyed thirty-one years' retirement from the age of sixty-seven, Ned remains in very good spirits despite his belief that, 'all of your

friends desert you when you're old. In the old days people looked after one another. Leave stuff outside now and it'll be pinched pretty quick.'

Ned lives alone now in a quiet lane in Calf Heath, near Wolverhampton, in the house he bought in 1963 ('I sold a few fowls to pay for it'). Proudly, he declares, 'I've never shifted a five-mile in me whole life, apart from time in the army.' Alice has been in a home for a few years, but Ned has three caring daughters and a 'lad' of sixty-three who works as a ranger. 'I took care 'e never 'ad anythin' to do with keeperin'. It's not like it used to be.

'Today the vermin's doin' untold damage. 'Course, it were a lot easier in my day when all sorts of traps and poisons such as strychnine were still legal. But there was never any anti trouble and we always patrolled the ground properly so that nobody ever got onto it. And you 'ad to be a very good shot. When it came to foxes I picked the vulnerable place every time.

'We used to have the hounds over but the huntsman knew what we were about all right. When 'e came by 'e used to call out, "Wiry day today then Ned!" because we kept a vixen and cubs in a wire pen and just let one or two out on hunt days. This were the South Staffordshire hounds, but in the end they 'ad to go because they cut the wire and trampled fences too much.

'Another thing that's wrong now is these damn hoppers. They want to feed broadcast in the wood — make the birds work for it.'

But while Ned laments many changes in keepering he is certainly not a bitter man: he takes a keen interest in everything around him and still writes in a fine hand. His main regret is that he cannot get out into the garden which kept him so active until the last few years. 'They told me I wouldn't last a six-month when I retired, but I took up mole poisonin', and I'd always do a day's beating when I could. Now this sherry's the finest thing to keep me going.' God bless you Ned — the whole of the civilised world owes you a great debt.

Unsung Heroines
Mary Shelton, Joan Abbott &
Peggy Simpkins : Sussex and Essex

UNSUNG HEROINES

The Women's Land Army was established towards the end of World War I, but really came into its own during World War II, when its gallant volunteers – better known as Land Girls – helped to keep food on Britain's tables. Although their work was an extremely important part of the war effort, in that no nation can march on an empty stomach, they were regarded with disdain by many members of the armed forces. 'Fighting' with a pitchfork rather than helping to man the guns was often seen as a soft option, and many Land Girls were thought to have volunteered in the hope of a quiet country life rather then having to put up with the regimentation of factory or forces which would otherwise have been imposed upon them.

Opposite:
A Women's Land Army Information Bureau in an Oxford Street store. A good number of volunteers came from London, and representatives from agriculture, industry and the armed services manned these bureaus aiming to encourage more women to join up

The truth is that while some 'fell on their feet' and had sheltered, relatively easy, incident-free wars, very many more were exploited by suspicious, ungrateful employers and worked extremely hard in unpleasant conditions for poor wages. They were subjected to unrelenting work in all weathers, with the constant risk of physical exhaustion, injury and even disease such as ringworm from cattle. Such rigours were especially arduous for the many women who came from towns and had no experience of country life or outdoor work. Duties such as driving a tractor and milking cows at 5am every day were indeed demanding for someone with soft hands and used only to office work or even no work at all.

The WLA was officially reformed in 1939, when Churchill called for a million volunteers, and by July that year some 30,000 had come forward. They were partly controlled by the Ministry of Agriculture but were entirely dependent on the goodwill of the farmers, and it took a great deal of effort to overcome widespread prejudice. At first there was confusion, as many girls were trained but there were insufficient jobs for them to go to. Uniform was

provided but was slow to come through, especially gumboots, so many of them had to start work in their own, inadequate clothes.

The 'girls' – minimum age seventeen – came from all classes, and about a third from London and industrial towns, and they either lived in hostels or were billeted on farms. They could not choose where to work, although there was sympathy towards individual circumstances and many did work close to home. Officially they all earned the same wages, about half of which went on rent. However, there was some zoning of pay and there is no doubt that some farmers were more generous than others or had their favourite girls. Furthermore, there was no official recognition of the girls' labours and no system of promotion.

Despite all this, most Land Girls responded magnificently to the nation's need. Many were lucky enough to have kind and grateful bosses, and even those who didn't were often exhilarated by the challenge and adventure. Furthermore, there was a wonderful camaraderie between the girls, so it is not surprising that many now look back on their WLA days as some of the most fulfilling in their entire lives.

Time for tea;
a welcome break
from harvesting
the barley crop for
this group of Land
Girls

As rationing continued after the war, feeding the nation remained a government priority and so the WLA was not disbanded until 1952.

The accounts which follow describe the experiences of three Land Girls during both war and peace.

PEGGY SIMPKINS

Joining the WLA was 'a natural choice' for Peggy Simpkins: she had grown up on a farm and was therefore well used to outdoor work, and was also accustomed to relatively primitive living conditions in their very old farmhouse. Christened Peggy Hawick and one of five children, she was born at Mayfield, East Sussex, on 12 September 1920. Her father owned a mixed farm which helped support his timber-hauling business, at one time requiring nearly a hundred

horses – 'all of which had names'. But when Mr Hawick became ill in 1929, his work suffered and he had to sell the farm. Only six horses were retained and the family moved to South Nutfield, near Redhill in Surrey, where Mr Hawick undertook less exacting work. When the war came, Peggy's brothers and sister all enlisted in the forces, while she joined the WLA. In 1947 she married 'a town boy' and they still live at South Nutfield, where Peggy keeps in touch with the land through her few chickens and one-acre garden. Her time in the WLA, from 1939 to 1946, was not always easy, but overall she looks back on it as an enjoyable experience:

'When I went for interview I found they couldn't get enough people and there was no training at all. The only advice I was given was "Don't fraternise with anyone". I was issued with a pair of jodhpurs, two green jerseys, five beige T-shirts, a green tie, four pairs of dungarees of the bib-and-brace type, two pairs of heavy shoes which you could hardly walk in, a pair of wellington boots and about four pairs of Boy-Scout-type, knee-length socks.

'At first the pay was one shilling [5p] an hour; by the time I left it was 1s/11d [9p]. We were also supposed to get post-war credits, but never did. We fell foul because we didn't get any gratuity like the forces did. The farmers paid us direct, and we always felt cheated because it was the same rate for all jobs. But we always worked like mad, as you had to get it all done. There were no fixed hours and the only regular time off was half a day a week and a whole day a month, though sometimes you got more.

'Getting frozen and wallowing around in the mud so that you could hardly get your feet out were things you soon learned to accept; one of the coldest and muddiest jobs was cutting kale for the cattle, which had to be fed regularly, night and morning. I didn't have a watch so I took an alarm clock out, hooked it on a kale stump and set it for when the next feed was due.

'Although we couldn't choose where to work, HQ were quite good and tried to keep us near home. My first job was on a poultry farm at Effingham and I was billeted in a nearby village house, from where I cycled in. There were about twenty of us girls there and we all had to clock in. The owner of the farm was a very particular man, a Japanese who was later interned. Every henhouse had to be cleaned thoroughly every day, every egg logged in a book and every chick from the incubator sexed. But I refused to kill and draw the chickens, so I got reprimanded.

'Then Dad became ill, and as my brothers and sister were away I had to be at home to help. So the WLA found me a job which I could do while living with my parents: I went to Hale Farm, South Nutfield, a mixed farm owned by Douglas, the motor cycle manufacturer. The place was literally run by Land Girls, but then Douglas engaged this awful dairy man who used to hit the cows on the back – I couldn't get on with him at all. In fact I hit him with a milking stool – after all, he hit the cows with it. Once again I was reprimanded, this time by Mr Douglas. Unfortunately there were no WLA officers to come round and look after your interests; and all you could do was contact HQ if you were desperate.

'We had Redhill aerodrome bang in the middle of the farm, and used to have a great time with the Air Force boys; they were always keen to date us, and often came onto the farm to help us with our work to make sure that we finished in time to go out. One evening, when they were giving a hand putting hay in the racks for the cows, the boss (Douglas) suddenly came back in his Bentley; so they jumped up into the hayracks and we covered them over. But as Douglas was standing there telling us what to do, the cows were pulling the hay out and patches of blue uniform were starting to appear. Luckily he didn't notice a thing and went away none the wiser. We had a good giggle about that.

Peggy in her WLA uniform

'Another time, when we were still harvesting at 11pm in the days of the old double summertime (during the summer months of World War II the clocks were put forward two hours to extend the hours of daylight and facilitate a longer working-day), one of the RAF boys drove a tractor into the double-sided barn and the floor collapsed. We were horrified, and just closed the door till next morning; then we got other tractors to pull the first one out.

'Although we got on well with the lads, the RAF girls couldn't stand us, probably because they were jealous of us going out with their male colleagues. When they cycled by they'd make nasty remarks such as "How utterly nauseating – all this shit!" But on one occasion we had the last laugh: there was this brook with a little bridge of old railway sleepers, and when the girls cycled by they'd put their legs up to

Jack-of-all trades:
Land Girls were
expected to carry
out all sorts of
running repairs

cross it. But one day when they came hurtling down the hill they didn't know the bridge had been washed away, and four or five of them fell in and got soaked. Then my friend called out to them: "Oh darlings, where are your battle bowlers [tin hats] now?"

'With the aerodrome nearby there were quite a few raids, and once machine-gun bullets rattled through the window and knocked a line of tiles off the dairy wall while we were working there. We were a bit shaken, but luckily no one was hurt.

'We often had a good laugh. At Hale Farm there were a lot of yearlings, and when they came into heat they used to jump each other. One day this Geordie Land Girl went in to feed them and one put its "paws" right up on her

shoulders, so she shouted, "Oh you stupid bugger – get him off!"; but we were in stitches.

'Then three of us were transferred from Hale Farm to Pond's Farm, Shere, where there were fourteen Land Girls and no men at all except when we had some Italian prisoners of war, and they were lazy and useless. The owner was always absent, too, because he had a business in town, so without us girls the place would have collapsed.

'There were a lot of cows there and we had to milk them in batches three times a day in shifts from four in the morning to late in the evening. Very often we went to dances in Guildford, but if you missed the last bus and had to walk home, if you were on early turn you'd have to put on your dungarees as soon as you got in.

'I had the odd accident, of course, as most others did. Once I was driving a Cleetrack — a machine with tracks like a tank — with mangolds on the back, but the load was too heavy for going uphill and the vehicle turned over backwards. Fortunately I jumped off before it fell on top of me, but the mangolds were scattered all over the place. Another time I was on my bike holding on to the tractor — we all did it — when I came off and the tractor wheel went over my leg. In no time at all my knee swelled up so much that my dungarees had to be cut off.

'When I started to drive a tractor the sort we had then didn't have brakes, and the first time I forgot the way we were supposed to stop it; so I went straight through a five-bar gate. Another time I was driving one at night when sparks came flying out of the upright exhaust and caught the load of sheaves alight. We had to jump down and pull them all off a bit quick.

'Then one day when I was cleaning the bull out, he got free and I was trapped in the pen with him. He went to butt me, so I leapt on his back and scrambled over the top railings; but when I dropped down it knocked the wind out of me for ages.

'You could never afford to lose concentration. One day we were out with the cabbage planter, with one driver and two girls each side at the back feeding the machine, so that we planted two rows at once. Unfortunately we were so busy gossiping that we planted three rows upside-down and had to do them all over again. When we got back the gov'nor wondered why we had been so long.

'After Pond's Farm I went to Lockhurst Hatch, Shere, to help a Mr and Mrs Sherman who were very old and ill, whose cowman had just died. They only had twenty cows and the ancient buildings were very run down, but they were a lovely couple. I was the only help there, and I lived alone in an isolated wooden bungalow in the woods; but I was never lonely. I had two kittens and took in a lost dog that gave birth to six puppies.

'The Shermans had this huge carthorse

'...sparks came flying out of the upright exhaust and caught the load of sheaves alight.'

Land Girls learning how to lay bait – here they are using sausage rusk – on a pest destruction course

called Captain, and he could be a bit intimidating if you didn't know him. One day my sister came to stay with me and was helping the old lady with buckets of water when Captain thundered up behind her. She ran for cover, but tripped over the low boarding across the barn entrance – there was water all over the place!

'One day we had a big thunderstorm, and when we called Captain he didn't come; so Mr Sherman and I went to look for him. We found him with two cows beneath a tree which had been felled by lightning, all three dead; it was very sad.

'Once Mr Sherman sent me to Guildford with the tractor to collect a trailer; when I returned I backed into the cart lodge with the ladders still up and they were smashed to smithereens – but Mr Sherman didn't turn a hair. He and his wife were so kind to me and gave me lots of presents. Once she gave me a very old blanket box, and lining the bottom was a news-paper for 5 November 1805, reporting the death of Nelson. It must have been in there since the box was made, and I still have both.

'Lockhurst Hatch farmhouse was a fantastic place, dating back to the thirteenth century. There were rough, uneven, brick floors in all the ground rooms, with steps down into the dairy where they still had all the old equipment such as big pans for making cream. There was no stove to cook on, but there was a huge fireplace which Mr Sherman simply stuffed with whole faggots of wood and put paraffin on. To cook over this he just had two pillars of bricks with three or four iron bars laid loose on top, and these would be moved apart according to what you put on and the amount of heat wanted. Pots were suspended from hooks in the side of the chimney. It was generally Mr Sherman who got the bacon and eggs going in the morning, and it tasted out of this world as you were always so damn hungry.

'Water had been laid on, and we had this huge stone sink in the kitchen-cum-living room. When we wanted to clean the floor we just threw down buckets of water, scrubbed hard with a brush and then pushed the dirty water out through the special hole in each side wall. It was incredibly primitive.

'But perhaps the most remarkable thing on the farm was the garden privy, which was in a huge hollow yew tree. All the owner had done was cover the top with wood, put in a seat and fix a door to the front. When you sat in it you could see the stars twinkling through the gaps in the wood, and there were chickens and owls roosting in the branches above! I was very happy at Lockhurst Hatch and only left after about eighteen months to get married.'

JOAN ABBOTT

Born in London, in a Highgate coaching inn on 16 May 1919, Joan Abbott [née Spring] 'moved around a lot' as her hotelier parents 'descended from riches to rags'. However, she soon discovered her fondness for outdoor life when she went to stay with her grandmother in Kent and was taken on walks to gather wild flowers along the cliffs and hunt for pretty shells in Pegwell Bay. After school she won a scholarship in art and textiles and 'had to work in London', where she earned eighteen shillings (90p) a week at Norman Hartnell. Then the war came and changed her life completely, as Joan now recalls:

'Everyone of my generation was devastated, many of us having just started a promising career. Firms were closing down everywhere and we were all made redundant without compensation. So I joined the Land Army to make my escape to the country, which I loved; otherwise I would have had to have gone into a factory, which I couldn't face, although some girls got quite rich doing this. I was in the WLA from 1939 to 1945, mostly in Essex, near Ongar and Kelvedon Hatch, but finally at Hartley Wintney, in Hampshire.'

It was especially hard for many Land Girls because the first three winters of the war were exceptionally cold, with temperatures far below average. Joan well remembers early 1940:

'I was in Essex and we had the worst weather I can remember, with four feet of snow and the water bowls in the cowstalls frozen solid; I had to take a horse and cart with eight churns onto a frozen pond, break three inches of ice to fill the churns with a bowl, and then struggle back to the farm on my own. Each day I also had to carry hay, roped on my back, to some outlying heifers which had been cut off by the heavy snowfall. Fortunately the snow protected them from the icy wind and they all survived.

Young woman, old machine! Joan had to master all sorts of equipment

'No lorries could get near the farm to collect the milk, so I had to take it to the main road – about three-quarters of a mile away – with a pair of horses sliding all over the place; it was a job to distinguish the road from the hedge. The snow became packed really hard, and it was quite frightening as I walked with the horses there and back. I did this for about a week. Many of the old farmhands had some surprises as to what we Land Girls could do.'

Of course, the farm environment has always been hazardous, as often weary bodies would take many shortcuts and risks. It has also always posed great danger to adventurous children, especially as the amount of machinery has increased. For example, Joan remembers when a three-year-old farmer's son fell in the threshing machine and had to have both his legs amputated. Even so, what you would not expect on a farm is to be attacked by another person, as Joan was – twice. As she explains:

'When I worked in Essex I caught a strong young lad kicking a calf because it wouldn't drink quickly, and its nose was bleeding. So I went for the lad in no gentle manner, but he fought me, twisting my arm and dislocating my shoulder. That night I ended up in hospital; the boy, from Glasgow, was instantly dismissed, however. Since then my shoulder has been "out" fifteen times, though thankfully not in recent years.

'Towards the end of the war I looked after an off-farm, where a gypsy family was camped on the edge of one of the woods. They did seasonal work and sometimes disappeared up-country for pea picking. When they went away they didn't leave much litter, just the odd fire patch – they could get a fire going in any weather, even heavy rain. But it must have been hard for them living in an old tent in winter. I think there were four children, and the oldest would sometimes help me with the cows, for a few coppers. But one day I caught them all stealing the farmer's mushrooms, and she went for me and knifed me down the arm. Fortunately the knife was blunt and I was only grazed.'

But these were exceptional incidents. As Joan herself is quick to point out, even during the war years people generally could go about with a greater sense of security than many folk have today:

'When I used to visit my parents in Surrey I would return about midnight and had a mile walk from the station to the farm. On my way I had to pass an Italian prisoner-of-war camp – but there was never any incident, and I had no reason to be afraid.'

But in the WLA Joan did suffer through sheer hard work: 'The biggest problem was sore hands as there were no rubber gloves in those days. We had terrible cuts on our fingers during mangel-pulling and had to plaster them with "Snowfire" and wear old cotton gloves in bed at night.' This must have been especially hard for the girl from Norman Hartnell, used only to fine fabrics. However, tough outdoor work had many compensations, not least the enhanced enjoyment of food:

'My favourite meal was breakfast. Having been up since 5am, I was always ready for three home-cured rashers, a one-inch-thick slice of fried bread with a duck egg on top, mushrooms in season and any potatoes left from the previous day; plus cereal or porridge to start, toast and home-made marmalade to finish. But perish the thought now.'

Joan and the other Land Girls also had plenty of fun. Indeed, she remembers one time when she laughed so much she got into trouble: 'In Essex I shared a room in a council house with another Land Girl; it was a small, very clean room, and in the corner was a narrow cupboard which always intrigued me.

'After a few weeks my friend said: "Why don't you open it?" So I did, and out fell over twenty hats. Well, the fun we had trying these things on made us hysterical. There were feather-trimmed hats, some with large bows, bunches of cherries, flowers as big as a lettuce, huge brims, high crowns, veils, and much, much more – Ascot wasn't in it.

'Eventually there was a knock on the door, and hats flew everywhere as we tried to hide them. Our landlady – the owner of the hats – had come to say that the people next door were complaining about so much laughter because the walls were very thin. I wonder what they would have said about present-day pop music.'

Left: Coping with brute power – a woman's touch

After the war Joan's husband, who had been a photographer in the RAF, returned to his pre-war job but could not settle. As Joan explains:

'He wanted to share in the "good life", so we left the city to work on a farm. I was glad to return to the country and we have never regretted it. Up to 1974 we worked on four farms in Somerset, living in tied cottages on the understanding that I would do seasonal work or help with the milking. My husband, who is now eighty-two, became a cheesemaker and later assistant manager of a creamery. We moved here, to Sturminster Newton in Dorset, in 1978, and we still enjoy gardening and country life.'

Right: Joan, on milking duty, with the head cowman at Beacon Hill Farm, Essex

*Thrashing at
Toplins Farm,
Hartley Wintney,
in about 1943*

MARY SHELTON
(née Chesson)

Mary Shelton has spent all her life in the country. The youngest of three children, she was born at Hammerwood, near East Grinstead in Sussex, on 3 September 1925. Her maternal grandparents were working farmers in Kent, her father was a cowman and her mother – one of sixteen children – took in washing from the vicarage; however, she developed asthma having fallen victim to the widespread influenza epidemic of 1918. Here Mary recalls her tough early life:

'Our food was very plain as we had so little money. Breakfast was often just bread broken up into a bowl of Oxo gravy, while kettle bender was bread and margarine broken into a bowl with a little hot water and seasoned with salt and pepper. In the spring, as a treat, we sometimes had a moorhen's or plover's egg. Midday dinners centred around rabbit, in stews, puddings, pies or roasted. Bacon roly-poly made with scraps and flavoured with sage and onion was quite tasty, and occasionally we had beef pudding, but again made from scraps. Suet puddings and dumplings were cheap to make and filled you up.

'Vegetables were all home-grown and what you didn't grow you didn't have, but sometimes, if swedes or turnips were grown for sheep a few would arrive in a sack by the back door. Tomatoes and cucumbers were unknown to us then, and I don't think I tasted either until long after I left school.

'We had plums in the garden and virtually lived on them in the autumn; like the rabbits, they were eaten in every possible way. Any surplus was made into jam, although I can remember Father selling some at sixpence a gallon. Occasionally we had cake or bread pudding, and we only ever drank tea or water.

'Clothing was either cut-downs or hand-downs. Every winter I was enclosed in hated combinations, given by a better-off house in the village – Mother would say: "If they're good enough for them, they're good enough for you". Most girls wore liberty bodices, which in winter had suspenders sewn on to hold up your black woollen stockings. Everything was darned, patched or mended and the seats of knickers or boys' pants often seemed to be more darn than original material. Boots and shoes were handed down too, and if they were too big, hard luck.

'Our well was shared by four cottages and in a hot summer it would run dry. Then my father and the other cottagers would shoulder a yoke with two buckets and walk nearly a mile down through a wood to a spring, where they would fill up and then carry their heavy load uphill the mile back. This would be done very early in the morning, before going to work at 5.30am, and then again in the evening after a hard day's labour which probably included working till at least 8pm if haymaking or harvesting.

'Any bathing which was done was in a tin bath in the kitchen, but it was not all that often. I think most people washed down as far as they could and up as far as they could, as my mother used to say. Our tied cottage had no sewerage, and Father emptied the contents of the earth closet into bean and pea trenches.

'My approach to wildlife was influenced by a country upbringing: thus, birds' eggs were taken for collections or food, but only one from each

nest; and pigeons or rooks were shot when they became too numerous. Rook pie, made with just the breast and thighs, was as tasty as chicken, and pigeons were roasted or casserolled to make a welcome change from rabbit.

'I did not receive any pocket money, but odd pennies were given by visiting relatives and my father would give me one shilling [5p] on the Saturday before Christmas, when we went into East Grinstead to do our Christmas shopping. That would buy all my presents.

'Father did not drink a lot, but when he went out on a Saturday night, Sunday morning always found a penny Bridgewater chocolate wafer on the chest-of-drawers next to my bed.

'When my father changed jobs he worked for a gentleman farmer at Ripe. This man had two sons at boarding school, and he had me taught to ride so that I could exercise their ponies in term time. Apart from Church Farm he rented several fields a couple of miles away, where he ran bullocks and dry cows; he suggested that I might like to ride down there each morning before school, to count and check them. I was also given the job of feeding the chickens morning and afternoon, collecting the eggs and cleaning the henhouses out on Saturdays. For this, at twelve years old, I received a wage of 2/6d [12½p] a month.

'One morning I found a sick cow with a dead calf, and the farmer was so delighted with me for raising the alarm that he doubled my wage to five

Left: Mary (centre holding the ball) at Hammerwood village school in 1934

Right: Thirteen-year-old Mary feeding turkeys at Ripe

shillings [25p] a month. In the summer, after school and in the evenings, I worked one of the carthorses in either a swathe turner or hay rake, for which I was paid 3d [1¼p] an hour. One year I set turkey eggs under broody hens and for each one that was ready for Christmas I received 6d [2½p].

'I remember a great many superstitions from those days. Warts were rubbed with the soft, fluffy inside of broad bean pods: the pods were then buried, and as they rotted so the warts would disappear. Our Granny Ridley once offered to buy my sister's warts for a penny, and it worked. In a thunderstorm, mirrors were covered and cutlery put in a drawer because they attracted lightning.

> ## COUNTRY SAYINGS
>
> *If you wish to live and thrive
> Let the spider run alive*
>
> *An old Sussex saw at corn-sowing
> time:
> One for rook and one for crow,
> One to rot and one to grow*
>
> *About carthorses with white feet:
> One white stocking, try him,
> Two white stockings, buy him.
> Three white stockings, doubt him,
> Four white stockings, do without him.*

After school it seemed likely that Mary, like most working-class country girls then, would have little control over the type of work she would do: 'But war broke out on my fourteenth birthday and saved me from a life in domestic service. In those days ladies from the big houses, needing servants, visited the school to find out which girls were leaving at the end of term. They would then visit them and their parents to decide which girl they would prefer. The hours, wages and uniform were discussed with the parents, and if all was agreed, that was it – you

went whether you wanted to or not. I was dreading it because I was quite a tomboy and longed to spend all my days out in the open air.

'I had already lost one job because I was rather sullen and rude, much to my mother's disgust: "You're not too old yet that I can't put you across my knee and give you a spanking!" Then my parents were about to move to Worthing as Mother's asthma was so bad and it was thought that the sea air might be better for her. So I went to stay with some family friends for a few days. The husband was a carter on a large farm and market garden estate in mid-Sussex; a few Land Girls were already employed there, and this made me ask if I could have a job.

'I was accepted, and when I started at fourteen I worked a basic 52 hours a week, rising to 65–70 in the spring and summer with overtime. Three-quarters of the time was spent hoeing, and I soon found out what a back-breaking task that was; sometimes I wished it would rain just so that I could have a rest. But on my first payday the boss came round and said that as I had worked very well in that first week he was going to pay me above the basic rate – 6d [2½p] per hour instead of 4d [1¼p]. So I received £1 6s [£1.30p], and I was so proud. I was very happy there and as soon as I was old enough, at seventeen, I joined the WLA.

'Although a lot of the summer work was back-breaking it was at least done in good weather; but market gardening in the winter was not at all pleasant. Daily market orders ruled our lives, and in spite of rain, gales, frost or snow, had to be ready for collection at set times. Often we were soaked to the skin day after day, slodging about in the mud cutting cabbages, digging leeks, carrots and so on. Each morning we had to put wet coats on again if they hadn't dried overnight, and in bitter frosts we'd be numb with cold while picking sprouts.

'By 1942, with fifty to sixty of us girls on the market garden, the foreman began to get worried about the time it took us to "spend a penny". We had to find a deep ditch or empty cattle shed, and

perhaps we did hang it out a bit sometimes because it made a welcome break. We also went in pairs, each acting as look-out for the other. So he and the boss came up with the idea of "tin huts" — about two foot-six square with a slanting roof, latched wooden door and wooden seat. But we had to supply our own paper, and there was a foot gap at the top and bottom of the door to make sure — according to the foreman — that they were too uncomfortable to sit in for long, "or else we would spend half the ruddy day in them".

'With imports almost non-existent, British growers strived to fill the gap, and onions became a much sought-after vegetable. In the summer of 1942 they provided us with quite a bit of excitement. One Saturday night a German plane dropped a string of bombs across the farm, including one in the middle of a field of onions which were almost ready for harvesting. On the Sunday morning a lot of local people, plus some from nearby villages, strolled out "to see the bomb holes". This was quite a normal thing in those days and generally the only bit of excitement we had. The children would go round looking for pieces of shrapnel for souvenirs.

'That morning the boss was also doing the rounds to see what damage had been caused, but when he came to the onion field he nearly had a fit. Not only were people walking across his precious onions to see the holes, they were also helping themselves to onions on the way back — pockets bulged and many men's caps were carried as baskets. The boss immediately tore round in his car and collected as many of the farm men as he could and had them stand guard on all the field gates to keep the people out. On that occasion he reckoned he lost more onions to the lookers than he did to the bomb, and the smell of burnt onions lingered in the air for days.

'The carter I lodged with really worshipped his horses; in his eyes they could do no wrong at all. However, one spring he was ill for a while and so I took them over as I was used to working with them. One day the foreman asked me to put Boxer in the fertiliser drill and spread manure over ten acres. I told him that the carter didn't like using Boxer for that job because the horse didn't like the smell and sometimes got very upset over it. But this was pooh-poohed and I had to get Boxer out.

'I set off across the field with Boxer's lead-rein unwisely wrapped tightly round my hand, thinking this would give me more control over him. All went well until we turned and the wind blew fertiliser into Boxer's face; he leapt up into the air with a huge snort and took off up the field. Unable to loosen the lead-rein from my hand and weighing eight stone to his one ton, I was soon pulled over and dragged along, with my arm nearly wrenched out of its socket – and this over a hard, dry ploughed field.

'Somehow I managed to get my hand free and roll out of the way of the iron wheel before we reached the hedge at the top. Boxer continued through the hedge and wrapped the drill round an oak tree before coming to a halt in the ditch, when the shafts broke. Luckily I was only very badly bruised and sore. But did I get any sympathy when I told the carter? Oh no! "What on earth did you let him go for?" he asked. I "could have hurt the poor horse, or even killed him!"

'Wednesday, 10 February 1944 was cloudy and dull, and the order for the day was "parsnip ploughing". For this we used an ordinary single-furrow plough, the horses walking one behind the other instead of abreast. As the furrows turned over the parsnips stuck out the sides and were picked out by the girls, roughly cleaned and put into boxes. The field was divided into 'cants' or lengths, so that each girl had her own section to pick. As the carter was fully employed watching the cut of the ploughshare – an inch out either side could result in slicing the row in half – he had a girl – me – leading the horses and turning them at the ends. We had nearly a full complement of girls, about forty in two rows, the horses ploughing out one row going up, and one coming back.

'Soon after dinner it came on to rain; we stuck it till about 3pm, by which time we were soaked to the skin, so the foreman called it a day. The carter and I unhitched the horses and set off back to the stable. We had just finished unharnessing them when we heard a plane coming down very low. "One of ours looking for Jerries, I expect," said the carter. But he had hardly

A WLA worker feeding poultry. Many women stayed on in these jobs after the war

NATIONAL SERVICE
WOMEN'S LAND ARMY

APPLY FOR ENROLMENT FORMS AT YOUR NEAREST POST OFFICE OR
EMPLOYMENT EXCHANGE

A recruitment poster for the WLA, dating from the First World War

finished speaking when these great thuds shook the ground. "By God, it's a bloody Jerry," he shouted, and we dashed to the stable door just in time to see this plane drop out of the cloud. It was so low we could see the pilot's face and it looked as if he was coming straight through the stable door. The machine guns rattled and the plane disappeared into the cloud again.

'Sadly, several people had been killed in the village. But what, I wondered, would have happened had it not rainedand us forty Land Girls had remained in two straight lines across the field, which lay between the village and the farm? Would the gunner have resisted the temptation to put his finger on the button?

'The first farm party took place on Saturday, 1 January 1944. The boss agreed to foot the bill for it if the employees formed an organising committee. Girls were allowed to take boyfriends or husbands, and vice versa for the men. It was held in the village Institute Hall. Extra rations were miraculously found, and several of us girls spent the afternoon making sandwiches while some of the younger men brightened the hall with borrowed Christmas decorations. A neighbouring farmer volunteered to bring his gramophone and his collection of Victor Sylvester records, and so we were well away.

'From 7pm small groups of people converged on the hall, some walking over a mile along dark lanes with only a glimmer of torch-light to see their way. Many wore wellingtons to get them through the mud and carried their shoes in shopping bags to change into on arrival. Conversation was soon buzzing, and included a lot of "So that's his wife then, is it!" "Who's that she's with then?" and "Didn't know young Sally was going out with the Smith boy." Some of the older men looked uncomfortable in their best suits, with collar and tie, usually kept only for weddings, funerals and christenings.

'Soon over a hundred people were sitting around the hall, waiting for our boss and his parents to arrive. It was like expecting royalty, and when someone called "They're coming!" the babble of voices suddenly ceased and everyone stood to clap. Our MC for the evening, one of the under-foremen, led the guests towards chairs specially placed for them near the gramophone, took their coats and then started the evening's fun. He thanked the family for allowing and financing the party, then invited the boss's mother, partnered by the neighbouring farmer who provided the music, to lead the dancing in the opening waltz.

'Parties then were so different from those of today. As well as dancing, there were games such as musical parcels, musical chairs and musical laps – very popular with youngsters. Team games included passing the matchbox on your nose, passing the balloon between legs, light the candle and tiddlywinks. Everyone was encouraged to join in, and those who didn't cheered the others on. A sing-song was included, and one of the local girls appeared in her father's cord trousers, smock and boots to sing some of his old favourites, such as "Buttercup Joe", "If I was a Blackbird" and "When the Fields are White with Daisies". She was a great hit.

'By 10pm some of the older men had left. After all, some were cowmen or carters and had to be up at 4.30am, even if it was a Sunday. The official ending was 11pm, and then – after a few hours' sleep – we returned to the hall to put everything to rights again. Everyone agreed it had been a great success, and it was the main topic of conversation for weeks.

'Three or four times a year we Land Girls had to take part in celebration parades. One, in 1943, was "Salute the Red Army Day" and we were asked to be at Hove at 1.30pm. There the parade would form up ready to march along Western Road and North Street to the Dome, where Mr Herbert Morrison, the Home Secretary, would address the audience.

'We knew where our position would be –

right at the back, as it always was! I suppose that as we were a civilian army we did not count for much, and we could well imagine the army officer who organised the parade saying: "Land Army? Shove 'em at the back." All the armed services took part and they, of course, had their own bands at the front; by the time we came along, behind the fire service, police, ARP etc, we could hardly hear the music. Eventually, however, we were off, and after a lot of shuffling we all actually managed to keep in step. Crowds eagerly lined the route as there was little other entertainment in those days, and everyone treated this sort of thing as a carnival. Perhaps such parades were as much a morale booster for the local population as a tribute to others.

'However, halfway along Western Road us Land Girls received *our* morale booster, because from a great crowd by one of the side streets an old chap suddenly shouted out: "Ere comes the gals that do the work: God bless 'em. Come on, give 'em a cheer." Then great cheers rang out, with much clapping. That dear old boy never knew how much that meant to us: I'm sure that our shoulders stiffened, our chins went up and from then on our marching was a credit to the WLA.

'I changed jobs in 1945 so that I could do general farm work and went to Goring-by-Sea, to Chatsmore Farm, which is now completely covered by bungalows and flats and a suburb of Worthing.

'One of my jobs was to work Gert, the odd-job horse. In the autumn many people within a mile or so would order a load of manure for their garden, and I made the deliveries. So I spent each evening in the stables cleaning up Gert's brasses and harness for the morning. Then, with the cart well loaded, we set off with brasses gleaming and ribbons flying for the drives and avenues of Goring and West Worthing.

'Sometimes I was asked to throw the load over a hedge or fence, but often it was just tipped on the grass verge. The charge for a load was £1 7/6d [£1.37½p], but invariably I was given a £1 note and a ten-shilling [50p] note and told to keep the change. This was very good going, because 2/6d [12½p] was a lot of money then; as I reckoned to do three loads a day, this gave me an extra 7/6d [37½p]. A week or so of this and I had enough money to buy nearly all my Christmas presents.'

Mary left the WLA in 1948, but continued to work on farms until she married in 1953. She then lived in Buckinghamshire, but was so home-sick for Sussex that she and her husband moved back into the county in 1960. They rented a small cottage on the farm of Mary's former employer. In 1963 they moved to another farm cottage, at Hassocks, still in Sussex.

In the twenty-five years to 1995 Mary raised over £40,000 for charity through events such as garden open days, coffee mornings, plant sales and Shire horse waggon rides.

Time for a picnic in the Suffolk sunshine for these WLA girls

Button Hooks
and Britches

Aubrey Charman : Sussex

BUTTON HOOKS AND BRITCHES

Aubrey Charman, a sprightly, almost hyperactive eighty-four, comes down the track to greet me from one of the oldest farms in Sussex. Great House Farm has stared across the fields towards Southwater, a few miles south of Horsham in Sussex, since the middle decades of the fifteenth century. In 1462 according to the date carved on an oak beam, the oldest part, still largely unaltered, was put up by a local yeoman farmer. What is laughingly described as the new part of this massive timber-framed house was erected a little more than one hundred years later, in 1575 (again the date appears on a beam) and this is still known as the 'new house'. What used to be an external door in one wall of the 1462 part of the house has been beautifully preserved since being enclosed in 1575 by the building of the new.

Aubrey Charman's family have been here since 1823 when his great-great-grandfather came to the farm. Though he knows little about this long-departed ancestor, other than that he was called James and that he was a good farmer, Aubrey still has the bill of sale from the farmer from whom the first of the Charmans took over the tenancy. Among the listed items are 'five cows in profit, three broad wheel dung carts, a cider press and four horses (three heavy).' Since the date of that sale, September 1823, no farm sale has ever been held at Great House Farm; which is no doubt why today it is still filled with the furniture and effects carried through the doors at that time.

'No, we've never sold anything,' says Aubrey with a laugh as he shows me round the house. 'But it's such an old place that I've come across all sorts of odd ancient objects since I've been here.' And just to prove his point, as we step down into the ancient flagged kitchen Aubrey picks up a tiny, beautifully made child's leather shoe. 'It was probably made early in the nineteenth century,' he says. 'Perhaps about the time my great-great-grandfather arrived.' Other objects include an ancient longcase clock, tables and chests-of-drawers made by local craftsmen in the sixteenth and seventeenth centuries, button hooks, old harness, leather britches, and tools and iron implements of every conceivable shape and variety. But where on earth have they all come from?

'A lot of 'em from the roof,' says Aubrey with a grin. 'This house has fifteen bedrooms, and the roof space alone would fit two or three semi-detached houses. It's enormous, and though each stone slate weighs more than a hundredweight there are so many massive oak timbers the whole thing has hardly moved in four hundred years.' We chat for a while in the kitchen which still has its flagged stone floor and massive lead pump. The pump is beautifully decorated with a floral motif raised in the lead, and was made when the house was built; and it still works. Before we get down to discussing the business of farming, Aubrey shows me the two oak settles built into the walls of the massive fireplace, above which a remarkable ancient jack spit remains. Built with a weight on a pulley, the jack spit had a crude, clock-like series of wheels and gears, and with the weight attached it will slowly turn the massive roasting spit above the fire. So ingenious is the design that the weight takes about fifteen minutes to reach the ground; during that time the housewife is therefore able to get on with other tasks, safe in the knowledge that here roasting pig will be evenly cooked on all sides.

My tour of the house ends in the sixteenth-century sitting-room in which Aubrey, now semi-retired, spends most of his time. This quite remarkable room, immediately above the cellar, still has every last inch of its original oak panelling; the walls are covered from floor to ceiling.

'My father and I were born in this house, and as I've said, we know little about great-great-grandfather other than that he was called James, that he came here in 1823 and he was a good farmer. In those days it was a mixed farm with hogs and sheep, corn and vegetables, and when I arrived in the world it was still pretty much the same with pigs and sheep and twenty cows, and we grew corn; we had about a hundred acres of corn. Now, however, we have ninety cows and no corn at all – you have to specialise now. My grandfather is buried in Southwater church and his seven children were all born here in this house. There were no midwives then, and there were still none when I was born.

'One or two village women would come up when Mother was about to have a child. The only doctor we had when I was young was in Horsham, four miles away, and that was too far. My grandfather's eldest son went away to Africa and became a butcher; my father was the second son, so he took over the farm. Dad was very clever; he was told he should have been a teacher.'

Aubrey is extremely proud of his father, and with reason. The old man was a talented mathematician, and studied a great deal at a time when few farmers would bother with such academic pursuits, as Aubrey explains: 'He *studied* farming far more than most. At a time when most farmers could get barely a couple of gallons of milk a day out of a cow, Dad was getting up to eight gallons which is as much as they can manage today. He had a book on protein, you see, and knew about its importance while everyone else went

on unthinkingly as they'd always done. He fed those cows on Egyptian cottonseed case which is about 42 per cent protein, very high. And linseed cake, which he thought was good too, and so it was. I still have his protein book, and it even tells you how much protein there is in an oak leaf.'

Aubrey's earliest memories are of the hard winters of long ago, and of leading two massive horses up an icy field. His father kept a team of Shire horses: 'Seven carthorses, I recall. I'd have been about ten when I first remember leading them. Always slowly, always at a walk. A carthorse never runs or trots, but they'll do three miles an hour and the smallest boy can lead and stop them when they're trained. Ours were trained by the farmworkers; normally we

Great House Farm dates back to 1462

had eight farm-workers, and two pupils who would generally have been eighteen or perhaps nineteen. We had farm cottages then, too, which have gone now, but each man had a cottage with the job in the early days, and we never turfed them out when they retired; they stayed till they died, or went into a home.

'Winters were undoubtedly worse when I was young, and summer betters than now – Father had always finished the harvest by the time we get started these days. We still have the dates the

harvest finished carved on our granary wall, and they go back more than a hundred years.

'In winter we always skated on the pond in front of the house for weeks on end; now, the ice is never thick enough. We used to skate late into the evening when the moon – or as we called it, the parish lantern – was out. There is an exception to that, however: 1963. That was a terrible winter.' As Aubrey remembers, all traffic came to a halt around Southwater in 1963, so deep were the roads and lanes in snow. The farm milk couldn't be collected, and after three days all the farm churns were full, because, of course, the cows had still to be milked. But Aubrey had the answer: 'With sixteen churns my wife and I toured every street in Southwater in the cart. I rang a big bell and shouted "Milk!" at the top of my voice, and people came out and stopped us, and my wife filled their cans and jugs as required. As they hadn't had a delivery for three days they were more than happy. We sold 160 gallons that

morning, and it was as if the clock had gone back fifty years to a time when we would have sold all our milk locally.'

The Charmans have always rented Great House Farm. They tried to buy it on two or three different occasions, but each time, according to Aubrey, the landlord's agent boosted the price to an exorbitant level. 'Sixty years ago it was valued at £25,000, but the agent, who was always on the grab, said we couldn't have it for less than £56,000. It's funny, too, because although we've been here a long time the landlord's family has been here even longer. Sir John Aubrey Fletcher owns it now, and it's been in his family since 1678.'

Aubrey is fascinated by the past, but this doesn't mean that he rejects the modern world and the modern machinery of farming. 'Horse ploughing was a skilled business, but so is ploughing with a tractor. An untrained man couldn't do it. You have to know what you're doing when you set the plough, although I would admit that with a modern plough once you've set it correctly it's pretty easy.

'The difficulties of the past may sound interesting today, but when modern alternatives came along I can see why people often grabbed them gratefully with both hands. Take matches – well, they weren't invented till the 1850s; before that you had to strike a flint to light anything, and getting a flame from a flint wasn't easy. We got round the problem here by never letting the fire go out – year after year it stayed alight, and there was a skill, too, in making sure it stayed alight. Every night when you went to bed you covered the glowing ashes with grey, burned-out ash; in the morning when you raked this grey stuff off, the red embers would still be alight and you could get the fire going again.

'We had two maids in those days who slept at the top of the house. They got up at six every morning – the same time as everyone else – and lit the big sixty-gallon copper we had for boiling water; and this copper had to be filled using buckets filled at the pump. That carried on until about 1940 when piped water arrived, but the well and the pump are still just as good as they ever were. So is the pond, and let me tell you, it isn't just any old pond: it was built about a hundred years ago chiefly for washing the farm horses' legs, which is why it's got a solid stone bottom. When they're ploughing, heavy horses get their legs badly caked with mud, in particular the long hair above the hoofs, and if it isn't cleaned off they get a terrible skin affliction we called farcy. So every evening at ploughing time they'd be tied nose to tail and led to the pond, and then they'd be driven round it for a few minutes until all the mud on their legs had washed off. The youngest ploughman normally rode the first horse round and round to make it go and the others would follow. We did this right through ploughing time until we got our first tractors, though I never heard of any other farmers doing it.

In the 1920s and earlier the farmhouse itself was a place of intense daily activity, as Aubrey recalls: 'My family consisted of my parents and us five children – I was second to youngest – but the house had other occupants, too. Amongst the staff would be a housemaid and dairymaid, who would help milk the cows and clean the dairy utensils. Every day two large pails of milk were put through the separator to separate the cream from the skim milk; the latter was fed to the calves until they were eight weeks old – all the female calves were kept to go into the dairy herd when they were mature at about three years old.

'The house had a set weekly routine: on Mondays the housemaid would light the big sixty-gallon copper fire with faggots, bundles of hazel sticks about six feet long and a foot wide, to heat the water for washing day. At about 9am every Monday two of the workers' wives would help to do the weekly wash, and that happened every Monday right through my childhood and beyond.

'There was also a great big baking oven in our kitchen, and here bread was baked every Tuesday: always Tuesday. Three faggots were pushed into the seven-foot-long brick oven, then set alight; when the embers were glowing red hot, about twenty big lumps of dough were placed above the embers, using a long-handled shovel called a baker's peel. Then the cast-iron door was closed to keep in the heat. Twenty minutes later, the dough would be baked into lovely crusty cottage loaves – the smell was wonderful, and we boys were often given a still-hot slice to

Aubrey and his brother Ronnie in 1922

A HORSE IN THE SIDINGS

'Horses were used for some odd tasks in my youth, things that people have forgotten all about. For example between 1850 and 1914 two huge shire horses were always kept at Horsham station to shunt trucks into sidings. These trucks might easily weigh twenty tons, but the horses were specially trained to lean against the trucks until they started to move. Very few horses could do it.'

eat. You didn't need butter or jam when the bread was fresh from the oven like that, made from home-grown wheat milled between huge millstones at the Southwater windmill, and later at Warnham water-driven corn mill. Some yeast would be saved to mature for the next week's bake. My mother looked after all the baking, and several of the labourers were given loaves as part of their wages.

'Wednesday was always butter-making day. My mother had been trained in this art before she was married, and so she was an expert, churning the cream into butter in what we called an end-over-end churn. It usually took two hours, and a man was always on hand to help turn the handle because it was hard work after a while. And by the time the dairy equipment had been scrubbed and packed away, another day had gone; but that's why different days were allocated to the different major tasks around the house and farm. Thus Thursday was ironing day, and Friday general shopping day.

'On Friday my father would harness the pony and bring round the trotting cart to deliver some of the butter and eggs to shops in Horsham. As we went round we'd buy the things that we needed, although when I was young you couldn't buy vegetables in any shops because everyone grew their own, so there was no market for them.

'Saturdays were busy because we had to get double supplies of hay and straw ready for the cattle for Sunday. No work other than feeding – both stocks and humans – was done on a Sunday, and most people went to church, sometimes twice; all the children went to Sunday School on Sunday afternoons, and there was always an annual outing to the seaside for them. I would say that until the first war most farmers and country people went to church on Sunday, and if they weren't there the vicar would want to know why. But generally people were pleased to

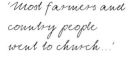

'Most farmers and country people went to church...'

go because most couldn't read and it was the only way they got to hear any stories; it was also the way village people kept in touch with each other. Remember, too, that if you lived in the country before the Great War there was nothing else at all to do except work. So Church was really a bit of a break from the routine.

'Twice a year my Father would kill a big pig for our own consumption. Outside our kitchen door there was a large square of flat bricks with a drain, laid out specially for killing pigs; it is still there now. A pig would be selected and a cord tied on one of its hind legs so if it tried to run away or misbehave it was easier to control, and it would then be driven from the sty to the back door. It was blindfolded, stunned with a very heavy hammer, rolled on its back and its main jugular vein cut. After being bled, it was scrubbed and all its bristles removed. It was hung up and cut into joints, some being hung up the chimney to be smoke-dried by the great log fire which was never allowed to go out. The belly parts were salted down in a huge chest that we called the brine tub, and about sixty pounds of salt would be used for the belly pork from one pig; the salt stopped it going bad. Belly pork was a luxury for the farm-workers when they came in to tea at haymaking time. To be honest, I think the way we killed our pigs was very humane even by modern standards; because they were blindfolded they never really knew what was happening.

'There's a funny story connected with pork that I ought to tell you. My wife and I were sitting in the dining-room one day in 1966 when a great big piece of soot crashed down the chimney and onto the dining-room floor. My wife picked it up and threw it out of the window into the garden; but then later that same day we saw the dog was taking a particular interest in it, so we went to investigate. And would you believe it, that piece of soot turned out to be a great big piece of bacon that had been hung up that chimney to smoke at least twenty years earlier by my father. We cleaned the sooty meat and tasted it and it was delicious.

'Eight farm-hands sat at the table for tea at five o'clock when haymaking was in full swing in the old days. They had homemade bread and cold belly pork, homemade cheese and butter, washed down with homemade cider. Only half an hour was allowed for this meal, as all hay was pitched by hand in those days. We have a big cellar and can still smoke our own bacon up the chimney. I remember long strings of sausages

hanging on hooks close to the ceiling along the beams; they would hang there until they were all used, and they never seemed to go bad.

Aubrey has records of his family's movements going back to 1749, but these only begin to include substantial details in the middle decades of the nineteenth century. His great-grandfather, for example, was the first warden of the village church, which was built in 1850. His father sang in the same church choir for seventy years, and Aubrey himself sang there regularly every Sunday for fifty-two years. When he stepped down it was in favour of his son who had already taken over many of the main tasks around the farm and who will, insists Aubrey, take the family dynasty into the twenty-first century.

Throughout his stories of the past Aubrey acknowledges that life in rural Sussex before and just after the Great War had changed little in centuries. He is particularly conscious of this because the lives of his own ancestors are so well documented. And in the same way that Great House Farm has passed from father to son down

'We had forty
apple trees and a
cider press...'

CIDER MAKING

'We had forty apple trees and a cider press, so when the corn was stacked in the
stackyard after harvest, the men were sent to gather the apples. The best eating
apples were laid out on newspaper, carefully and individually in the attic. The
sour apples were crushed in the cider press and all the juice collected, treated
with yeast and other ingredients, and put into forty-gallon barrels. We usually
made over one hundred gallons of cider each year, as this was the drink sent out
to the men working in the hot sun during the hay and corn harvests. The cider
barrels were stacked in our cellar and I still have some thirty gallons maturing
now, seventy years after they were first put down there. These days the farm-
workers prefer tea, which is surprising because they always seemed to enjoy the
cider so much.'

the generations, so too were many other local businesses and trades handed on from one generation to the next. The trades of wheelwright and farrier, for example, were often carried on by men whose great-great-grandfathers had started their own businesses. As Aubrey recalls:

'Before the first war there were two blacksmith's shops in Southwater, one run by Mr Gardner and one by Mr Piper. Piper also made waggons and waggonwheels, and many times I have watched him and his men make a cartwheel rim out of iron. This would be heated in the forge until it was red hot, then forced onto a newly made wheel; the heat would make the metal expand, but even then it would be a tight fit and would have to be hammered on. As soon as the rim was fitted, five or six buckets of cold water would be thrown over it to make it shrink; so you can imagine how tightly it finally gripped the wheel. These wheels were so tight and well-made they might run for fifty years with perhaps only two changes of rim in all that time.

' I also remember John Piper buying one particular group of oak trees; when he cut them

In the days when horses were used for agricultural work even the smallest villages could boast their own blacksmith's forge

down he sent one to be cut into paper-thin veneer because he knew that this particular tree had a lovely flower, or pattern on it. This was in about 1933, and do you know, that oak tree went to veneer about forty rooms and cabins on the Queen Mary.

'Piper also made coffins for the village people, and would arrange the whole funeral including organising a farmer to transport the coffin in a waggon to the church. In fact the last villager who died and was taken to church in a waggon was my mother. She died in 1944, and I remember my father washed his newest four-wheeled Sussex waggon and took her in it from the farmhouse to the church. Even by then this was unusual because motor hearses were already in common use.

'...the last villager who died and was taken to church in a waggon was my mother...'

'When I was six I remember coming out of Southwater Infants School and seeing the Horsham fire engine for the first time: drawn by heavy horses, it thundered past the school and we raced after it all the way down the road to Cripplegate where the village windmill was on fire; but as the windmill was all wood it had virtually vanished up in smoke by the time the engine arrive.'

The Cripplegate windmill was a very interesting structure, and was probably one of the last of England's movable wind-driven mills. These movable windmills were built on oak skids as much as thirty feet long, and as many as sixteen oxen were harnessed to them when the mill was sold to another village or if it had to be moved for any reason.

'Oxen were used,' remembers Aubrey 'because they were slow and steady, and would never rush, and that meant there was little danger of the mill being pulled over when it was being dragged across hilly terrain.' The Cripplegate windmill that Aubrey watched being destroyed by fire all those years ago was so called because it stated life at Cripplegate, one of London's gateways. Centuries old already, in 1810 it was towed slowly by oxen from London to Rusper village about six miles north of Horsham. In 1823 it was moved to Southwater, again using oxen. But if oxen were slow, the same thing couldn't be said of horses. 'Contrary to modern belief, horses could be very fast indeed. You'd be surprised at the distances a good horse used to cover in a day – not cart or farm-horses, but a good trotting pony. I'll give you an example: my uncle had a fine horse, and three or four times a year he'd harness this horse to the dogcart and trot up to us from his house about twenty-five miles away. The horse could do twelve miles an hour, so it only took him about two hours to get to us. He'd spend the day and then drive back in two hours, and in spite of a round trip of fifty miles and a good smart pace all the way, the horse would never get in a lather.'

Farmers are marvellously innovative when it comes to avoiding waste, and Aubrey's ancestors were no exception. Thus when a giant cask of homemade cider was spoiled when air leaked into it, Aubrey's father fed the forty-five gallons, little by little, to his pigs. Each time the pigs emptied the trough they very quickly became completely stupefied, and fell asleep until their next feed. 'This went on for six weeks, and for the whole time those pigs were completely drunk,' says Aubrey with a grin. 'But the pigs grew so quickly on this diet that my father contracted a Horsham brewer and bought spoiled beer from him regularly.

'Animals are strange things, though. One of the oddest occasions I can remember was when a big sow we had became ill with pneumonia and apparently died. We dragged it onto the stable-

manure heap, and being so heavy it was quickly half submerged by manure; Father and I planned to take it to the carcase man the following day because we would at least get a few shillings for it. But when we went to look for that pig next day we found it was alive and well and back in the pig house! All we could think was that the heat from the manure had driven the pneumonia out of it and revived it.'

Many of the everyday items of food that we now take for granted were difficult, if not impossible, to obtain earlier this century. Other items such as fish were a rare meat for inland families like the Charmans. 'Over the years from 1920 until about 1936 we children would listen out for the sound of a bell ringing on the main Worthing Road. Immediately we heard it, my mother would give me a shilling and tell me to run up to the road because it was the mackerel seller, a man with a big horse-drawn cart piled high with thousands of mostly mackerel and herring. He would have started early that morning on the south coast, and gradually worked his way towards London selling his fish at every village along the way. We usually got thirty herrings for a shilling, and sometimes more if there were only a few left, because by the time he reached us, the fish man would usually have had enough and would not be wanting to go further. If he did, he had to go up Picks Hill at Horsham which was very steep; in fact it was much steeper than it is today, and to get up it you had to hire two extra horses at the foot of the hill at the toll gate; they were kept there specifically for this purpose. You can still see how steep the hill originally was if you look at the two sides of the cutting the council made to reduce its steepness.

'Between 1915 and about 1935 there was another oddity on the road, one which almost everyone forgets these days: the steam engine. The steamers, as they were known, needed a lot of water so village ponds near the road were kept as free as possible of rubbish so they could fill up as they went along.'

Aubrey would be the first to agree that in the old days the countryside produced many eccentrics. They were usually tolerated, however quirky their behaviour might become, but it is wrong to think that they were always amusing; some were probably simply reclusive. Aubrey remembers one noted Southwater character whose reputation as an eccentric was based largely on the fact that he was extremely antisocial:

'Bernard Green died in 1979. He would have

been about seventy-five, I think, but I remembered him from when he was twenty and he came to work for my father. He was a most conscientious worker, but nothing would induce him to get to work before nine o'clock and as that upset all the other farm-workers who started at seven, we had to get rid of him. When he left he rented about twenty acres of land and reared stock. But he would help any farmer at harvest-time. He was often seen digging potatoes late at night by the light of a lamp, but you'd never see him doing it during daylight. He never mixed with the villagers, and lived in some poverty in a cottage in New Road. He was often seen returning from his cattle well after midnight. When finally he was found dead he was in his bed with an overcoat and boots on, and all around him were scattered cattle sales cheques going back years which he'd never bothered to pay into the bank. Although he lived in Southwater for more than sixty years I don't suppose he was known to more then twenty people, and he had no friends.

'Animals can be eccentric, too; each one has its own character, and occasionally you'll get one that is remarkable in some way – like our mare Dolly. She was used as a trace horse: when we were carting mangolds or whatever from a very wet field, the waggon would sink into the mud; so using a special chain harness we would add Dolly to the horse already harnessed to the waggon. When the load had been pulled across the field to the hard road, the man in charge would unhitch Dolly, hand the chains over her back and turn her round. She'd then set off on her own across the field precisely to the front of the next loaded cart, and she would do this all by herself twenty times a day. She was a lovely horse with a marvellous nature, and she worked for us for twenty-three years before we pensioned her off.

'Another horse we had wasn't so amenable. She used to be in a terrible hurry to get out of her harness and start feeding when we tried to unhitch her in the evenings; she got so bad that she'd sometimes break out of the harness, and we knew that eventually someone would get hurt. We cured her by putting a coat over her head before unhitching her and leading her to within a couple of feet of the stable wall. Of course, she bolted as usual, but this time she hit the wall and knocked herself out – but she never rushed again.

'Horses could be marvellous. Every morning our seven would be tied together, and entirely on their own they would leave the stable in line and walk eighty yards down to the pond to drink before returning to the stable for breakfast. They always did the whole thing on their own, at the same pace and in the same time. It was a marvel to see.

'Horsham market was started in 1852; it has long gone, but we used to go by horse, or on foot driving the sale animals, and it was a fair sight to see. There would be sheep, cattle, chickens and rabbits everywhere, and you would always see a number of Jews, who came down from London to buy poultry and rabbits.

'For as long as anyone could remember, and certainly until the end of World War II when new hygienic regulations made it impossible, most villagers kept a pig or two in a sty built at the bottom of the garden. They bought the smaller piglets, known as "dolly" pigs or "runts", from a farmer's litter, and reared them on boiled scraps, milk, curds and buttermilk. In the autumn they would go "gleaning" which was a family affair, to collect corn-heads spilled at harvesting. I've known a family collect several bushels of corn-heads which were fed to the pigs for several weeks. When half-grown, the pigs were sent to the butcher for killing, and he would buy half, while the other half was taken back by the cottager to be smoked in the chimney for use during the winter. The same could be done today,

Opposite:
The beautifully straight furrows of a newly ploughed field form a striking pattern. Ploughmen took great pride in their work and ploughing competitions were a regular feature of rural life

except that modern law does not permit the smell of a pig in the garden in housing estates. The great thing about keeping a pig was that it didn't need much space and you could feed it on anything; we'd feed ours on dead chickens and dead rabbits with the feathers and fur on, bad cabbage and apples, damp corn going mouldy and absolutely any waste vegetables from the kitchen. They thrived on everything. I even remember one farmer whose land was infested with rabbits: every evening he took the Land Rover and his gun, and shot up to thirty rabbits which he then fed to his pigs, as meal at that time was very dear. For two months those pigs lived on unskinned, uncooked rabbits and what is more, looked very well on it. Pigs will eat almost anything, even bones, and can successfully convert any waste foods.

'Nowadays most farmers specialise in one or two products in a big way, where seventy years ago they would have kept a few of all types of

livestock, including geese, turkeys and farmyard fowls. My grandfather and his father kept large black lop-eared pigs which were known as Sussex pigs. They were easy to control because their ears covered their eyes, which meant that if they tried to run off they would bang into things because they couldn't see. Our breeding sows were driven out every day to graze grass, and in the autumn walked to the woods to feed on acorns. As boys, my father and brother used to take the pigs out to certain fields before they went to school each day, and they would fetch them back in the evening, after school.

'On one occasion, three of our sows were due to farrow at the same time, so one shed was filled with straw. The sows were brought in that night and they made a cosy hole in the straw. The next day they had all farrowed, so they were trough fed, near their young. Three days later the little pigs had all appeared and were running about, and there was a record number: fifty-one, seventeen per sow. The sows were sisters and happily suckled each other's piglets, so no one really knew the correct mothers or how many each mother had had. My father assured me these facts were true, so pigs have not improved in performance today since the average for the best herds is now ten and a half piglets reared. Black pigs have all but disappeared because modern housewives don't like the black pigment caused by the skin; also the Middle White, snub-nosed pigs which were very popular thirty years ago as they were good doers and very fat are now almost extinct, as people have gone off fat.'

Like many farmers and farm-workers who grew up during the early years of the last century, Aubrey built up an immunity to TB, the disease which was once endemic in British cattle; in fact, either you became immune or you died.

'Our cows were first tested in the spring of 1920, and twenty-seven out of thirty were found to have TB; under the law, these had to be slaughtered. To my father and I this was a great disappointment as they *looked* perfectly healthy. It wasn't a total disaster, however, because we were given money in compensation for our loss. With this in his pocket, my father went to the north of England and bought replacement cows which had passed all the TB tests.

'Twelve months later, after the cows had been housed all winter, a second test was carried out for TB, and imagine our disappointment when twenty-five out of thirty cows failed. My father promptly called in the vet, who phoned the head of the ministry's veterinary department; we received a visit from the ministry, and were told that we had to build an outside yard so that the air could blow through night and day. We could use

clay soil all our cows must be housed for the five long winter months even today, but they are kept in open yards and we haven't had a case of TB in any animal for thirty years.

'To encourage farmers, in 1920 the Government paid an extra fourpence per gallon on milk proved free of TB. But as a child I had a glass of milk for supper every night, and I must have drunk many a gallon of tubercular milk. Because nature builds an immunity to most diseases in children, I have remained very healthy, although I must admit I've never been tested for TB. I think cattle now are more healthy than

The Charman family in 1947, Aubrey standing at the back (far left)

the old enclosed cowshed for milking only; but should turn the cows out again into the outside yard as soon as fresh straw had been spread.

'What had been happening was this: a cow with what might have been dormant TB germs breathed against the wall of the cowshed, and in the hot, enclosed atmosphere the next cow caught the germs. She then passed it on to the next cow, and so on until virtually every cow was infected. Remember, the cows spent five months in this cowhouse, and evidently the temperature was so hot the TB spread very rapidly. On this

most humans because they get tested for things so often. It is still every two years for TB.'

Amongst the most interesting medieval survivals that Aubrey remembers were the faggots used to light ovens and heat coppers. Faggots were bundles of wood about six feet (2m) long, tied in the centre, about nine inches (23cm) in diameter. For centuries in Sussex and elsewhere all bread was baked in ovens that had first been heated with faggots. Two or three were set alight in the oven, which was usually a great brick-built thing, or a smaller opening, with a door, in the

THE FARMWORKER'S SMOCK

Aubrey's memories of animal husbandry, and of the everyday life of farm and village in the early twentieth century are remarkably precise, and when interviewed he was one of the few still alive who can remember seeing men wearing that most English of farmworkers' garments, the smock: 'For more than two hundred years all agricultural workers in Sussex and many other areas wore a smock — it was actually a kind of overcoat. It went out of use just after the Great War in this area, but I can remember the men wearing them. The Sussex smock was a long bell-shaped garment which had no buttons but had to be slipped over your head. They were rather heavy, especially when dressed with tallow — the fat from which candles were made — to make them waterproof. Nevertheless, if you were ploughing all day in the rain this waterproofing was a great asset. Most workers and farmers kept a second, clean white smock for attending church.'

A rabbit is dug out of a burrow with a ferret still hanging on to it

brick side of the chimney. The faggots were allowed to burn down until they were just red-hot ashes, then the bread dough was placed on a tray on a long-handled shovel and put into the oven. Up to forty loaves could be cooked at once. One or two bakeries in Southwater were still using faggots up until about 1930; then gas came in and other heating methods were used.

'In Southwater in 1930 there was a thirty-four-acre piece of hazel woodland which stretched from Church lane up to Shipley Corner. This was coppiced regularly every five years, in four-acre blocks, to supply faggots for our local baker, and for one or two other bakers in Horsham. Now the whole site has been built on, the Southwater baker carries on his trade in the same building, but using a modern oven.'

For Aubrey, one of the greatest losses to the late twentieth-century countryman is the rabbit. Before the arrival of myxomatosis in the 1950s — 'it was introduced deliberately,' says Aubrey — most landowners had a ferret or two for catching rabbits, which represented a good and, most importantly, a free meal. A ferret would be put down the rabbits' bury after nets had been placed over every escape hole that could be discovered. 'The rabbits nearly always fled at the first whiff of the ferret, and as they shot out of their bury holes they were caught in the nets — though it was only occasionally as easy as that makes it sound. We caught a lot, but we also lost a lot. In Horsham's weekly market I used to see about three hundred rabbits for sale regularly. And rabbit skins were bought by the rag-and-bone men who came round every week. I was told the rabbit hair was used to make trilby hats.'

The attitude of country people to animals was clearly a lot less sentimental in former times, but most country children always kept pets of various sorts, and then, as now, most farmers were unlikely to be without a dog. Aubrey remembers one or two rather more unusual animal companions: 'We had some marvellous pets over the years. My wife once reared an orphan lamb which became completely domesticated.

Carrying sheaves of corn. The boys in this photograph, taken in 1936, were from the National Children's Home and Orphanage in Frodsham, Cheshire

People say it can't be done, but it can. The lamb came when it was called, would climb the stairs and jump on the bed, and it slept with the dogs. When we used to walk across the fields to the pub it came with us – we used to give it beer in a dish which it loved, and chocolate. Eventually it grew so big and greedy it became a terrible nuisance, and ate all the flowers in the garden. When it was three we had to sell it, and by then it weighed more than 150 pounds.

'At the moment, as well as my golden retriever I've got two cats. They sleep with the dog, and when the dog and I go to check the cows the cats come along with us – it must be two miles across the fields and back, but every week they make the journey. Animals are funny things. When I was in my thirties I had a dog that always ran up and down the furrow all day long when I was ploughing. Hour after hour it would run, never stopping and hardly ever even slowing down. I reckoned he must have run a hundred miles each day.'

There's no doubt that roads, housing estates and modern farming practices have dramatically reduced the amount of wildlife in Aubrey's part of Sussex. Animals and birds that were once common exist now only in small pockets, and one or two species have disappeared altogether. 'In the 1920s I remember seeing quail and corncrakes running in my father's corn, but there's hardly a corncrake left in Britain now. I even caught one once. It had got caught in the binder and tied up in a sheaf of corn, so I fished it out and put it in my pocket. Soon it began to struggle, so I took it out and showed it to a friend who was nearby. Just as he took a look the bird's head flopped down and my friend insisted it was dead. I wasn't so sure, so I put it on the ground. Soon one eye opened, then the other and next minute it ran off. That was my only experience of an animal feigning death to escape trouble.'

Before the widespread use of chemical fertilisers, most of which arrived in rural Sussex in the years following the end of the World War II, farmers had to rely on muck-spreading and marl. 'Everyone know how good muck is on the land, but few people realise about marl. It's a sort of blue clay which you find perhaps fifteen or twenty feet down, and when it's spread thinly on pasture land it sweetens the grass beautifully – by that I means it makes it far more palatable for the animals. We had our own marl pit, and every winter the carts would go back and forth to it all day long. Cartloads were spread over the more distant fields where no manure was available. The first half-decent alternative to marl arrived here in about 1910, in the form of sulphate of ammonia from the gasworks.'

In a world without television and radio, language and patterns of speech were little diluted by outside influences. For most of the inhabitants of Southwater as late as the 1930s London was still a remote place, and many villagers would have spent their entire lives within the few square miles bounded perhaps by Horsham four miles to the north. This insularity produced a distinct Sussex dialect which has all but vanished.

'It's the fact that people are able to travel about more, and they hear different accents on television. That's what's got rid of it, but I can remember from my very early days, bits and pieces of the local way of speaking. I'll give you an example: when I was about ten I asked the carter if I could lead one of the horses up the field, and I can still remember exactly what he said: "Keep they wheels in the lowses, don't knock no gaat posties and don't scat yer legs on they lawyers and don't get in the dick." It was a rich, wonderful sound you don't hear today – oh, and lowses are ruts, lawyers are brambles and a dick is a ditch.'

Aubrey is ambivalent about the changes he has seen in his lifetime. While he agrees that much that was good has vanished, he has a pragmatic attitude which accepts that things have to change. 'My great-grandfather would have made changes from the way his father farmed, as I've accepted my son has made changes from the way I did things. Life is like that and so is farming. You can't get the past back.'

THE ROLLS ROYCE OF CHICKEN HOUSES!

One of Aubrey's strongest memories from his youth has only an indirect connection with farming, but it is a story he still loves to tell: 'When I was seventeen I saw a Rolls Royce advertised for £30. My total savings amounted to £17 at the time, but I wrote to the advertiser anyway and offered him what I had, and to my astonishment he took it. My older brother drove it down from Leatherhead. It was a Silver Ghost built in 1912, and because it had a 45 horsepower engine I couldn't afford to tax it for the road; road tax in those days was worked out at £1 per year for every unit of horsepower. So all I could do was drive it round the meadows. A few years later I stripped the body off, wrapped chains round the rear axle and used it to roll and harrow the meadows. Then I got fed up with it and we left it in a shed for years. Eventually I sold the engine to a man who needed an engine for his motorboat, and I used the chassis as a chicken house. It's not every farmer who keeps his chickens in a Rolls!'

Mine Hunting Host

Jack Crook : Devon

MINE HUNTING HOST

For much of his seventy-four years, Jack Crook has lived for horses and hunting. He has also enjoyed more than the odd stirrup cup and there have been many times when the mixing of such interests has produced a cocktail of misfortune. Jack recalls:

'One day I rode over to the Rising Sun and got tanked up on too much scotch. On the way back I tried to jump this very big fence, but the horse came back on me and I gashed my head. Down at Newton [Abbot] hospital I had to have four stitches, but when I asked for an anaesthetic the doctor said: "I think you've had enough already."

Opposite:
Hunting has been a lifetime's interest for Jack (centre)

The Hunt often met at the Jolly Sailor

'I also used to go to other boozers in me horse and trap, for a couple of hours from about six in the evening. One night I was over at Kingsteignton with Tony Skedgell when this woman called out to us: "Do you know this is a one-way street?" Tony called back: "Yes, and we're only goin' one way." So she phoned the police and they phoned my wife, Gin. Although that woman who reported us didn't know our names, the police knew there was only one mad bugger about here with a horse and trap.

'One of our local policemen was a bloody nuisance, always comin' round to hide behind the wall by the cellar just as I called time in the bar. So one night I chucked some water over the wall, pretending that I didn't know he was there, and out 'e came in a rush.

'One year I was privileged to lead Newton carnival on my horse, and as I rode through the town this huntin' friend saw me, dashed into the nearby supermarket and came out with a can of beer to keep me going. Then I held the whole procession up while I drank it.'

The son of a horseman and born at Tiverton on 20 September 1924, Jack soon became very interested in most country pursuits. As a boy he worked for Uffculme Co-operative Wholesale Society for a few years before joining the Great Western Railway in 1941, as a footplate fireman. Eventually he qualified as a driver, 'but it was a real case of dead man's shoes unless you were prepared to move away,' so in 1967 he took redundancy money and became the tenant of the Heavitree Brewery's Jolly Sailor at East Ogwell, near Newton Abbot. The pub had been neglected for some time.

'I'd known the pub before as I used to come

THE JOLLY SAILOR

EFFORDS TRANSPORT

The publican
with his friends at
another Devonshire
pub, the Setting
Sun, Torrington, at
the turn of the
century

out 'ere helpin' a local farmer with the harvest. They say it got its name from the days when the press gangs used to visit to pick up more labour. There's certainly always been a lot of Navy chaps hereabouts, and we're not too far from the sea. But we never knew how old the building was. Apparently it was two cottages knocked into one in the 1920s – one ol' chap always said 'e was born in our bedroom. The walls were ever so thick, all cob and stone, so they must have gone back a few centuries.

'When Gin and I went there we wouldn't move into the livin' quarters because it was so filthy, so while the place was done up we stayed in a caravan for seven weeks. Poor Gin – that's an old family name, by the way, and nothing to do with pubs – well, she spent ages cleaning this iron bath which had become black, but when she got to the bottom she discovered it was cracked, so she'd wasted all that time. Then we acciden-

tally dropped some liquid on the floor and discovered that the carpet was not brown after all, but red. I shot rats out the window and discovered loads of others dead under the floorboards. In them days the takin's was only £60 a week, but we soon got up to £150 with new attractions such as a skittle alley in the old pig barn I bought.

'There was a lot of labour about in those days and most of our customers were workers from farms, the council, the waterworks and so on. Some of them were great characters, including Reg Mathews, a poacher known as Greybird who never did a day's work in his life. He was always borrowing a pound and you rarely got your money back.

'Edward Stone was a real boozer. One night, when there was a lot of snow, someone came in and said there was a pair of boots out in the car park. When I went to investigate I discovered there was someone inside the boots – completely buried by the snow! It was Edward Stone, who'd been in such a state that when he slipped he couldn't get up again. And the more he struggled the more he covered himself over. 'E'd 'ave been dead by the morning if his boots hadn't been spotted.

'Then there was Bill Cann who used to get up on the table to sing, but one night 'e forgot 'e was up there and stepped right off with one hell of a bang. He never did get back up after that. Bill Cann and Jeff Thomson each drank ten pints of farm cider a day, so we had no problem in getting through forty gallons every week.

'We always made our own amusement, but now there's just two tellies in our old bar. We used to 'ave a good sing-song most Saturdays, especially with a huntin' crowd in. It was always the tradition with the hunt to finish up in the evenin' where you started off in the mornin', so they'd come back to the pub on days we held meets there – generally two or three times a year each for both the South Devon and the Dart Vale. Luckily we never had any antis in as we had too many supporters around, but there were a few out on the moor I had to put my whip round. The pub meets stopped in about 1987 because the area had become too built up, but we were able to continue with hunt supporters' club meetings.'

Jack started hunting with the South Devon and the Dart Vale in the 1950s, when he was still on the railways. In those days he did not own his own horse but would 'borrow anyone's that needed exercising'. Later he whipped-in to the Dart Vale for three years and not only had his own hunter but also stabled two others. Generally, he hunted three days a fortnight, but insists that his passion did not interfere with the running of the pub.

'I'd never go off without leaving everything completely ready for opening by nine o'clock in the morning. Nowadays they don't know the meaning of the word work – you go in many pubs and they're still moppin' up at eleven o'clock. Course, with all the food laid on now it's much more difficult to get time off. Also, now it's hard to find somewhere to play a simple game of darts, euchre or table skittles because they want every table to eat on. But there aren't many landlords can say they've cooked breakfast on a shovel over the fire. This was what us railway chaps always used to do, so one day I had to do it for my customers in the bar.'

Jack no longer rides to hounds, but remains a keen ferreter and roughshooter. And at his East Ogwell home he remains close to both foxes and the Jolly Sailor. He told me: 'I can still see a vixen and four cubs here any night at the moment. I just go over with a few scraps and whistle 'em up on the green. Also, Gin and I still go down the pub for a game of cards two or three mornin's a week, but I'm afraid most of our old friends are gone now and we'm the last of the boozers.'

Jack behind the bar of the Jolly Sailor

Lumberjills

Berta Gillatt, Doris Streatfield &
Eileen Rawlinson : Timber Girls

LUMBERJILLS: THE TIMBER GIRLS

The need for women in the forests began as soon as war broke out in September 1939, but the Land Army girls were slow to volunteer for woodland work. By 1942 so many of the men in forestry had been called up that the need was even more urgent, and in April that year the Women's Timber Corps (WTC) was set up quite separately from the Land Army, answerable to the Ministry of Supply's Home-grown Timber department rather than to the Ministry of Agriculture. That separation seemed to work well: by July 1943, when recruitment ceased, there were more than 3,000 lumberjills in the woods and at the sawmills, and they worked right through the war and beyond it. At its peak there were more than 6,000 members, including those in Scotland. The WTC was finally disbanded on 31 August 1946.

The Land Army girls had been encouraged to train for timber work on a four-week course. Margaret Vidler (née Carwardine) remembered her training in Yorkshire only too well. At seven on that first morning they were bundled into the back of an open lorry and bounced into a clearing in a pine forest, clambering out in their hard army-issue boots and standing about while a second lorry was unloaded of their tools.

'This is a four-and-a-half pound axe, see,' said a man with muscles like rope. He demonstrated the technique. 'When you swing it, you gotta slide your hand down the shaft like this ... Let the blade fall, see. That's the secret. Don't try to hack.'

That was Margaret's first surprise: surely they didn't expect girls to cut down trees? She had volunteered as a timber measurer.

He continued with the lesson. 'Now, you put the scarf in the tree the way it must fall. Nice big chucks like this – the slices you cut out are called chucks. Neatly and effortlessly, he sliced out a huge crescent of wood. 'Now, when the scarf is in, you go round the back with a cross-cut. You have to kneel down – right down, mind, this timber mustn't be wasted. Every scrap counts.

There's a war on and we don't want no waste. So you kneel behind the tree, one either side, and you cut just above the roots. You pull, see – *pull, pull, pull*: this saw's a puller, not a pusher, as you'll soon find out.'

As his bemused students swung their first axes, cries of 'Cuckoo! Cuckoo!' rang out from the watching men. A cuckoo, they soon learned, was a tree that snagged in the branches of a standing tree and therefore could not fall.

Jessie Bailey, as a WTC member, remarked aptly when the Corps ceased to exist: 'Of all the jobs which women on the land have undertaken, it is the work of the Timber Corps which would probably have startled our great-grandmothers most. Land girls like Bo Peep and the Pretty Maid who was going a-milking and the Goose Girl have been friends for many generations; but there have been no nursery rhymes or fairy stories about maidens who hewed down forests, nor cautionary tales about young ladies who cut off their fingers owing to carelessness with a circular saw.'

Bonneted Bo Peeps the lumberjills certainly were not! They tackled every sort of job connected with woods and trees: they drove tractors

and locomotives hauling loads of timber up and down impossible gradients, and they even steered motorboats towing rafts of logs across distant Scottish lochs, as well as measuring and felling trees, slicing them up and loading endless telegraph poles, pit props, railway sleepers and potential packing cases and charcoal.

The earliest of the training camps was in Gloucestershire at the Parkend Forestry School, Lydney in the Forest of Dean. Later the girls were also trained in Yorkshire at Morlands Camp,

Wetherby, and in Suffolk at Culford, Bury St Edmunds.

For many girls, it was a sudden rite of passage from the security of home to hardworking independence in all sorts of out-of-the-way forests and mills. They came from every type of social background; they came from all over the country, very often from the cities with no experience of the countryside, let alone forestry. They grew up fast, and they were invariably nicknamed Timber.

Photographers did little to dispel the notion of women volunteers being pretty little things messing about down on the farm. Despite this cheeky image the work of the Women's Timber Corps was tough

BERTA GILLATT
(née Winn)

Berta, now living near Banbury, has been a prime mover in setting up WTC reunions and gathering material for the museums. A small, merry, pretty and energetic woman today, she was living in Birmingham in 1942 and working as a comptometer operator. Like everybody else, at the age of seventeen-and-a-half she registered for war work. She did not like the idea of either the nearest factory or the armed forces but she 'had a thing about trees'. In May, she was interviewed for the new WTC. Towards the end of that summer she received her uniform: one felt hat, one WLA badge, three cream shirts, one green pullover, two pairs of fawn breeches, two pairs of dungarees, two overall coats, one three-quarter-length great coat, one mac, two pairs of brown shoes, a pair of black boots, leggings, and an armband for the six-monthly service flashes. In September she found her way to Morlands Camp for her four-week training, along with two hundred other girls. They all slept on unmattressed plywood boards covered by a blanket and sheet – an unforgiving base for muscles aching from unaccustomed manual labour. Her first day's work at Wetherby was loading at the railway station into a truck taller than she was, and it was almost a relief to have to rise from that unyielding bed early enough for an outdoor roll call at 6am.

Berta, with her comptometer experience, was allotted as a measurer – a role which involved not only measuring felled timber (length and half-way girth) and calculating its cubic content with the help of a Hoppus Ready Reckoner, but also counting pit-props, measuring cordwood, burning brushwood, selecting telegraph and Admiralty poles, keeping records of outgoing goods from sawmills, calculating wages and buying private woodlands.

Her training successfully completed, she was given her new green beret and the brown bakelite badge which bore a fir tree surmounted by a crown, and surrounded with the words 'Timber Corps' and (irritatingly to some) 'WLA'. She was posted to Cinderford in the Forest of Dean. 'A wonderful place' she enthuses.

Her first job was in Micheldean Wood. She worked on several other sites in the Dean but her favourite was Chestnuts Wood, Little Dean, where they measured felled timber, pit-props and cordwood.

'There was a sawmill run by 47 Battalion of the Royal Engineers – all Scotsmen – helped, or hindered, by the Italian prisoners-of-war. Their job was to roll the timber down the ramp; we measured the timber at the sawmill and checked it off before it was dispatched into lorries as railway sleepers and planks. There was a little wooden hut where we did all the office work, including the returns and the wages. I discovered that some people could not read or write. They had to sign with a cross, but they could still tell you if there was anything wrong with their wage calculations!'

There were everyday problems in the woods. 'By the side of the sawmill were two little cottages and one day a lovely lady at their gate, Maisie Gardner, asked if we'd like a cup of tea. I was delighted – we only had cold tea from the bottle, and she offered us as many hot cups of tea and coffee as we liked.'

There were occasional problems with the Italians. Berta remembers a knock at her office door one day: it was a handsome Italian barber. 'He had the biggest wad of money notes in an elastic band and a great big thick gold wedding ring on the top. He said, "You, me, five minutes up the woods and it's yours." I said, "Get out of here!" ' He was not the first, or the last, to try it on with this eighteen-year-old; she had already fended off a 'big fat man in Italian naval uniform.' As Margaret Vidler remarked, you learned to take care of yourself 'for it was no use screaming rape to the lonely trees.'

Other Italian memories are associated with food in those wartime days of rationing. 'Every day those Italians had a slice of gammon, an egg, chips – that was their lunch, every day, and all we had was endless cheese sandwiches and cold tea. They had coffee made with all milk, drunk out of soup tins. At one stage in Chestnuts Wood the Italian cook came into my office with a plate of egg and chips and said, "You like, you have". After that he gave us that every day'.

Opposite: A WTC forester measuring timber in the New Forest

Gladys (Clarke) Bainbridge and friend Ngaire

There were other foreign voices in the woods. In the Dean she had to calculate the hours of a pair of charcoal burners who were Danish sailors, escaped to England and on curfew, living in private billets and reporting to the police once a week. 'They looked so forlorn. It was a filthy job and a lot of the Timber Corps girls did it because the Italians refused. If the girls were at a hostel, they got an extra ration of soap for that job.'

From Chestnuts Wood, Berta was transferred to the beautiful acres of the Westonbirt Arboretum, with a billet in the town of Tetbury. Then she moved to Dorset, where she worked in Wareham Woods, with an office at the railway station, and also on a delightful site overlooking Lulworth Cove, with 'a very distinguished gentleman, Fabian Hayes Turner, as a sort of fore-man. Instead of the proper forester's clothes with leather bindings and so on, he always wore a great big wool cloak.'

For a while she was put in charge of a group of forestry girls based at Puddletown in Nissen huts heated by smoky tortoise stoves. She did not like Puddletown. It was a bad place to be based: there were three pubs, one small post-office shop and nothing at all to do in their spare time. The camp was 'cold, dirty and horrible.' Most of the girls were from Newcastle. 'They were the biggest, toughest, roughest lot — appalling language, drank like fishes, banned from two of the three pubs there. Awful crew.'

Berta married at eighteen-and-a-half and proudly gave her occupation as 'Measurer, WTC' on her marriage certificate. They were proud of their corps, and quite offended that they could only get WLA armbands, ties and coat flashes. But they did find private supplies of what looked like a suitable insignia: a pair of crossed axes. Berta bought hers in the Army & Navy stores in Gloucester and sewed it on to the sleeve of her greatcoat.

Heather Crisford and Flo Cryer

BETTY PAGE

Betty Page lives in the Hampshire village of Selborne. She is a straightforward, practical sort of woman who does a great deal of charity work now. At the beginning of the war she was a chestnut-haired nineteen-year-old living in Wrecclesham, Surrey. She considered joining the armed forces but her father told her she would come to a nasty end and her brother,

too. We had to take shelter behind those huge trees. Then of course Southampton was bombed.

She enjoyed the sawmill and was doing well on the job as a measurer, but after a difference of opinion with a resentful forewoman, she walked out. Her brother had been right about her rebellious nature.

She found herself a new posting in Cumberland. 'It was marvellous up there. Apart from worrying about my two brothers, I really

'They poached tiny trout for breakfast ...'

already in the forces, said that she was too rebellious by nature to knuckle under to a bullying NCO. One day two women came to the door looking for lodgings; they were in the Land Army but were doing forestry work. Betty was immediately interested, and in February 1940 she went to the Forest of Dean for her month's training at Parkend.

Betty's first posting was to Thetford, in East Anglia. Her second was in the New Forest at an Ashurst sawmill, and that was a happy time of very hard work. 'It was the time of Dunkirk, though, and I remember all the trains loaded with injured people coming through the station with red crosses on them. It was then the German air force was hotting up and they used to strafe those trains – and strafe us in the Forest

had a happy war.' She had lodgings at Loweswater and then, with two sisters, took over an old World War I army hut right on the edge of Crummock Water. They poached tiny trout for breakfast, grilling them over an open fire by the lake; they watched the buzzards and heard the evocative call of the curlews. They cycled for miles and miles to measure for timber fellers, who were paid on piecework by the volume they felled. Often the bike ride was eighteen miles each way, and often the forests were on very steep slopes. 'We used to wear shorts and got as brown as berries. We had Land Army uniform basically – green jerseys, knee breeches, thick woollen khaki socks and heavy brown shoes.' The corduroy breeches were 'sort of khaki-ish or washed-out mud colour' and they had been issued with khaki Land Army felt hats rather than the WTC's green beret. The clothes and hat were far from waterproof. 'Nothing kept the rain out – we used to get so wet! But it was lovely. We had terrible winters up there. I was always a bit chesty and got a terrible cough and cold in that army hut; one very cold night, with crisp snow on the ground, I went outside in my pyjamas with nothing on my feet and I danced about in the moonlight – and it cured me.'

She then went to a sawmill at East Witton in Wensleydale, right under the fells, and there were some hair-raising incidents when articulated lorries laden with timber careered out of control down the slopes. There was also the problem of being on the flightpath of enemy planes, on their way to bomb Liverpool, which would dump unwanted bombs on the way home. Betty was blown out of bed one night, and on another was 'blown into a basket of wet washing.'

The sawmill was closed down when the local timber supply ran out, and they moved down to the Earl of Swinton's estate at Masham. Then she went to Westmorland and stayed in a gamekeeper's cottage. The keeper was a Scot, 'a dreamy person,' who taught her a great deal about wildlife and how to identify various birds and animals. The conifer forests were full of birds, especially tits, and deer. He showed her for the first time a goldcrest's nest, and all his patient

'The conifer forests were full of birds, especially tits, and deer.'

teaching would come in handy later in life as well as being a great pleasure. 'That is all I remember about Westmorland – I remember nothing about the work at all.'

The next posting was right up on the borders near Rothbury, Northumberland, where her only real memory is of chain-smoking to keep away the flies on the long walks home in those busless days. By now it was 1943 and she was posted to a sawmill at Crowborough in Sussex. She lived in a very old caravan on site and found herself right in the path of the doodlebugs of 1944. 'They used to fly over the sawmill and the anti-aircraft shrapnel would land on top of the caravan. At the peak of it all, they were falling all around us – this doodlebug was coming straight for the huge crane on the sawmill and we just watched, aghast, but there were two Spitfires around and one of them came down and just tipped the doodlebug's wing. It landed a quarter of a mile away instead. If it hadn't been for that Spitfire, I wouldn't be here today.'

Such dramas apart, she did not feel part of the war at the sawmill: the atmosphere was more one of making money than contributing to the war effort. Disenchanted, she parted company and left the Timber Corps. But that was by no means the end of her forestry career: in 1947 she joined the Forestry Commission at its new Alice Holt research station and worked her way through a variety of jobs there over the next thirty years, the most interesting being collecting specimens for the entomology department's research into larch sawfly. 'It would attack the young shoot and go into the twig, sealing itself in behind a little transparent window.'

She retired in 1976, but her interest in wood continued: she produced some beautiful, simple carvings, one of which is in her local church, and liked nothing better than a spot of joinery. Of her days with the WTC, she said: 'It was a great life. I was in heaven. All that fresh air and weather and wildness and sheer hard work. Up in the forests and on the fells it really was my kind of life. It seems like only yesterday . . .'

DORIS STREATFIELD

Doris was born and bred in London, but was evacuated in 1940 to her grandparents in Lincolnshire. On an impulse, she enrolled with the forestry branch of the Women's Land Army at the age of seventeen-and-a-half. She took a bus and alighted at a crossroads in the middle of nowhere, to be met by an organiser who took her to a billet down the road in the small hamlet of Hanthorpe, north of Bourne.

She had a shock on her first morning in forestry. She couldn't ride a bike and there was no other means of getting about. Not that there was a bike for her that first day: she and her fellow lumberjill set off pushing the friend's bike. 'Oh dear, oh dear. Gum boots, bib-and-brace overalls, thick socks, haversack with my lunch and to drink a bottle of cold tea. The miles we walked seemed to be eternity.' What had she let herself in for?

They at last reached Kirkby Underwood and walked on beyond it to a large green hut which would be their assembly point every morning. Then they tramped further, through the barley fields and into a new plantation, where they sickled away the long grass to give the young trees light. 'My goodness, what a back-breaking job! Up and down these fields we toiled and I must confess many a young tree lost its top.'

Poor Doris. Her next trial was the winter. 'You can imagine how we girls suffered – we were all town-bred and not used to the wide open spaces. On one particularly bitter day I was so cold when I returned to the billet that my colleagues had to prise my fingers off the handlebars of my bike. My landlady made me sit with my feet in a bowl of hot mustard water, saying I wasn't strong enough for this sort of work and I ought to go home. I gritted my teeth, determined not to lose face.'

After eighteen months in Lincolnshire, Doris and two friends decided to transfer to the newly formed Women's Timber Corps. They were not popular: it seemed to cause all sorts of bureaucratic problems, but in the end 'we swapped our

'...but there were two spitfires around ...'

A charcoal burner in the Forest of Dean stacking short lengths of timber ready for firing

pork-pie hat for a green beret and a brown badge and we thought we were the cat's whiskers.'

The threesome considered themselves to be old hands at the job by now, but they were sent off to Wetherby for their month's training anyway. Their first posting was to a Gloucestershire sawmill. 'Goodness me! We were dropped off in the middle of a common, really isolated this time, with just two cottages – one of them was our billet.'

The sawmill was manned by Spanish prisoners-of-war in the charge of New Zealanders. The girls found cordwood for the charcoal kilns alongside the sawmill; they measured trees and marked them up so that the prisoners could saw them into railway sleepers; and they rode with the men on the lorry taking timber to a match-making company in Gloucester.

In the end town-bred Doris survived all that the woods threw at her and she stayed 'in the Timber' for four years. Now living in Bracebridge Heath, Lincoln, she says: 'It was really a great experience and although we had some rough times we also had some good times. I wouldn't have missed it for anything.'

EILEEN RAWLINSON
(née Burton)

Eileen travelled from Cardiff in October 1942 to Culford Camp, set in the midst of the Forestry Commission's softwood plantations near Thetford in Norfolk, for her month's training in forestry. She learned the art of the woodman: felling, trimming, sawing, stacking and carting, stripping bark and lending a hand at the sawmill. Culford's corrugated iron Nissen huts had been used as a work camp during the Depression. 'The men had helped to plant the forests which now we were to help cut down …'

Eileen had rarely ventured beyond the borders of Wales before. 'I was to have my eyes opened, ears assaulted, muscles hardened and mind broadened to take this life in my stride. Once embarked on these new ways, we loved it all. We were doing our bit for King and Country and we did it with enthusiasm. But who'd believe we actually felled trees?'

Their felling tools were axes and cross-cut saws, the latter often wielded while they were on their knees. Being a resourceful bunch, they invaded Bury St Edmunds and bought up every supply of horse knee-pads they could find in the shops.

Eileen was only 5ft 2in tall and used a four-and-a-half pound axe. She also learned how to sharpen it on a grindstone and how to 'hone a keen blade with a carborundum stone.' At the end of the course she was put into a group of nine forest workers posted to a site near Ashford, Kent. They worked mostly in beech coppice, where the fellings were 6–8in in diameter and each girl was expected to cut twenty-eight to thirty a day, clean and stack them, burn the brushwood and clear the underbrush. They also felled some larger oaks, on average about two foot in diameter, and prepared all the timber for extraction either by tractor or by horse. For three weeks in April and May they debarked the oaks for the tanneries, peeling off the bark like the skin from an orange.

Felling was an art, of course. They would begin by trimming the protruding tree roots at ground level and would put the 'fall' in the tree, cutting only six inches above ground level to make use of as much of the trunk as possible. Down they would go, on to their horse knee-pads, sawing as they had been taught and inserting steel wedges to keep the cut open. 'Before the final bite of the saw, a warning cry of "Timber!" sounded; then the saw was drawn in its final sway and the wedges were finally clouted before the tree came crashing down in all its thunderous glory.'

Like many others, they had the frightening experience of being strafed by German fighter planes as they worked and they had to bolt for cover behind the trees. But otherwise the summer of 1943 was a glorious one and they worked in suntops and shorts in spite of the midges.

Eileen's next posting was in Shirley Hills, near Croydon, felling tall Scotch pines for telegraph poles and working in the beech and larch woods. 'In the spring we witnessed one of nature's tragedies. High amongst the tree foliage were both red and grey squirrels, but came the summer time and the red squirrels had vanished from our wood. We witnessed the killing of the red squirrels by the grey: the high-pitched screams of the chase were a frightening sound, and to see the bodies of the red squirrels as they came hurtling to the ground was deeply upsetting. We assumed our presence in the wood and the air raids over Croydon were upsetting woodland life.'

From Shirley Hills she moved down to Heathfield, Sussex, to clear chestnut coppice wood, all by axe – very hard work. Then they felled Scotch pines in what was then known as 'bomb alley' in a direct line from Eastbourne to London, and most of their time was spent falling flat on the ground. 'When one of our airmen patrolling over open country saw a V1 rocket on course for London, he'd chase it and put his plane's wings under the rocket's, tilting it so that it then fell like a stone. The pilot would emit a whoop of success, then perform a victory roll

BARK PEELING

The barking season had just commenced, and what he had heard was the tear of the ripping-tool as it ploughed its way along the sticky parting between the trunk and the rind – A milking-pail of cider stood near, a half-pint cup floating on it, with which they dipped and drank whenever they passed the pail.

Each tree doomed to the flaying process was first attacked by Upjohn. With a small bill-hook he carefully freed the collar of the tree from twigs and patches of moss which encrusted it to a height of a foot or two above the ground, an operation comparable to the 'little toilette' of the executioner's victim. After this it was barked in its erect position to a point as high as a man could reach. If a fine product of vegetable nature could ever be said to look ridiculous it was the case now, when the oak stood naked-legged, and as if ashamed, till the axe-man came and cut a ring round it, and the two Timothys finished the work with the cross-cut saw.

As soon as it had fallen the barkers attacked it like locusts, and in a short time not a particle of rind was left on the trunk and larger limbs. Marty South was an adept at peeling the upper parts: and there she stood encaged amid the mass of twigs and buds like a great bird, running her ripping-tool into the smallest branches, beyond the furthest points to which the skill and patience of the men enabled them to proceed – branches which, in their lifetime, had swayed high above the bulk of the wood, and caught the earliest rays of the sun and moon while the lower part of the forest was still in darkness.

'You seem to have a better instrument than they, Mary', said Fitzpiers.

'No, sir, she said, holding up the tool, a horse's leg-bone fitted into a handle and filed to an edge; 'tis only that they've less patience with the twigs, because their time is worth more than mine.'

A little shed had been constructed on the spot, of thatched hurdles and boughs, and in front of it was a fire over which a kettle sang.

Thomas Hardy, The Woodlanders, 1887

and be off to make the next encounter. Most of the airmen had no idea we were in the vicinity. Our wild gesticulations and prancing eventually drew the attention of some of them, but their thrill in the chase still caused us to dive for cover and clamp our hands over our ears.'

Later that summer she was transferred to the Cothi valley in west Wales and worked over a wide area of Carmarthenshire, living in a mountainside hostel with about thirty Land Army girls through a bitterly cold winter. But the spring in that valley was lovely. They were in Carmarthenshire on VE Day and travelled by lorry to Cardiff to join in the parades and turn their thoughts to civvy street.

DELLA GARDNER
(née Smith)

Della left school in the summer of 1937 and worked in Canada House in Trafalgar Square. Her company was evacuated to Bromley, Kent, in September 1939 and she soon decided to enrol as a timber measurer in the Women's Land Army. She trained at Lydney in the Forest of Dean, surrounded by endless rows and rows of trees –

'Even his little old sister, who smoked a clay pipe ...'

a good introduction to the sense of isolation that many new forest workers would experience. Her first posting was in Buckinghamshire, where she was billeted at Stokenchurch, near High Wycombe. The foreman lived on the village green in a tumbledown cottage and had little idea of management, however good he might have been with timber. 'Anybody who wanted a job was on his books. Even his little old sister, who smoked a clay pipe and never ventured out of the cottage, was on the payroll. In the winter a large number of gypsies joined our ranks; they spent their time burning up the vast quantities of brushwood. The men were paid on piecework and it was our responsibility to keep records of their work, and to do all the clerical work involved in dispatching the thousands of pit props.' She also helped with the manual work, travelling on the lorries to unload the props into empty coal trucks at various railway stations, and she learned to drive a brightly painted 'fairground type lorry' with gate-change gears on the right-hand side of the driving seat.

They felled their way through the Chiltern Hills, Ibstone, Turville, Fingest, Skirmett, down into the Thames Valley, working in beautiful surroundings from Henley, through Hambledon, Aston, Medmenham and Marlow. They exhausted the supply of softwood in Buckinghamshire and Della was posted to Preston in Hertfordshire. Unusually for the time, she was under a trained forester. His staff included men whose age group had not yet been called up, and also a group of Italian prisoners under armed guard.

'We reduced plantation after plantation to a flattened mass of timber,' Della recalls, a pattern that was followed all over the country at that time of great demand for home-grown timber. They worked around St Pauls Walden, King's Walden, Breachwood Green, St Ippollitts ... She was billeted with the butler's wife on Captain Brassie's Node estate. Fellers from a wide area were concentrated on the village of Codicote, and thence they felled plantations in Kimpton, Whitwell, Wheathampstead and Ayot St

Charcoal burner's hut in the New Forest

Lawrence, Weston and Walkern, constantly on the move, swathing through one plantation and on to the next almost before the trees had hit the ground. 'Huts were erected, tractors, lorries, drums of oil, axes, saws, wedges, tools of all descriptions were brought in. The men worked in pairs, each felling a strip in the dark wood until gradually the light was let through the remaining trees. The trees were cut close to the ground to allow the tractors to be driven through the wood. No part of the tree was wasted.'

Gradually the girls themselves had to carry out more and more of the work as the men were called up. In the summer of 1944 Della went to Hertford to take charge of the felling of 200 acres of hornbeam coppice in woodland owned by the Abel-Smith family around Bramfield, and its conversion into charcoal. (She would settle in Hertford after the war and still lives in Bengeo.) There were about thirty girls in her charge, from all over the country, and a squad of Italian POWs. The girls felled the trees, working on piece rates; the felled wood was stacked and measured in cords, then it was loaded by the prisoners on to trailers, which the girls hauled out to the kiln by tractor.

The kilns, 'like huge stove pipes with removable lid and chimneys', were in low rows, with saw benches on rail tracks so that they could be moved alongside the kilns. Seven tons of wood, sawn into short lengths and thrown into the kilns, would yield one ton of charcoal. 'The kilns were filled, fired in rotation, and sealed with sand to prevent air entering and burning the wood to ashes. After twenty-four hours the white smoke from the chimney turned to a blue haze.' The charcoal was ready. It was left to cool and was then sacked up and loaded into lorries by the girls, who drove their loads to the goods station at Hertford, where the sacks were transferred into the empty coal wagons and sent to Courtaulds factory in Manchester as an ingredient for smoke-screens when Allied troops were crossing the Rhine into Germany.

On the eve of VE Day in May, 1945, the whole group went up to London and joined in the celebrations in Trafalgar Square. The last kiln at Bramfield was fired in the spring of 1946 and the work of the lumberjills came to an end.

✳ ✳ ✳

And so those women who had come from so many different places and different backgrounds, left behind their invigorating outdoor life – a life that could be alarmingly tough, but in which they found a great companionship that, in many cases, has lasted for the rest of their lives. Many of the elements of each story are shared – the lack of money and food, the varied billets, the homesickness, the labour, the cold and the wet, the isolated surroundings, the endless acres of conifer forest, the village dances, the laughs, the lasting friendships, the prisoners-of-war. There were tales of great stoicism, such as that of Gladys: she had taken the butt end of 200 telegraph poles being loaded into railway wagons all day and, without telling anybody, gave birth to a baby girl two hours after her shift was over. There are memories of rogue equipment, like the ancient sawmill steam engine which would run out of control, shuddering and pounding and whirling the bench saw crazily while everybody took to their heels.

They had not been the first of the lumberjills. Their predecessors in World War I have received even less recognition. Ernest Pulbrook, in his book published in the early 1920s, dismissed them in a few words: 'Women also assisted in forestry work, which became a great industry in woodland districts, mainly carried on by Canadians and Portuguese, and later by German prisoners. Settlements of log huts, more familiar to the backwoods of America than the ordered landscapes of England, sprang up in clearings and on hillsides, and coverts once sacred to the pheasant were transformed into deserts of mud mottled with tree stumps and mountains of sawdust.' He published a photograph of a pair of girls standing

Laura Simpson, Forestry Corps, 1918–19

on a sledge-load of timber, holding the reins of a fine pair of working horses as they hauled the wood out of the forest. The driver looks for all the world like a female Ben Hur in a chariot race, or perhaps Boadicea.

Laura Simpson, who was born in Derbyshire in 1898 and lived at Basford, Nottingham, died in Rotherham in the spring of 1993. She was one of those pioneers who joined the Women's Forestry Corps and was stationed in a tented camp in Gloucestershire in 1918–19. She would have had some marvellous stories to tell.

Endless memories, endless tales from women proud to call themselves 'Old Woodlanders'.

Timber! WTC workers felling trees in the New Forest

The Farmer's Boy

Leslie Buckle : Sussex and Kent

THE FARMER'S BOY

Leslie Buckle did not come from a keepering family, but his father's farming occupation was certainly instrumental in determining his future. Leslie was born on 4 October 1921 at his father's Mead End Farm, Sway, in the New Forest, then still a very unspoilt and remote corner of Hampshire quite unlike the tourist trap of today.

*Opposite:
Peeling potatoes for the stew. Gypsies were regular callers at the Buckle household selling reels of cotton, bootlaces and wooden pegs*

It was a place frequented by gypsies, who often came around to play their wind-up wooden organs in the road. And on the rare occasions when the family had a few spare coppers young Leslie would be sent out with a penny or tuppence for the music-makers.

One day a gypsy woman came to the Buckle door selling reels of cotton, bootlaces and wooden pegs with pieces of cocoa tin round the ends. On her back was a grubby infant wrapped in a blanket, and her eyes lit up when she saw five-year-old Leslie walking most uncomfortably behind his mother. Casually, she asked what the trouble was.

Leslie told me: 'I had a boil on my bum: it had been there for a couple of weeks and was so painful I needed at least three cushions before I could sit down. Going to the loo was a real problem.'

'Anyway, the tinker said I should be given the liquor from boiled dock root. So that's what we did – and 'orrible brown stuff it was too. To our amazement the boil came right up and burst within twelve hours and I soon made a full recovery.'

It was in those New Forest days that Leslie first came into contact with a shotgun, though it was not used for sporting purposes. His father was the local horse slaughterer, but he would only undertake this unpopular task if allowed to use his twelve-bore.

Leslie also helped his father take the horse hides to Sway railway station, but this was a pleasant task because he was always rewarded with a penny, which he put into the Nestlé's machine to buy 'one very thin slice of chocolate.'

A few years later the family moved to Sussex, Leslie's father becoming the tenant of Huxwood Farm on the Idsworth Estate, near Rowland's Castle, on the Hampshire–Sussex border. Their cottage was right in the middle of a keeper's beat and not surprisingly it was not long before ten-year-old Leslie was helping the beat-keeper with simple chores such as setting traps and feeding pheasants. Indeed, the experience made such an impression on the lad that he decided there and then that he wanted to be a gamekeeper.

Sometimes he went beating on a Saturday to earn 3s 6d, and if he was lucky enough to carry a

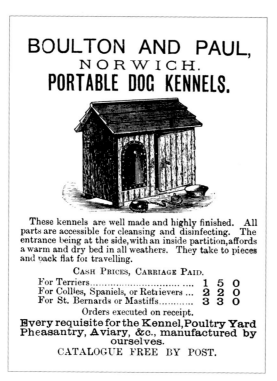

spare cartridge bag for one of the Guns a shiny, silver half-crown would probably come his way too. At the time all the beaters had to take their own sandwich lunch, but the men were given beer by the estate.

Knowing what he wanted to do in life, Leslie lost interest in school long before the leaving age of fourteen and matters came to a head anyway in the summer, when he was still thirteen. When he announced that he was to play Prince Charming in the school panto his father decided enough was enough. There would be no more 'time wasting' and young Leslie could leave immediately.

At first the lad had to help his father on the farm, and in those days everything was horse-drawn. 'On the farm itself we had a mixture of all sorts — cattle, pigs and so on, but not a lot of anything, including money.'

When he was fifteen, Leslie went to work as a keeper's help for Countess Howe who owned the Idsworth estate, where he had first been so attracted to the keeper's life. And it was close enough for him to travel home to his parents' house each day.

Most unusually, the Idsworth keepers were not allowed to keep dogs: that was a job for estate specialists, as with Lady Howe, the shooting took second place to her great passion for field trialling. The estate kennel contained about sixty labradors, pointers and setters, and there was a full-time gundog trainer, Mr Gaunt, as well as two kennelmen and a girl assistant.

'In those days it was only the upper set that went to field trials,' said Leslie, 'though there were keepers' trials.' These were always two-day events at Idsworth and Lady Howe always bought the winning dog. Apparently keepers could only enter if they agreed to let Lady Howe buy the winning animal. And although she always had black labradors, when a yellow dog won in 1938 she had no hesitation in paying a hundred guineas for it — an enormous sum in those days.

On his first day there, Leslie accompanied the headkeeper to a hut in the woods where they collected a bag of whole maize – no problem for the pheasants to deal with in October. Then they marched around the beat together, feeding birds along the way, and thereafter Leslie was left alone to get on with it. His other duties included setting vermin traps, but whereas the other keepers had new or sound ginns, Leslie had to make do with old ones, putting blocks of wood under the weak mechanism so that they would spring better.

In those days there were many more stoats and weasels to be dealt with as there were so many more rabbits and other prey for them to feed on. But the keepers did not resent these pests too much as selling their skins was just about the only legal way they could supplement their modest income. Grade I stoat skins fetched 1/6d each. They were tagged and, when there were enough, a batch was sent to Friends, the fur and feather merchants, who also took jays' wings for fly-tying and hat decoration.

Eventually a 12/6d postal order would arrive, 'but that was only enough to buy one boot' remembered Leslie. 'So then you had to wait ages to gather enough to buy the other. Horse-hide boots were the only really water-proof ones. The hides were tanned in the Black Forest by Krupps and we bought the boots from a firm in Scotland, but as far as I know you can't get the like of 'em now.'

Tips were very modest on an estate where every shoot was a field trial. But Lady Howe did give boy Buckle £5 at the end of each rearing season, as a special thank-you for work well done, before she went off to Scotland for grouse shooting. 'When she gave it to me I really thought I was a millionaire and couldn't get home quick enough on my bike. Apparently she gave me the same as the other keepers and the head always told me to keep quiet about it as I was only a lad and the men might object.'

'My old BSA was a damn good bike – Father bought it at Havant market for sixteen shillings. The headkeeper had a little van and I can still remember its number plate – COT 643. We always made sure we knew all the local number plates so that we knew when strange vehicles were prowling about. Every other car contained someone out from Portsmouth trying to knock our pheasants off. But there was only one local trouble-maker. He was the poacher and was caught every other year, but he didn't mind if it was at the end of the season as he used to say that getting put away for a few months helped the winter along. Earlier on he was more careful as most of his business had still to be done.'

When he was eighteen Leslie became a keeper's help on the Little Green estate, working for Sir Philip Reckitt of 'Reckitt's Blue', and 'Reckitt and Colman Mustard' fame. As it was close by he still lived with his parents, 'but instead of going up the lane, I cycled down it.'

The move brought more money: at Idsworth he started on fifteen shillings a week and ended on 22/6d, but at Little Green he started on thirty shillings. He had heard of the job on the grapevine and secured it through the influence of his father, who was known to the estate.

In addition, he was given a yearly clothing allowance of £8 10s, which bought the traditional 'salt 'n pepper' three-piece tweed suit, two pairs of longjohns, a pair of black leather leggings and a matching cap. That was in 1939.

At Little Green the shooting was on a much grander scale than Leslie had been used to, and eleven keepers were employed to provide eighteen consecutive days of double-gun shooting, Sundays excluded, beginning in late November. The concentration was on pheasants, though there were a few early partridges as well.

During the entire three weeks Leslie had to load for the estate's agent, Mr Orr. 'He never missed a day's shooting and got more out of the estate than both Mr Reckitt and Mr Colman, who came into it later with Tommy Sopwith. Orr was sloshed most of the time, only ever grunted and never tipped me, but then he was a Scot. He even had his own chauffeur, housekeeper, butler and boot-boy as well as all the free shooting anybody could ever want.'

In complete contrast was the headkeeper, a kind man who had so much responsibility yet could not read or write.

The beaters were paid 6/6d a day, which was rounded up to £2 for a six-day week to encourage them to stay on.

At Little Green there were two hundred pheasant coops to a forty-acre (16ha) field, and the three keepers working a field thought they were doing well to average fourteen six-week old poults to a coop, having started with twenty chicks. All the birds were reared under broody hens.

Throughout the rearing programme the birds were kept as wild as possible and grew up almost wary of man. 'That's why they flew so much better in our day,' says Leslie. 'Not like the pathetic things you have to teach to fly today.'

When the pheasants were given their first feed of the day at 7am, the shutters were removed from each coop and laid alongside so that in the evening they could be picked up quickly to shut the birds in again. In the morning the birds would not even come out of their coops until the keeper had moved away, despite the calling of the hens. And when the time came to shut them in for the night it was essential to creep up and pop the shutter over in a flash, otherwise the chicks would scatter in all directions. But some always managed to slip away on the first circuit of the field and it was often necessary to go round several times, trying to remember which coops remained to be dealt with. This often went on till 10pm or later, despite the fact that the keepers had to be up to let the birds out again at 7am.

Leslie Buckle, aged
nineteen, in his
keeper's uniform

But those were far more labour-intensive days – one of the major chores was moving all the coops every day so that the birds were always on fresh grass. And on each occasion young Leslie also had to swing the scythe right across that forty-acre field.

Even on the day the coops were moved into the woods the routine had to be adhered to. The poults were taken off at dead of night so that they would settle down better in their new surroundings. A sack was slid under each coop and the four corners tied together at the top before it was loaded onto a horse and cart. The entire operation had to be completed by 6am so that the birds had time to settle before the first feed at 7am.

When all the poults were accustomed to the wood, first the hens and then the coops were taken away, one or two at a time, until eventually the pheasants were living entirely wild.

In 1939 Leslie returned to the Idsworth estate as a beatkeeper, but the war put a stop to rearing and in 1941 young Buckle was called up in the Navy, in which he became an ack-ack gunner. He sailed on HMS *Cairo* to Scotland, Gibraltar and Malta, but on his second Malta convoy they were sunk by a U-boat and had to jump into an escort vessel. *Eagle* and *Manchester* went down with them.

Leslie was taken to Gibraltar before coming back home on HMS *Nelson*, being transferred to Rossyth and then sent on a special train to Portsmouth. 'My parents knew that the *Cairo* had gone down, but none of us had been able to send word that we were alive. And I knew that we would not be able to telephone from Portsmouth, so when the train went through our village I scribbled a message on my lifebelt and threw it out of the window. Luckily it landed on someone's garden path and they contacted my parents to tell them I was all right.'

Life on board *Cairo* had certainly provided variety and adventure, but perhaps the most interesting trip for Leslie was that to Murmansk in Russia in February, 1942. They took back a party of Russians who had been studying production in British factories, and they returned with a cargo of gold bullion – payment to the USA for arms supplied.

There was further action, too, on a minesweeper and then on HMS *Belfast* on D-Day.

When he was home on leave in 1942 Leslie married one of his childhood sweethearts from Idsworth. 'During my courting days I used to call in regularly for a cup of cocoa at 9.45pm after my keepering rounds, and I always gave her mum a rabbit and a couple of swedes. With the occasional game of darts in the evening that was the limit of my social life in those days.

'Apparently I always stank of skinned stoat when I went a-courtin', but of course I did not notice it like they did. And years later when I was at another estate and happened to skin a stoat my wife said "God, what's that smell?" "Oh, isn't it horrible," I replied. "No, no, I like it," and she

Opposite:
Leslie Buckle
outside his keeper's
lodge at Stansted
Park in 1988

added – "It reminds me of you years ago when we were courting."'

After the war Leslie was unable to return to his old job as it had already been taken by somebody else. So he took a position as a single-handed keeper at Uppark, near Harting, Sussex, for Admiral Meade Fetherstonehaugh – and once again it was his father's farming connection which had paved the way. As a married man, Leslie was greatly attracted by the rent-free cottage which went with the job.

There was very little rearing in those days and all Leslie had to do was look after a few wild pheasants and control the rabbits. In fact, although he had a very fine pair of Boss twelve-bores, the Admiral did not even shoot. So the only rearing Leslie did at Uppark was of a hundred or so turkeys for the Christmas market, but even though it was his idea the profits went to the Admiral. Mind you, he did have a bird or two for himself.

At the time, food was still rationed so the turkeys had to live wild and fatten on beechnuts. But Leslie also gave them clayder (goose grass), eggs, onions and chopped stinging nettles 'for the iron.' Each evening the birds went to roost in the beech trees. And this peaceful regime of turkey rearing combined with roughshoot keepering continued for eleven years.

Then came four years as headkeeper for gamefeed manufacturers F. C. Lowe & Sons (run by the Voucher brothers) at Otterden in Kent. The shoot was leased from the Wheeler family and Leslie had two underkeepers plus his eldest daughter to help him continue with the open-field rearing system, at a time when most other estates had changed to the Cotswold System. Lowe's made feed for open rearing so this was not surprising: 'we were probably the last estate in the country still using the system.'

In 1960 Leslie was invited to become head-keeper for Frederick Edward Neuflize Ponsonby, tenth Earl Bessborough at Stansted Park, Sussex, and Leslie was pleased to accept as it meant both he and his wife could return to their native haunts. And there he stayed.

At first there were four underkeepers and they put down 7 or 8,000 birds a season. In later years, in his so-called retirement, Leslie worked with only one pensioner and two lads, yet still put down some 5,000 birds. He regrets the trend which has made keepers more like poultry farmers, but there is no way that so many birds could be reared by so few men today using the old methods with broody hens.

Poaching has always been a considerable problem at Stansted as more and more people own cars and swarm out from neighbouring towns such as Portsmouth. But Leslie has always enjoyed great support from local police and there have been only two occasions when he was in some danger.

'The first happened on a Sunday morning, when a father and his two sons knocked me into a ditch. I had blocked the road with my Land Rover and one of them came at me with a spider wheel-brace. I was knocked out for a while and when I came to, one of the men was still over me thumping me for all he was worth. But I managed to get my thumb inside his mouth and heave him off.

'I was just beginning to get the better of my attacker when the other keeper came back from phoning the police. He came up on the father who was watching his son grapple with me and smashed him on the head with the butt of a .22 rifle. The old poacher had a big, grey overcoat on and I'll never forget the sight of him as he crumpled unconscious into the hedge, the huge, bloody collar coming right up around his face. I thought we'd killed him. And on top of that my keeper colleague seemed to go berserk, swinging at everything and everybody within reach, smashing the windscreen of the poachers' van.

'Meanwhile, the other son had driven my Land Rover off down the lane and crashed into a fence-post, so we had to go and retrieve it to get the old boy to hospital. But when we came back we found that the other son had somehow managed to get his father into their Mini van and driven off with him.

'We gave chase down the track and the little van soon got stuck in some water, but while we were so intent the poacher who had been put in the back of the Land Rover jumped out and ran off.'

'Then we drove in front of the van, but as we did so they managed to start the engine and reversed down the lane, only to find the police waiting for them. I can tell you it gave me great pleasure to see them all handcuffed – though at the same time they handcuffed the keeper who had assaulted the poacher with his gun.

'The trial last two days at Chichester Crown Court and the poacher who attacked me was given four months suspended for two years. Later they came up for the poaching offence at the magistrates' court, where they were all fined and had their guns confiscated. The police decided not to prosecute the other keeper for his assault.

'On another occasion, at about 5pm I heard air-rifle shots coming from the pheasant pen just opposite my house. And when I crept over I saw a man and a woman killing the birds. He was the marksman and she the picker-up with a canvas holdall.

'When they saw me they made a run for it. There was no way I could catch the fellow as he was much younger than me and had light shoes on whereas I was lumbered with wellies. But I caught the woman and then the fellow came back. He aimed his gun at me, but I told him not to be so stupid and as I walked towards him he fled again.

'I asked her what was in the bag. She said I was not going to see and hurled it into the bushes over the fence. Then I walked down the road with her so that I could at least see their vehicle and get the number.

'We were only about twenty yards along the main road when the fellow came back, and as I turned he hit me and knocked me down, but I was still conscious. Then the girl put the boot in and called out "Give it to him, John!"'

'My main thought was to get the gun away from him and we fell struggling onto the bank. I managed to grab the gun and held it away from him with one arm while I held him back with the other. With a great effort I was just able to toss the gun up and away, but it hit the top strand of the barbed wire fence and bounced back into the road. And all the time I was shouting for help.

'Then the girl picked up the gun, but luckily enough a car came along and stopped, and my wife appeared from the house. She immediately telephoned the police.

'Then came another car with a petty officer in and he turned out to be quite useful, pinning the man against the fence until the law arrived. Very soon there were police all over the place – cars and motor bikes in all directions. They were marvellous, the local boys from Westbourne.'

As a result of the attack, Leslie had to go into hospital for two days so that a surgeon could ease out the dent in the side of his skull and relieve pressure on nerves. This injury surprised them all as he had not been rendered unconscious. In recent years, however, the injury has been troublesome.

The airgunner was given a suspended sentence and fined. The woman had to pay damages to Leslie – 'Every month I had a cheque for a pound or two in the post. She had been in all sorts of trouble and was a real gangster's moll. I also received £750 from the Criminal Injuries Board.'

Despite these setbacks and a not unexpected degree of gun deafness, life at Stansted has been very satisfying for Leslie and he has enjoyed serving the Earl, born 1913. 'Lord Bessborough is a good and keen Shot but, like me, he is understandably slowing up a bit now.

'We still manage some fifteen days shooting and enjoy a constant stream of interesting guests. We have had King Constantine, and one of my favourites was Lord Hailsham, who came almost every year, usually on Boxing Day, and stayed for a couple of days. He was a real gentleman and always wrote to thank me as soon as he got home. We really got on well together.'

Today Leslie continues to judge gundog tests, but not trials as he is too busy in the winter, though he does trial a dog sometimes. And he is extremely well organised by his second wife, who works in the estate office and does much of the shoot's paperwork.

As far as he knows, Leslie is not related to the famous nineteenth-century Buckle keepers of Merton, Norfolk, but he does have a younger brother in keepering at Alton, Hampshire. He does not have a son to follow in his footsteps but his three-year-old grandson has already learnt to set snares and loves playing with grandad's ferret. He will have a lot to live up to.

A good gundog was worth its weight in gold

Good Yeoman Stock

Kenneth Liverton : Sussex

GOOD YEOMAN STOCK

'I always wanted to be a farmer; there's nothin' to take its place', seventy-seven-year-old Ken Tiverton told me at his Woolbeding, Sussex, home which has its origins in the eleventh century. But then, that is not surprising when both his father and grandfather were also tenant farmers before him. And now his only son follows in the family tradition. 'Mind you, my two brothers weren't too interested, but they came back to it after the war.'

Young Ken Tiverton with horse and cart

The family's roots are in Devon, 'but it was hopeless to get a farm early this century,' so Ken was born – on 15 March, 1915 – at Carms Hall, Fareham, Hampshire, where his father had to be content with running an estate. 'From Fareham we went to live at Staines, as Dad took on a milk business when I was five, and when I was eight he got North End Farm, at Liphook, in Hampshire.'

'Everythin' was so quiet then – only the odd car or two chasin' around. No tractors – all horses. Most places it was quite safe to be on the road. Only trouble was when the occasional horse and trap bolted.

'Nothin' was ever wasted then. As soon as a horse dropped his fuel, out ran the old ladies with their shovels; some always watched the milk trap and as soon as the horse cocked his tail out they'd go.'

It was also a time when farming was more sympathetic towards wildlife and Ken always found time to give nature a helping hand. One incident stands out from the days when he first started to help his father on the farm. 'I was runnin' a light pair of harrows over some corn 2–3in high, to get rid of the weeds, when I saw a plover up ahead on its nest. So I carried on till the horses drew close, walked over, picked up the eggs, put them in my pocket, marked the spot with a stick, carried on down the field, came back and went over the nest with the harrows. Then I stopped again and dug out a depression with my hand, where the stick was, put in a few bits of stubble straw as lining and then the eggs. I then worked up and down a bit and the bird came back and sat on the nest. I was very pleased about that.

'You see, in those days you really saw wildlife. Once you got your first furrow made and the horses were set in you could relax and watch everythin' around you.'

Of course, in those days farm boys were always expected to help out after school, ' and before we went in the morning we had to milk two cows each, by hand. Us boys were only allowed to deal with quiet cows, but I did have a bit of trouble one morning. I was sitting on the stool, bucket between my legs, as usual, and it was very warm and sunny with a lot of flies about. I suppose one of 'em stung my cow so she picked up her foot and bumped my bucket. I grabbed the bucket and stool but immediately she picked up a foot again and put it straight down on my foot, breakin' the arch. And I daren't let go of the bucket. Anyway, you didn't go to the doctor in those days, so I just had to put up with it. I've had a troublesome callous under my foot ever since.'

The milk was cooled and put into seventeen-gallon churns for daily collection by a lorry with solid-rubber wheels, which took it to Petersfield. 'You don't get milk like it now – they kill everything in it with treatment. When I was a boy it was good for making cream, cheese and butter, and mother was always busy.

'She made wonderful clotted cream. Now the doctors say it's bad for you, but I bet I've eaten more Devonshire cream than anyone else. Mother took a pan of about two gallons of our fresh milk in the morning and let it stand till evening, when she'd put it on the old range on a low heat, gradually brining it up over half an hour or so but never letting it boil. Then off it came and back in the larder. Next morning she'd go round the edge of the pan with a knife and take the crust off into a fair-sized basin. My father always said I'd get sick of it, but I never did. In those days the wife had to be able to cook and store anything, as there were no fridges.'

Ken left school at the age of fourteen to help his father on the farm, 'working all the hours of daylight and for no pay. I 'ad to catch rabbits for

my pocket money. I made and set my own snares – got good at it, too, eventually having about fifty down. After a while we met this chap who was in with the Navy and said he'd take as many as I could get. They were all hamstrung then and all I had to do was tie them up in dozens, label them for House & Son, Gosport, and put them on the train in Liphook – imagine doing that today. Then I'd be sent a cheque, but I had no bank account, so father had to bank it and he said, "We'll have to go halves on this" – times was really bad on the farm then. I think we got about 6d a rabbit.

'I also used to do a lot of pigeon-shooting. They used to play havoc with our flat pole cabbage – damn great things which was fodder for the cows. We 'ad about four thousand plants up from Devon each year and planted them about a foot apart. They did well coming from that red Devon soil into ours.

'One day when I was 17, Mum and Dad were out and I was in charge. There was a small field by our cowshed and in there was a lot of dandelions, which I spotted an ol' woman pickin'. Well, being in charge I thought I'd better do something about it. But I didn't like to just go out and say something. Anyway, in the cowshed we used to keep an old bull, so I went down and untied him

and let him out the side door into the dandelion field. As he went out I crept along and looked out the cowshed window. Well, 'e came round the corner and went "Brrr". She took one look and was off, and there was a barbed wire fence there which she got all hooked up in.

'When she was gone, I just put a bit of cake in the yard, I called out, "Come on, Bill," in came the bull good as gold and I tied him up again. I'd never do that now.

'A couple of months later I was walkin' a pair of horses up the lane when I saw the same woman. I said, "How are you?" and she said, "You've got some nice cabbages there; do you mind if I have one?" So I said "OK" and she said, "You won't let the bull out this time, will you?" Well, I had no idea she knew what happened the time before and I felt as small as anything.

'In those days we had a herd of about twenty-five to thirty shorthorn; it was all short-horn then, but now it's all Friesian and you can't find a shorthorn anywhere, but you get more milk from the Friesian. A cow used to cost about £10, perhaps £15 for an exceptional one. When father took on North Farm at the auction he only paid £100 for everything – cows, ol' plough, everythin'. We had a full-time cowman even though all the family helped with the milking.

'Also, in the summer we had to have help with the haymaking and then with pullin' up and trimmin' the mangels, which were stored behind the cowshed for cattle-feed. They were built up in a triangle and covered with straw; then we dug a trench round the bottom and earthed up over the straw to keep the straw on and the mangels dry. The cows always came in the first week in September; father was strict with that. They stayed in till the end of April, being fed hay and mangel and bedded on bracken.

'We used to go over to Holleycombe to cut the bracken by hand, at Sir John Hawkshaw's; he was our landlord and we had the right to it free. We brought it back in a waggon with a pair of horses. And we had another strip just down the road here at Redford. The bracken was put in a rick and thatched in, about the end of August.

'We had pigs too, about twenty breeding sows – mainly large whites. In the evening we'd let them out for the acorns and you wouldn't see them again till next morning; they used to wander miles. They were also fed our own mix of barley meal and crushed oats, all grown on the farm.

'One old field of ours had a stream runnin' through the middle and you couldn't do much with it, so we decided to cultivate with the old sows. We had this local carpenter – damn clever chap, could make anything – build a big shed for the pigs, twelve feet wide and twenty-four feet long. He made it in the yard and we took it down the field in sections it was so heavy. The carpenter suggested anchorage for it, but father said no – it was big and heavy, and in any case it was sheltered by the wood.

'Then one night we had an awful gale, and when I went down to feed next morning the sows were lyin' where the shed had been, but the shed was away across the field more or less intact, only a board or two broken. Unfortunately, the wind had blown from an unexpected direction. So we had to take the shed to pieces again to move it back into place. But this time it was anchored down properly.

'We used to run a boar in the field with the sows all the time, and as soon as we saw one or two getting' heavy, we'd shut them up at the farm and give them better food. Now and then one had eight, but mostly we had litters of ten; that was good then. But they were in good condition runnin' out all the time.

'Most of the pigs were sold live at market, but we also killed a few for home use. Every village 'ad a pig sticker then and it was a special day when he came, with a big staff on hand. We had to hold each pig on its back while he stuck the knife in its throat. That was one job I always hated – poor old pig squealin' away.

'The joints were salted down in big pottery containers and put in the cellar. Once a month mother went down and rubbed more salt in. They were big pigs we killed then, about five or six months old, not like the little squirts you get now.

Between the wars this bull was one of the Liverton family's prized possessions

*Opposite:
Today the sight of herds of cattle roaming in the high street would be a cause for concern, but at one time this cattle market scene would have been commonplace*

'We used both Chichester and Petersfield markets. I was at Petersfield the day it closed — must have been thirty-five years ago. Chichester was on alternate Wednesdays to Petersfield; they had dairy cows, but Petersfield was mainly killing, except for calves. If you bought a cow at Chichester the only way to get it home, unless you had your own lorry — and they weren't much cop — was by rail. We'd put a cow and calf on the rail at Chichester and the head carter would take an ol' dung cart down to meet them at Midhurst. He'd load the calf aboard and the cow would follow the 6 miles home.

'We'd get down to Chichester for 9.30 and Petersfield for 10. There was a bar in the yard open all day, but I couldn't go in till I was 20. But I didn't want to anyway because of an earlier incident. After pheasant shooting had finished each year, each tenant farmer was allowed a day's rabbit shooting on his farm and we'd get about twenty Guns out. One day Dad couldn't go and I went in his place. At lunchtime the hot water ran out for tea so I was tempted to take a glass of beer for the first time in my life. Unfortunately, it must have been off and when I went home that night I felt done in, so I went to bed early and later on I brought it all up. After that I never touched it for years.

'When we first started on the rabbit shoots we shot about fifty, but then I started to soak strips of paper in Redoline and stuff them down

the holes the day before. This kept the rabbits out and we got the bag up to about 150.

'We were very lucky in having the help of a one-armed dog man from Fernhurst. He had a lot of spaniels and terriers and the way those dogs obeyed him was remarkable. Those ol' dogs loved him, but he always asked us not to bring any other dogs so that they wouldn't get distracted. He never charged us, but we always went round with a hat and he'd end up with a pound or so — that was a week's wages for most of them.

'In those days we had an old Ford van — used to frighten me to death. No dashboard then, of course. There was a box by the steering-wheel and Dad was always rooting around inside it to

sort the ignition out – sparks flyin' everywhere. That must have been the late 1920s.

'Us boys used to like market days at Chichester because we always hoped to see Old Man Alley, who had the knacker-house at Liphook. As soon as we spotted him, we'd point him out to Dad, who was always busy talking to someone else. But we'd keep on until we got them together for a word or two. The reason was that as soon as he shook hands with us in dropped two shillings, a florin; he was always good to us boys.

'We had a lot of screw cows then. You couldn't sell 'em at market because they'd cock their tails up and out would come a stream of water – some sort of disease. But Old Man Alley always took them. One day I was up at his yard and asked his man where they all went. He said the boss took 'em up to London, to the East End, because the people up there were so poor they'd take anything.

' I don't know what Dad got for those cows and it was a job to tell the prices paid at auction. At first I couldn't understand the auctioneer's gabber at all. The only time you 'eard the price was when the hammer went down, and it would soon go up again if he heard another bid.

'The same man who made our pig-shed built the two houses for our two hundred laying hens. The eggs used to go to market till the price

went right down. Then a neighbour took some to sell around the big houses at Haslemere, where fresh farm eggs were so welcome he soon sold out. He did so well, the following week he had to take a pony and trap up, and after that he took our eggs for years.'

Ken became closely involved with horses when the carter was leaving 'and I took over his team. First day I went out he played a trick on me. We were going out to do some chain har-rowing, to level out mole heaps on grassland. When he was backing horses into place he delib-erately twisted the chains which fixed to the har-rows on the side I couldn't see. Then he said, "See what you've done."

'The first time I went ploughing I was nearly finished come dinner-time. But when I saw father he said, "It's because your plough is not set right: it should carry on up the field if you take your hands off the reins." He showed me how to set it properly. We had five horses – mainly Clydesdales and a Shire. I loved ploughing.

'In those old days we only grew a few cereals – oats, which we crushed for the horses and cows, and barley ground for the pigs. Under the agreement with the landlord you only had cer-tain fields under arable to supply your cattle and horses, but not for sale. So father was pleased when the War Agriculture ordered that a certain acreage of grass had to be ploughed up for corn.

In those days he paid ten shillings an acre rent and we had about 125 acres.

'I used to plough all day long, from 8 till 5 to get just an acre done. But there was always something to look at, and no noise.

'The first farm machines I can remember were the traction engines and thrashers. You hired the driver as well and he came out from Petersfield to do all the farmers in the area, as there was only a small quantity of cereals grown. He also towed his hut and elevator and the whole thing was like a circus coming along the road.

'I've also cut corn by hand, with a scythe about four feet out from the hedge so the binder had a clear run and the horse wouldn't trample it down. There was no waste then; every bucketful was useful.

'We bought our first tractor, a Fordson, in 1932, when I came back from twelve months at Sparsholt Agricultural College. It was second-hand and comin' off the flints the tyres was nearly bare. Our binder was Massey Harris. Nowadays you only get the odd binder where they want wheatstraw for thatching as the combines chop it all up.'

Sheep, too, have figured prominently in Ken's life. Traditionally, local farmers had Kent store lambs up for the winter. They had to come off the marshes, where they would otherwise get bogged down, and Ken's farm could accommodate them well as there was a lot of autumn grass with the cows coming in early. They usually had about sixty up by train from Midhurst, 'but once we had to walk about 12 miles with them, back from Northchapel Station.

'There were always other flocks of sheep on the road then, but we never did get mixed up, even though it took most of the day to run them home. I used to fetch them with my dog in the early 1930s; he was the best I ever had. One day when I got down to Midhurst to collect the sheep the agent said, "Where's your men?" – all the others had half-a-dozen. He was quite worried about it. But I said, "Don't you fret, Bob'll keep 'em apart." So they unloaded the lot and away we went – me walking in front all the way and the dog behind. After a while we came up to a big flock with six men and two of their sheep came back, but Bob soon cut 'em out, and the same happened with a flock behind.

'I always remember this chap came hurtling down the hill on a bike with no brakes. I shouted at him but 'e smacked into the bank and rolled back down on the sheep.

'We used to have the sheep from the end of September till the end of February or early March. At first the owner used to pay us about 3d a week per sheep, but the last lot we had was 6d. Whole trainloads came into the area then. You had to have good fences to keep them in as they were used to roaming over much larger areas on the marshes. They didn't take a lot of looking after really. Just a bit of hay – all loose then, no bales – if it was snowy. You had to watch for foot rot though, any cases being trimmed out and a mix of Stockholm tar and salt being put on. After we had

Top: Ken Liverton's uncle milking at Endicott Farm, Cadbury, Devon, early in the twentieth century.

Above: In their younger days, Ken Liverton (pillion) and his brother took a motorbike holiday to Devon

wanted to buy his farm of 125 acres, but the executors said the whole estate had to be sold in one lot. And farms were cheap then, too. So then I decided to start up there, at Woolbeding, in 1942.

'Farming was a reserved occupation, of course, but I did sign on for the Air Force. In the end I volunteered for the Home Guard and we used to be on duty up here at the Duchess of Bedford's hangar. She used to fly a plane but was killed.

'One winter night I was in charge and there used to be two of us on duty and four sleepin'. But it was too cold in the hangar so we moved into the cottage alongside. We went up at 9 and my younger brother Cecil was with me. He was a good cook and we decided to have a good cook-up. But first we went off to Midhurst in the car for a drink and to bring back some beer. There we met two girls we knew in the pub and invited them back for a meal.

'We'd just finished our cook-up when a chap came runnin' in to say that the commanding officer had just arrived, so one girl slid under a bed and the other went in a cupboard. Fortunately, the CO was quite a lad. In he came and said, "You've got a good sentry there – well done. And that's a fine smell. Been cooking?" Then he settled down and started to tell us such a good yarn the girls started gigglin' and he heard them. So out they had to come and he said, "What's two lovely girls like you doin' in there? I wish I'd known you were there before." After that, we all had a nice evening together and the CO even took the girls home.

'It was very tiring then; after all night on duty I had to go home, milk the cows and then go hay-makin' all day. There was never any set hours; if the weather was right you had to get on with it. Haymakin' was a lot of hard work – all by hand then, but some people had a horse rake, going round clearing up what you missed with a prong.

'When I first took this farm I didn't live here. I was very lucky because there were four land girls workin' here on the thrashin'. They were supplied by the War Agriculture; it was an

the lambs, they went back to Kent for fattening on grass and selling. 'Once we had the sheep on the golf course up at Holleycombe. On Boxing Day I used to go up to feed them first before going on to a shoot at my wife's parents' farm at Lurgashall. But one Christmas I went, I had the shock of my life. There were sheep lyin' all over the place and I had to kill six with my knife, they were mauled so badly. And wool – you've never seen anything like it. I rang the police, but they never found the culprits; they thought there was a pack of dogs gone wild. It was the only time I ever had sheep worrying, but it upset me so much I never had any more sheep there.

'When Sir John Hawkshaw died, father

alternative to going in the forces. And when it was wet and we couldn't thrash, they came up here and scrubbed out and painted the rooms, so we had a lovely start. I only had pigs there then.

'But when I came up one evening I was confronted by a sentry, who called "Halt!" I said, "What you doin' here?" and he said, "It's been taken over." "No", I said, "it's my house; you can't do that." So I called for the CO and he said it had been taken over, as there was no one living there. But he let me through and I went to the barn where I had two ton of seed potatoes stored. Well, the soldiers had their kit all over 'em and were layin' across the sacks. So I soon said they'll have to get off and sleep on the floor.

'After that first day they were quite nice and let me come and go. They stayed about a week, but you daren't ask them where they came from or where they were going. They was all gettin' ready for the second front then.'

In the following year, 1943, Ken got married; his wife died in 1979. They had three children and now their son runs the little seventy-five-acre farm. There are a few sheep, but the main concern is the riding stable, in the care of Ken's daughter-in-law. His son also works on other farms.

Fit for his age, Ken still drives the tractor a bit and manages occasional fencing work. He is obviously a restless spirit and seems ill at ease in the peaceful atmosphere of his black-beamed living-room, where only the gentle tick of a Horsham-made grandfather clock breaks the silence when his toddler grand-daughter is not there climbing all over him.

Ken's great energy is obviously inherited. 'Grandfather went out on his eighty-first birthday to see what he could kill with twenty-five cartridges. He shot while another man worked the ferrets and he came back with a pigeon and twenty-five rabbits – two came out of one hole together. He was delighted. This was down on Pitt Farm, Cadbury, Devon, and I was so pleased I was down there then; he died the following year.'

In earlier years, Ken once went down to Devon for a holiday, travelling pillion on his

brother's BSA motorbike. 'We pulled into this petrol station – single pump with rotary winder – and this proper Devon bloke said, "You be foreigners." We said, "No we're not", and he said, "You don't come from Devon". That must have been in the late 1920s.'

But the fact is that Ken is of the type who could never be called a foreigner in any county. Dig gently beneath that façade of an accent to find the true character of the countryside, that good yeoman stock whose line is apparently endless. He may have been on local television and on the BBC's *Songs of Praise*, but his abiding place is as a pillar of village life. Not for nothing was he a churchwarden for over thirty-five years.

Farmer Ken Liverton in 1991. Being a sheep man, he always had a collie

BEYOND LIVING MEMORY

April Tasks

Feeding cattle in the yard still continues, from deficiency of grass. Fields intended for mowing are cleared of stones, bush-harrowed, and shut up; all ditching, hedging, and draining, better done last month, but if unfinished, to be concluded. Water meadows, which have been eaten, closed at the end of the month. Sowing still continues of spring corn, peas, tares, sainfoin, flax, hemp, mustard, rape, poppy, rhubarb, and other medicinal plants; at the end of the month planting mangel-wurzel, carrots, and swedish turnips. Early potatoes are planted. Hops are poled, and the ground between the rows dressed. Evergreens are planted, as holly, yew and the fir tribes. Poultry broods are now numerously hatched, and demand much of the good housewife's cares.

Dairy Time

Abundance of grass now [May] plunges the housewife into all the cares and nice processes of the dairy, skimming, churning, and cheese-making. The farmhouse is now an affluent place, abounding in all the good things which may be made from milk; rich cream, sweet butter, curds and cream, syllabubs, custards, and so forth. Where there is a dairy, at this season, fetching up cows, milking, churning, scouring utensils – making, pressing and turning cheese, etc. leave no lack of employment.

 Osiers are now peeled; and it is a pleasant sight to see groups of young and old seated in the open air, at this employment. The garden demands various operations of weeding, training, and putting in flower-seeds. The children of the poor have an easy and pleasant occupation in gathering cowslips for wine. Poultry broods, as last month, demand attention; corn is weeded, and rearing calves turned out.

   William Howitt, *Book of the Seasons*, 1830

They Were Good Times

Dennis Lindup : Clwyd, Bedfordshire and Warwickshire

THEY WERE GOOD TIMES

'As a boy I used to buy tuppenny packets of seeds from the local shop and grow flowers to take to the market. I used to get 6d a bunch for them, or something like that, for pocket money and did quite well, so I decided to go in for gardening; but it wasn't easy in those days.' Dennis Lindup, the son of a blacksmith, was born on 16 December 1916, at Sweeney Mountain, three miles from Oswestry, in Shropshire. It was difficult to find gardening work: *'Chaps going into gardening always reckoned on getting into glasswork first if they could. Anyway, when I was fourteen, my father got me into Brogyntyn Hall. He had met the head gardener a few times, and there came a vacancy, and I got it.'*

Opposite:
Dennis in the
Carolean Garden
at Packwood House

Dennis was fortunate enough to have a bicycle and would set off every morning on his four-mile ride. 'I had to be there before seven in the morning so that I could fetch milk for the bothy and the head gardener and be back by eight o'clock. There were four in the bothy and I had to cook the breakfast, and I had half-an-hour for that. Bacon and eggs was mostly what they had. I had about an hour to wash up, then I had to go down to the Hall to see the cook, to see what vegetables she wanted. I had about an hour for that, especially if there were celery and leeks to dig up and savoys to be cut. Potatoes came in in the winter and there was a place to keep those. In the early part of the winter there were grapes and apples and I took them down to the house-maids. Then I would come back and wash flower-pots or crocks or something for a short time, and sweep up the greenhouse. I always found a job to do.'

The bothy was a comfortable house, with one room and a kitchen downstairs, and four bedrooms upstairs. At the back was a range of green-houses, the potting shed and a couple of other sheds. 'They used to have a woman come in, the second keeper's wife, to cook some dinner and I would have to wash up after that, too. There were always things to do. I would tie carnations sometimes. Then about half-past four I used to get some sticks and coal for the head gardener and do any other things that wanted doing. At half-past five we left off in them days, and I would bike home. The girls in the house had to be in by nine o'clock, so it was no good coming back to see them! Anyway I got caught once. The kitchen maid went down to where the keeper's wife did the bothy and after that I brought her home. That started the romance off and I saw her every day for about three years. She left, and of course I left; she went to Cheshire and I went to Chirk Castle. It was all done more or less by letter, and after that she became my wife.'

One day the head gardener at Brogyntyn had told Dennis there was a job going at Chirk Castle, Denbighshire, and had asked if he would like to try for it. 'He gave me a note. It wasn't a long way away, about seven miles. So I went there and found Mr Jones, he was the head gardener. He said "I've had thirty-two letters, and I've had a lot of callers. I can't make any promises." So that was that.' About a week later, however, Dennis was

told that he had got the job, so off he went to work at Chirk under Mr Jones.

'I had only been there about three months and there was an apple fight going on. Yes, four o' them, and he caught 'em, one pinching the apples out of the fruit room, the other picking them off the trees. Then the one had the sack you see, so they advertised; but they only got two replies and one of them was a student. Mr Jones didn't think much of students.' It was unusual to advertise for new staff — they were more frequently found by recommendation. If an estate

at nights. He used to go all over the country, they reckoned, but he'd call and he used to have his dinner. And he'd know what time to come!'

After the lad had been given the sack for apple fighting, Dennis was put on two months' trial working in the greenhouse, and felt himself very fortunate to be able to keep the job when the trial period was over. He continued to work in the greenhouses and with the fruit and carnations, and he used to go to the house in the morning to help with the flower arranging. 'A couple of times I did the dining-table on my

was known to advertise a lot it would get a poor reputation; workmen would become suspicious of the conditions offered and it would be considered not worthwhile to seek employment there.

'In some places it was by word of mouth, but then of course there was the old man who went round selling pictures, "Picture Jack" they called him. He used to come round and he'd have his dinner in the bothies and then he'd move on. Of course, he'd have a natter with the head gardener and get a pound or something off him. The foreman and the head gardener, they got a lot of information of these places, off this old boy, what was good and what wasn't good. He wouldn't get much for his pictures, so I don't know how he did for lodgings or where he slept

own!' Dennis laughed heartily. 'The first time, I decided to do the table with pyrethrums, but I'd not seen the dining-table before,' and Dennis remembered being amazed. 'It was set for eight, and I'd got four vases to do, and there was a great big gold cup and how many knives and forks and glasses, I don't know. And there was me, with the pyrethrums dripping water all over. I'll get murdered, I thought.' Dennis could hardly tell the story for laughter. 'The rain had tumbled down with a thunderstorm just as I was getting near the Castle. Anyway, nothing was said and I got away with it.

'I had some fun at Chirk Castle. We used to go out on the lake at about eleven o'clock on a Saturday night when it was moonlight. There

was another lad out of the bothy, the keeper's son George, and me, one would have the canoe and two the rowing boat, and we used to race across the lake half the night. Well, there was a place out there where you'd hit the ground, it was a sandbank or something, and the thing was to avoid it. Some say it was where the river came in, but I don't know. The river might have been the boundary, because the pub in Chirk itself was closed on Sunday, but the one at the bottom of the bank was open on Sunday. The servants were only allowed to go to dances in Chirk.' Traditionally, public houses in Wales always closed on Sundays, whereas in England they opened.

After Dennis had been at Chirk for a year and nine months the foreman recommended that he, along with three others, should move on to Woburn Abbey, in Bedfordshire. He was very surprised when he had a chauffeur to meet him on his arrival at Woburn Sands, and remembers the head gardener was a gentleman. 'We worked under a foreman; they had forty-five gardeners working there.' He found his experience of working under glass invaluable, and got on very well there working in their great range of greenhouses.

The bothy comprised accommodation over the cart sheds and was not particularly cosy.

Garden Rollers.

No. 795.

Best Quality. New Design, with Rounded Edges, Double Cylinder, Solid Ends, Planed Centre Joints, Steel Axles, Balance Handles, and Painted in Good Colours. Compare weight of our Rollers before ordering elsewhere.

Sizes.	Approximate Weight. Cwt. qrs. lb.			Cash Prices. £ s. d.		
14 by 14	1	3	6	1	6	6
16 ,, 16	2	1	0	1	10	0
18 ,, 18	2	3	9	1	15	0
20 ,, 20	3	1	8	2	2	0
22 ,, 22	4	0	21	2	5	0
24 ,, 24	4	2	16	3	3	0

Rollers only delivered Free to any Railway Goods Station in England or Wales.

Hope Cottage, North Hayling, Hants.
DEAR SIR,—I beg to acknowledge the receipt of Lawn Mower. It is a well finished article and dirt cheap. Marvellous value.—I am, yours sincerely,
JAMES KELLY.

They had a woman to cook for them, though they cooked their own breakfast. 'We paid our bill for our food dividing it out between five of us. When Christmas came round we were given 7s 6d. At Chirk Castle we were given 3lb of meat each, and the girls got a pair of black stockings.'

Unfortunately, Dennis's time at Woburn was interrupted when he had to go into the Royal Air Force, but the wage of fourteen shillings a week that he earned whilst serving his country was made up by the Duke of Bedford to the sum of 35s, the agricultural wage he had earned at Woburn. Dennis thought the Bedfords generous and was impressed that Whipsnade Zoo was given to the nation by the Bedford family.

Sadly, Dennis's most vivid memory of Woburn is of when he was leaving to go off to war, and it is not a good one: 'A chap did himself in while I was there, who'd been there forty years. I went in the bothy and there were four of them there, one or two had been in France, in the Great War, and they were having their meal. They started teasing me and made out I would be in the ground and started singing "When the poppies bloom again, When we go marching over you'll know it's us you hear." Well, he got up and went out. There was a well at the back with a slab on it – all the time I'd been there it had never been altered. Well, I got up, too, and went out to see the head gardener; he always came out at two o'clock after he had had his dinner. He asked if a taxi at half-past five would be alright, and said that George would take me round the garden as he had to go somewhere. Well, we passed the well and George commented "Some lads have been playing here." We went further round and someone asked "Have you seen Harry?" Then again, two or three time, like. Then someone saw his hat and cigarette were floating on the water. They put a stone on a line and it was about twenty-five feet deep. So they sent for the fire-brigade, but I'd left before it came because it was half-past five. The bombs had upset him, and when they started on me it had upset him again.'

Dennis decided not to go back to Woburn because he was anxious to get a position in the neighbourhood of Craven Arms where his wife's people lived. He had about eight weeks' de-mob leave in which to look for a new job, and seeing an advertisement in the Gardeners' Chronicle for a gardener wanted at Packwood House, decided to put in an application. He was given an appointment to meet the head gardener, Mr Weaver, who took him to meet the owner, Mr Baron Ash. 'Ash and Lacey had made their money in the Great War on barbed wire, millions of miles of it. Before that they made cow troughs from corrugated and sheet iron.' Mr Ash and Dennis got along well together and Dennis got the job; then he plucked up courage and asked if he would be able to keep some chickens. Mr Ash replied that was a fair question, and gave Dennis permission to use the spinney. Dennis and his wife were delighted when he got the job: 'We went to two sales in the same day. We'd got the house, but had no furniture.'

The poultry were a great help to Dennis and his wife because food was still rationed. It did not cost much to feed the chickens because in the harvest fields there was often loose corn around

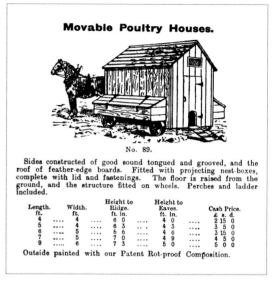

Movable Poultry Houses.

No. 89.

Sides constructed of good sound tongued and grooved, and the roof of feather-edge boards. Fitted with projecting nest-boxes, complete with lid and fastenings. The floor is raised from the ground, and the structure fitted on wheels. Perches and ladder included.

Length. ft.	Width. ft.	Height to Ridge. ft. in.	Height to Eaves. ft. in.	Cash Price. £ s. d.
4	4	6 0	4 0	2 15 0
5	4	6 3	4 3	3 5 0
6	5	6 6	4 6	3 15 0
7	5	7 0	4 9	4 5 0
9	6	7 3	5 0	5 0 0

Outside painted with our Patent Rot-proof Composition.

under the trees where the machinery could not reach. Dennis soon got to know the farmers, too – and some of the local authorities: 'One day I was on my bike and I'd got some crushed maize and I was stopped by a policeman. He pulled up on his motorbike and said "What have you got in that bag?" "I've got some maize," I said, and rattled it, like. "Where have you come from?" "Packwood House," I told him. "Well, I might as well kill two birds with one stone. Does anyone go fishing in that lake? Do you think I'd get permission?" "Well, you might get a chance if you ask, but it's not up to me, kind of thing." So off I went, and he didn't bother me no more. When the local bloke came, he said someone had been pinching coke at Hockley Heath.

'The local policeman used to come in for a smoke and a chat. I learnt my driving with him, going around houses at night looking to see if there were any burglars about.' Perhaps it is in the nature of policemen to kill two birds with one stone?

Packwood House is renowned for its yew trees, but they were not without problems and developed a scale disease. Some men came from Pershore College to look at them and it was decided that it was due to bad drainage; but Dennis thought they had been over-sprayed, or perhaps the chemical was too strong. New drains were installed some three feet deep – but

Packwood House.
In the foreground
are the famous
yews which
represent the
Sermon on the
Mount

then it became necessary to water in summer. Fortunately there was a pump to bring water up from the lake. 'And it's all very well to be a conservationist, but if a brook isn't cleared out it will get full of sedges and a field will not drain properly.'

The yew garden was laid out by John Featherston between 1600 and 1670 and is said to symbolise the Sermon on the Mount, with fat yews and thin yews, tall yews and short yews to represent the multitude. The one in the corner was an old beauty, and the old gardener always called it Bessy Braddock after the Liverpool MP. 'She was awkward to cut and we had to put ladders at angles to get over her.'

Clipping of the yews commenced on the same Monday in late summer in each year, and it took seven men fifteen days. Eventually an outside firm was called in, 'but these blokes didn't work in wet weather so it might take three weeks, and it took something like £1,800.'

Dennis remembered the yews being cut at Chirk Castle, but he had had no special training. He says, 'The gardeners learnt from each other,

and we did it all by eye. When clipping some yews we had to go up forty-two rungs of the ladder – the highest yew was about thirty feet.'

Dennis tried all sorts of ways to cut the yews, and even experimented with a fork-life truck, 'but you had to have someone to move it and you couldn't get to some places on the terraces. With a ladder one man can work alone.' When cutting by hand they would cut as far as they could reach and then move the ladder round the tree; they started at the top and worked their way down, and would then work from a shorter ladder or a pair of steps. Eventually Dennis devised a satisfactory method of clipping the yews using ropes and garden forks: 'We tied the ropes three parts up the ladder to keep it in place, and then tied them to forks stuck into the ground so they wouldn't slip. When cutting at height you had to be careful holding your shears, not to go in with their weight. Nowadays of course it's all done by electric cutters.' String was used to hold the yews in shape, as wire might cut into the wood, and if these strings broke, Dennis would sometimes have to get up inside the trees to re-tie them.

'On one occasion someone came down to take photographs of us clipping the yews, for an advertising brochure, and they brought a new green baize apron along for me to wear. I wore it for the pictures, but it was away again afterwards. Never mind, the gardeners did get two new shirts each.'

Dennis finds it a most satisfying job to cut the yews: 'They looked beautiful in spring with the fresh shoots'; then he went on to joke about a lady visitor he had heard remark: 'They must look dreadful in winter when they have shed all their leaves!' The visitors were often amused by the peacocks. 'By the door there was a foot-scraper, and there was a mirror on the wall and people thought it was to see if their boots were clean before going into the house, but in fact it was for the peacocks – when a peacock saw itself in the mirror, up would go his tail.'

Packwood is also renowned for its Carolean Garden. The cost of the 4,000 tulip bulbs needed for planting it up in the early 1960s was £80, and they had to be taken up each year – as their quality deteriorated they were transferred to other, less conspicuous places. 'We would do this job on nice days in early autumn, and it took three men a day to plant the bulbs. They would drop a line and make marks for the holes evenly along it, then drop them in.'

Dennis grew a lot of herbaceous plants. 'I changed the borders every two years. Two years bedding out and two years herbaceous. No design, just put the lupins and tall delphiniums and dahlias at the back, anthusia and daisies, then polyanthus in front for springtime. When we planted it up we used to put a lot of pea sticks in the border. We used to cut them just below the plant, then put them in the borders before the herbaceous came up and let the plants grow through. I'd seen it done at Chirk. It

Cutting the grass early in the twentieth century. The ponies wore leather shoes when walking on the lawn to prevent hoof marks

looked a sight at first, but they were good support for the plants.'

Dennis is the first to admit he has had a couple of disasters. 'I got caught by an early summer frost one year and lost 810 dahlias. I was up that night at ten o'clock talking to an old gardener and we decided it was OK, but when I woke up in the morning at half-past five, I looked out of the window and everything was white, even the hosepipe was frozen. The grass was burnt where I trod, and you could see it for five or six weeks after. I'd got some cuttings, and I had to find some other stuff to put in, but I didn't have the blocks of colour and it spoilt the effect. After the war, everybody got cameras and it didn't matter what was in the garden as long as it was colourful.'

Some disasters were not of Dennis's own making. There were squirrels that stripped the sycamore trees of their bark, and there was the Hunt, when perhaps as many as a hundred horses might have gone galloping through, chasing foxes and trampling all over the daffodils. Least forgivable of the vandals were those who stole ornaments from the gardens. There was an old seat that was taken away in the night and found at Sotheby's, and a statue that was moved off a bed and taken across the park. This was discovered by the footprints left in the dew. 'Now Packwood is locked up like a fortress. You can't get in there now, it even became difficult to get

into our own cottages. There are spy holes and all sorts of things.'

The winter was a busy time. Early on there would be leaves everywhere, particularly from the huge beech; so heavy were their boughs that they weighed down to the ground, and had rooted themselves. Leaves would be swept up in the morning before they had a chance to blow all over the place.

If there were three or four damp, foggy days the men would spend time slug catching. 'It takes some to fill a four-inch pot. We would put in bran and camphor and they would go for the bran. We'd put rows and rows across the garden and catch thousands of them.' In 1993 Dennis caught six hundred slugs by this method in the little garden of his own home.

Pea sticks were collected in winter, and when the weather was really bleak, time was spent washing pots ready for potting up chrysanthemum cuttings and young carnations. In early spring the box would come out of the frames ready for planting along the edge of the herbaceous borders a little later. The gravel paths might need attention, too, because if children had kicked them about the camber would probably have been lost and they would need rolling. 'Once they had an old-fashioned roller with shafts and a pony to pull it and the protective shoes were still there in the house' [when Dennis left]. These shoes were made of leather and fitted over the pony's hooves; they were also once used to protect the lawn when the ponies pulled the lawn-mowers. During the Great War, anti-gas boots made of rubber were issued for horses, to be worn in the event of an enemy gas attack.

Later in the year the lawns took a lot of mowing and they tried to mow them in a day. 'We had a Dennis, now they have a sit-and-ride. In the war we had a hand-mower because there was a shortage of fuel and a shortage of labour. They had blokes come up from a local home and they would mow all day for ten Woodbines [cigarettes]; one would push and one would pull. We even had some geese to help keep it short. Later on we did get a drop of petrol for the Dennis.'

Labour too, became something of a problem. 'There was a girl and a gardener when I first went and there were three of us for twenty years, but when one retired he wasn't replaced, so veg was cut out and they did without flowers in the house, and I put in beech or laurel and gourds.'

In earlier times Packwood House had been very proud of the decorations inside the house, and Dennis was a founder member of the Solihull Flower Club. They would sometimes hold their exhibitions at Packwood House. 'They might have three or four thousand visitors on a Sunday afternoon to see a flower show. We had a flower room and at one meeting we had a draw with no end of good prizes, so I said to Henry, "We'll have a do in that Henry, we'll have ten tickets each." They were one shilling a ticket. We came back into the flower room and one lady said to another in a haughty voice, "I've sold 2,000, how many have you sold?" Well, there was us, we'd spent ten bob. We laughed and laughed.

'As the club got bigger they went to Chelsea and won this, that and the other, and they fell out. They had learnt a bit you see, and they all went off and started separate clubs in their own villages. I'd helped quite a bit, this way and that, and the lady president asked "Is there anything you want?" and I said, "We could do with some new greenhouses." And that's how the new

greenhouse came about and I don't think the National Trust know about it to this day.'

The National Trust took over in 1941. 'We weren't told. None of us. The head gardener heard it given out on the news. He said to the housekeeper, "They've given us away, they have. Lock, stock and barrel, to the National Trust."'

Dennis had been happy working for Mr Ash who had treated him very well, and after the Trust took over completely, Dennis would still get letters from Mr Ash. 'He regularly sent me £100 to go on holiday and at Christmas, and sometimes it would be £150. When he was

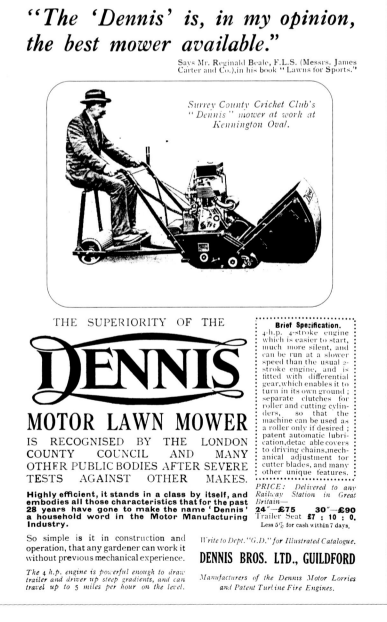

seventy-five years old he sent £350.' Dennis is very grateful because he feels he may not have had the house he has now if it hadn't been for this money that he and his wife saved. 'The National Trust treated me well, too. They left me alone and I was allowed to buy what I wanted, but there was nothing outrageous. I didn't cost them nothing. I gave them more than they gave me.

'Every three years the Trust had a trip, and one year we went to Ireland, another to Sheffield Park and we went to Wisley and the Chelsea Flower Show. There was a trip to Powis Castle and another to Nantwich. Then we met all the other head gardeners and Graham Thomas, the National Trust's garden advisor, would take us around. Sometimes they gave us a book of the place and another time we had to buy them. We

had lectures in the evening, but some of them rushed off to the pub. I knocked around with them from Cornwall and we had some fun with the head gardener from Trelissick, Jack Lilly. Once we stopped at The Feathers, in Ludlow, and we wanted bed and breakfast and it was £22 10s. Jack called out "Who's the boss that owns this place? Fetch him here! It would be cheaper to buy it!"'

They were good times, Dennis recalls. 'I had a party when I retired and they presented me with a silver salver, and I got the British Empire medal. So now I'm enjoying myself and keeping busy helping neighbours and friends. I've cut cypresses, beech hedges and yew, and I have my allotment. I go visiting gardens, and last year I went on a trip to Holland to the bulb fields with a lady friend and we had a lovely time looking at all those colours.'

A Keeper's
Chequered Past &
The Netter Netted

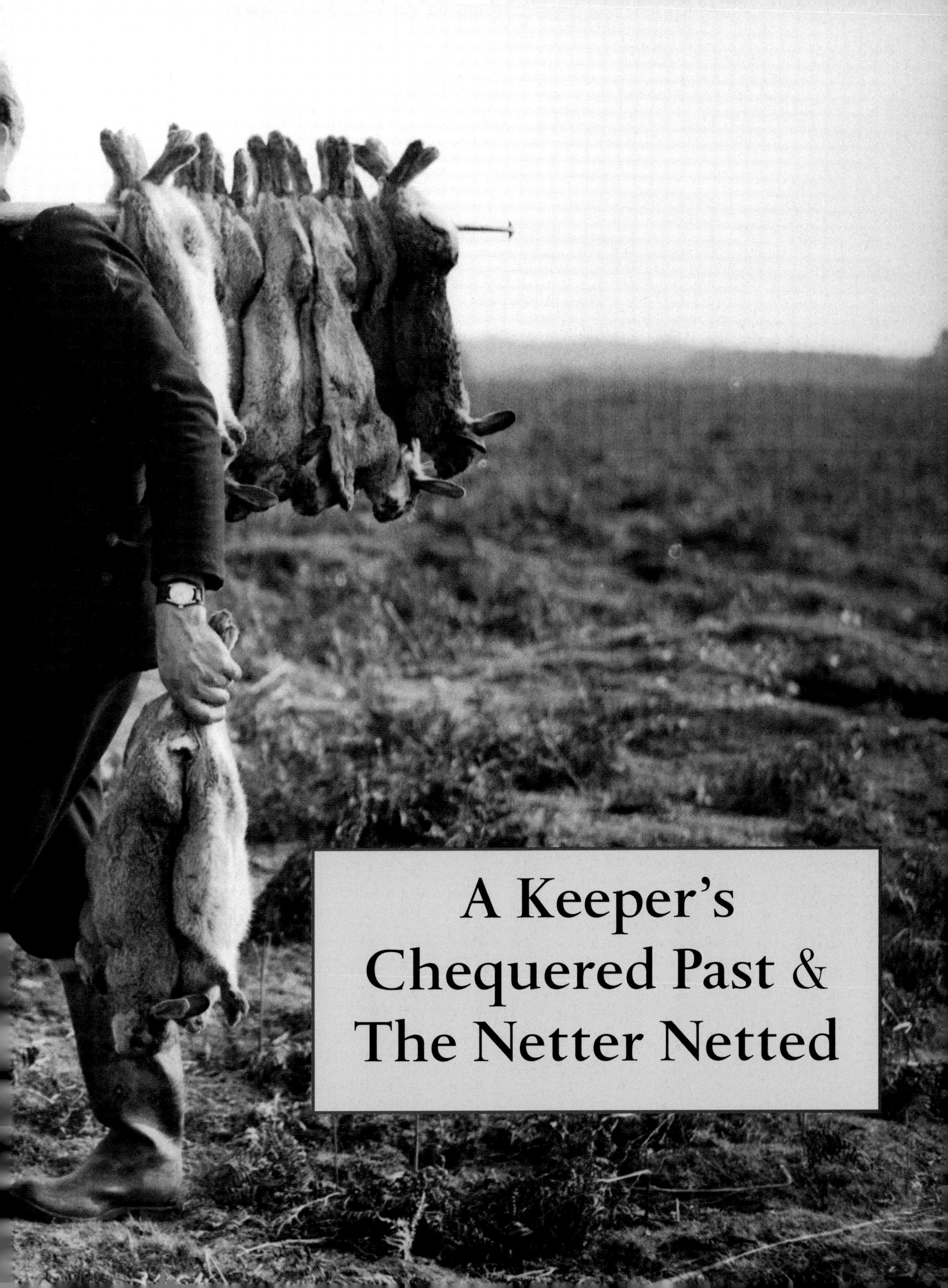

A KEEPER'S CHEQUERED PAST

Dick Townsend was not born a keeper. Like many before and since he started on the wrong side of the coverts, but it was to prove a good grounding for him when later he became a distinguished and fearless poacher catcher. It is an old saying that poachers make the best gamekeepers, although Dick saw the light at a youthful age.

'Between the ages of twelve and fourteen I did a bit of poaching myself, climbing down the drain-pipe when my poor mum and dad thought I was in bed fast asleep. This is where I had an early start at night life. I could use one of three things to get my prey: the air-gun if I was well out of the way, my catapult at certain places, and my favourite, the bow and arrow which made no sound at all, many a time I have taken a pheasant less than a hundred yards from the keeper's house and him none the wiser. However, I had to

make sure the wind was in the right direction so that his dogs did not get my scent.

'One dark night I had to come home by road. In our village they used to hold whist drives before the war; these would run from 7.30 to 9.30 and then there would be dancing from 10 until 1.30. My mother and father took part in these, my dad "on the door" and my mum helping with refreshments, which meant they were never home before midnight and this gave me a chance to poach without worrying about being missed.

'I left my house at about 8.30 and took the old route through the gardens and over the Park to one of the outlying woods. I noticed it was quite misty as I entered the wood and after being in it for about half an hour and getting four birds, I realised just how thick the fog was coming down.

'I managed to find my way out of the wood fairly easily, as I knew every tree and there was a ride to follow, but when I got to the Park it was a different story. There were no landmarks to help, everything was blank and I could see nothing. I started in the direction I thought was right, but got nowhere. I had completely lost my bearings. A lump came into my throat and I could feel tears coming. I was really scared not knowing what to do and wishing I had stayed at home, when suddenly I heard music. The lump in my throat disappeared and my eyes dried, for now I knew exactly where to go. The main drive to The Grange came out exactly opposite the dance hall which was only a hundred yards from my house.

'As soon as I knew exactly where I was I hid my birds and came home by road. I dare not risk

getting lost again so I picked up the birds the following morning. I have often wondered how long it would have taken to get home had there been no dance on that night; it was one of the thickest fogs I have ever known.

'Apart from poaching I made quite a bit of money by catching certain wild birds alive. It all depended on the species as to what price you were paid. There were very few birds which came to our Norfolk woods and streams in those days that I could not catch.

'I caught them in various nets and traps and a decoy bird would be used sometimes. My two favourites were the ride net which you would hang across a ride in a wood, and the other, the best of all, was a bridge net. On the estate there were quite a few bridges over various streams which were fairly high and you would get all sorts of birds and wildfowl flying underneath. The net I used was made like a funnel; I made it myself. I would set it over one end of the bridge and then go back to the other side for some distance, making sure to keep well away from the stream so nothing was disturbed until I started netting downstream towards the net. I have caught mallard, teal, widgeon, coot, water rail, snipe, the odd woodcock, kingfisher, penny wagtails, moorhens by the score and many other species by this method, I once caught 43 head in one setting, 31 moorhens, 7 mallard, 2 teal, and 2 snipe.

'Another way of earning money was by snaring rats round the farmers' cornstacks. All my gear was home-made and came from my own ideas. I was born with a gift and was never happier than when I had the challenge to catch something. I used to go to Woolworth's at Norwich and buy threepenny rolls of wire and in the evenings would make all my rat and mole snares. One thing led to another and the head warrener on the estate contacted my schoolmaster to ask if he would allow me to go with him and the other warreners on their big "roughing-in" day to shoot rabbits, and how delighted I was when he agreed. It was nothing for three or four men to shoot 250 rabbits on one of those days.

'When I left school I really wanted to be a gamekeeper, but the people on the estate were no fools and knew my reputation. However, I wanted the job so much that I plucked up courage and went to see the headkeeper.

'I shall never forget that day as long as I live. His wife came to the door (he was having his dinner), and I heard him shout, "Who is it?" His wife replied, "It's that boy Dick from the village." Then in a voice loud enough to wake the dead, he shouted, "Not Dick the bloody bird-catcher!" My heart dropped and I nearly ran off, but he came to the door and asked me what the hell I meant, being round there. I explained to him that I wanted to be a gamekeeper, and asked if he would take me on as his "lad". He said, "You really take the biscuit: you've had nearly as many birds off this estate as we have, and now you come for a job!"

'After an interval which seemed like a week he said with a deep sigh, "Well, I'll see if you are a man who can keep a promise. While I am keeper here you will never poach another pheasant off this estate." I promised him I wouldn't, so he told me I could start work Monday at 12/6d a week, with no time off. No one could have been more satisfied than I was. I did not want any time off, and remember well that in the first three years I had only three days off from work.'

THE NETTER NETTED

Chippy Smith of Tamerton Foliot, Devon is a traditional old-timer and part-time keeper responsible for sending me a number of wonderful tales; he was involved in a lovely story, told in my book Poacher's Tales, in which he and a pal fired the crazy muzzle-loader at a roosting pheasant, although now Chippy is pretty sure that it was, in fact, a flock of starlings. Now over eighty years old he has been persuaded to send a couple of reminiscences, this one about a night with the long-net.

'Many years ago we worked for the Air Ministry in the construction of a new airfield. We had access to a large area of fields and woods and were on good terms with the local farmers so we knew where the rabbits were lying out.

'Having a long-net at home I decided on my next weekend to bring it up and see if we could thin them out. My pal at the Ministry had never been long-netting before so we had a dry run in the daytime to work it all out and explain the setting drill.

'On the night the wind was perfect for this particular wood. Having set the net I explained to my pal where he had to go, dragging a tin full of small stones to move the rabbits. On his return to the net he would work from the far end taking out the rabbits and I would meet him half way along. The net was 150 yards long. All was ready so I whispered to him to set off and drive them in.

'I stayed at my end holding the top line waiting for the bumps which showed that rabbits were hitting the net. After about twenty minutes I heard a helluva noise and began to scan the skyline expecting to see a flock of bunnies making for the wood. It was my pal chasing straight towards the centre of the net with two large dray horses in hot pursuit of him.

'I started to shout, "Mind the net!" but no use: he came on hell for leather towards the wood. He hit the net full tilt and ended up totally meshed, lying in the brambles while the two Shires just stood blowing and staring down at him.

'I said that he should have ignored them: they would not have hurt him. He replied "With them bloody great feet they would have shoved me into the ground."

'Sad to say we did not pick up a single rabbit that night."

Boys and Girls and Gardens

Bob Gates : Banstead and Westonbirt School

BOYS AND GIRLS AND GARDENS

Bob Gates first taught gardening to boys in an approved school at Banstead, then moved to Westonbirt School for Girls where he spent most of his career. Bob's father had had a horticultural contracting business in Liverpool, after being in the navy; he was called up again before the outbreak of war in 1938. Bob left school in 1940 and found a number of jobs, before joining the Navy himself in 1943.

When the war ended, Bob joined the staff on the estate in Charlbury of OV Watney, the brewer, starting at the bottom as glasshouse journeyman. The head gardener was Mr Buckle. 'There was always great competition between him and the nurserymen at Cirencester about growing cyclamen – they used to vie with each other to get the best plant. Mr Buckle even used to lock the potting-shed door so that you couldn't see what he was putting into the compost! He used to look after the cyclamen as if they were babies, you know.

'Mr Buckle used to grunt instead of saying good morning and after about three weeks I had had enough of this. So the next morning I went "Hrmph." "What did you say Robert? You didn't

say good morning." "Well," I said, "I thought that was the way you wanted to be spoken to." He stumped away, but he always said good morning after that.'

Fuel was very short after the war, and consisted mostly of wood. They started to grow quite a lot of tomatoes in pots, to Mrs Watney's disgust, as previously they had produced tropical plants like bananas and pineapples, guavas, cotton and ginger. These were grown in a stove house, which was almost like a botanical garden, but because of the fuel shortages they had to change the produce they grew. There was three-quarters of an acre of greenhouses. 'We used to put a sheet down under the vines and thin the grapes out with scissors, then they used to sell them to the

bakers for gooseberry tarts. You couldn't tell the difference. The earliest gooseberry tarts in Charlbury were really grapes. I used to pinch a few grapes sometimes, and the head gardener came up to me one day and said, "Look, if you want to steal grapes, take a tip from me, always use scissors, then I won't know. When you pull them off, I can see the little bits hanging down."'

They had a nuttery at Charlbury, rare today, which was never mown. In the spring it was absolutely beautiful, full of wild flowers which were indigenous to the area; although Bob feels that an artificial wild garden such as that at Highgrove is very difficult to maintain.

After this practical training at Charlbury, Bob moved to another private estate before going to Wisley as a student. He considered it to be excellent training. Bob had enjoyed his sport in his leisure times at Wisley and decided that he wanted the opportunity to continue, and to find a job which would involve looking after sports grounds.

In fact the job he obtained was as instructor at Banstead Hall, at Banstead in Surrey. It was a short-term approved school catering for about eighty boys aged fourteen to eighteen, and Bob liked it when he got there. There were cricket and football pitches to look after, and Bob played sport every day. Physically the boys were worked very hard. 'If they were on punishment, they couldn't go out, and I used to have them all. I've had as many as seventeen or twenty boys in a line with spades, digging. And people used to come and watch. We had this huge field across the road from the school, and people used to like watching: the ground was going over like a plough, you see, because they were all in line, one behind the other, which was the old-fashioned way of digging – they went across the field. Of course you shoved the lazy ones in the middle, so they'd get their feet chopped off if they didn't keep moving. It was lovely to see this soil just going over, like ploughing. I believed in digging for them, some of these chaps were big and strong, they wanted something to prove themselves, and they didn't mind the digging. You would always have at least

Experts in the construction and planting of

ROCK GARDENS :: :: DUTCH GARDENS
WATER GARDENS ITALIAN GARDENS
FORMAL GARDENS JAPANESE GARDENS

PULHAM & SON
————————*GARDEN CRAFTSMEN*————————
71 NEWMAN STREET, OXFORD STREET,
LONDON, W.1

BY APPOINTMENT
TO H.M. KING
GEORGE V,
H.M. QUEEN
ALEXANDRA,
H.M. THE LATE
KING EDWARD VII.

GARDEN
ORNAMENTS
in *"PULHAMITE" STONE.*

FIGURES :: SUNDIALS
BIRD BATHS :: VASES
FOUNTAINS :: :: ETC.

LISTS ON RECEIPT OF REQUIREMENTS.

————————

NURSERIES ... BISHOP'S STORTFORD
WORKS ... BROXBOURNE.

six or seven and they were competing all the time. When I left they went and bought a machine, which spoilt the point of the thing.

'The boys were there for attempted murder and things like that. Mainly they were East End lads. Great youngsters, great sense of fun. The approved school system in that day [1949] was based on the public school system of points and houses. Smoking out of hours meant losing four points right away. And there were other things, too: if they lost twelve points in a fortnight then

Westonbirt House

their pocket money would be reduced, and they wouldn't be allowed home at the end of the fortnight. If I caught them, I would say, "take your pick, four points off, or a clock across the backside". But there was no animosity, it was finished with and they could go on. Of course I got reported for it, but they still sent me all the difficult rag-tags. You couldn't do it today, now they have called the analysts in. Mind you, you have all these different drugs today. I used to like the

East Enders, they have a great sense of humour, and they make jolly good gardeners, too. We used to have plant diaries just like we did at Wisley – twenty-one plants out on the bench on a Monday morning. They would come in and look at them, and write down what they thought they were. They were good at remembering them, the common names, not in the Latin so they didn't lose interest.'

Under instruction they grew all the vegetables that the school used, and lots of fruit too, such as blackcurrants, which they bottled. They looked after the greenhouse. They also had a hundred varieties of apples, and won prizes with them. Flowers were grown for the local florists. In due course Bob became a senior instructor, and he also met and married his wife Joy while at Banstead.

In 1958 Bob went to Westonbirt School as head gardener, and he stayed for more than thirty years till he retired in 1991. The house at Westonbirt is huge, in the florid high-Victorian manner, and the gardens are superb. The Westonbirt Arboretum, which is open to the public, is just across the road and is managed quite separately, although the wealthy Holford family started the collections of plants in both places.

'I didn't find it too awe-inspiring. Though I

JOBS FOR THE BOYS – FLORAL DECORATIONS

In the old days the men used to do all the flower decorations in the house – it is a fairly new idea to get girls to come in and do them under contract. At Charlbury the greenhouses were a long way away, so they used to have a horse and cart to take all the cut flowers and pots to the house; cherries and lilies for instance, would be forced in pots. Bob learnt decorating in a grand manner from the head gardener. 'They had carpets of Cyclamen hederifolium at Charlbury over the autumn and spring, and the secretary there came out one day and picked loads of these things, and put them in little paste jars. Ol' Watney was absolutely furious.' It wasn't 'done' to pick flowers without asking, and the paste jars were completely inappropriate.

didn't like the building at the start. In the bad weather it looks like Alcatraz. Once the sun comes out it's transformed, with those gorgeous browny, creamy, orange shades; it grew on you. The garden is very under-rated, I think. It was designed for a lot of people. It was on the grand scale. To see it you must go up into Holford's sitting room. Then you see what the grand design is. It was designed to have leisurely walks and little surprises.'

This is the third house at Westonbirt, and before it was completed in 1872, RS Holford had already started on the garden design which we can see today. Formal lawns and terraces lead down to the fountain pool, with views across the ha-ha, which hides the road, to the farmland beyond. The other axis leads from the church to the dell with its pond and statue of Mercury. A knot garden, pergola walk and an Italian Garden with architectural features complete the more formal eastern side of the property. The west provides a more informal aspect, with irregular clumps of trees, a lake, grotto and rockery. RS Holford was a pioneer collector of trees, shrubs and flowers from around the world, and Sir George continued his interests with a particular penchant for orchids and exotics. At one time three thousand amaryllis were grown in the hot-houses, and his camellias were famous.

Bob Gates never wanted to be a working head gardener. He was a Head Gardener, a manager of thirteen men under him, in the mode of the old private gardens where he had started his training. 'Head gardeners were very important people, they were gods. They were very respected and the boss would consult the head gardener on anything and everything. Of course coming to Westonbirt you had a lot of people who didn't realise that the head gardener was really something in his trade. The teachers didn't recognise the head gardener as anything other than an outside worker. I would never succumb to this, so I wasn't always very popular. I always got on well with the headmistresses and the bursars. And the men, we discussed things every day, we didn't have problems there.

'Running a place like this wasn't always like running an ordinary garden. The garden itself was twenty-two acres; with all the school sports grounds, and twenty-four grass tennis courts, a hundred and fifty acres in all. We used to mow a hundred acres a week. Also, the golf course became more popular. When I came you could fire a shotgun up every fairway and you wouldn't hit anything – now you'd have a job to get round it on a Sunday afternoon. We made a lot of money on the golf course, and that helped pay for the garden.'

As time went on of course men retired, and mechanisation became more prevalent. When Bob left, he had only three men to help him instead of the original thirteen. 'Strimmers revolutionised Westonbirt because of all that edging – we had two miles of edging altogether. It used to take a man the best part of three days to do the Italian Garden alone with clippers. It took two hours with a strimmer! And electric hedge clippers – though I still think that hand-clipping a hedge with shears is more accurate if you want to do it really well. The others are so quick, you know, even if you put up a string or little guides. You can make a better job with shears. But we don't have many hedges at Westonbirt.'

Bob thinks that he had one of the first strimmers, which was an electric one run off a generator. 'Innovations in machinery came from America, and amateurs had them first. In the early days some of the engines were terrible, we were always repairing them. But the new ones are superb, worth every penny. I never think machinery is expensive. If you had a strimmer, you needed a certain amount of skill, but it gave you more time to do the more skilful jobs.'

There were four men in the kitchen garden and two in the greenhouses. 'In the prospectus of the school in the 1950s, it was said that they grew their own vegetables. One of the Lyons family

A view of the gardens

(the catering people) wanted his daughter to come to Westonbirt, and I took them round the kitchen garden and showed them that we did actually grown them. We used to buy main-crop potatoes, but grow everything else. Miss Scott-Smith, who was the headmistress when I went, asked me why we didn't grow peas and beans. Mind you, I hadn't been there five minutes. "Well, I don't know," I said, "perhaps it's the

shelling of them." "Never mind about that," she said, "I'll get the sixth-formers to shell them." And they did for a bit!'

Bob used to sell the surplus produce in Tetbury and Malmesbury. Marketing by head gardeners was a practice probably started during the war, and in Bob's opinion it ruined a good number of private gardens, when it continued after the war. The owners might have no idea of marketing, and the traders would come in and take all the best. Or the owner would give away all the choice flowers to her friends, leaving the head gardener unable to make the garden pay, as he should have done. In the end Bob stopped the practice at Westonbirt. He also stopped his staff from making wreaths and hanging baskets because his men were making items for the florists and funeral directors at a price which was simply not viable.

The lake is a feature of the garden: 'It was part of the design. On the very old maps there were ponds for the vicarage there. Then when they built the present house, the lake was put here for a very good reason, because you get the reflection of the house in the lake when it's full. It's very well thought out. Anyway, the lake got algae in there – it made a blanket. It used to

CHRISTMAS TREES

Bob sold about five thousand Christmas trees a year. 'I used to have this lovely lady, a didicoy, a dealer – Mrs Hughes, very rich, but she couldn't write. She was very good, she used to take all the roots out when she lifted the trees; if you just cut them off, the ground with the roots in is no good to anyone. She used to come with all these notes. One year her daughter came when her mother wasn't well, and she wrote me a cheque. One year the Governors wanted a higher price for the trees, and so I went to Mrs Hughes, she went higher but couldn't go any more, and I thought she was quite right not to pay more. So I stopped doing it. Pity. It was an income coming in from ragland, and the school used a fair number of the trees, too. She was as honest as the day was long, that woman. She was strictly on the line.'

bubble up from the bottom. Terrible! We cleaned the lake out, scrubbed it, filled the holes. The water authorities couldn't give us any information. The water was high in oxygen. They suggested rainbow carp to eat the algae, which they did, but they couldn't eat it fast enough. The lake is built on the old riverbed, and the river is now culverted. When it was made, it would have been made with puddled clay. This was built on streams, and in 1870-something they had to concrete it – the date is on the bottom of the lake. But in 1975 we had those tremendous floods, and I reckon these just scoured the old river out. The lake bed is hollow underneath, and I reckon myself that all the effluent is lying there and just seeping up, particularly as the concrete is getting old.' (In fact the lake has recently been cleaned out and repaired and so it is clear once again.)

'I wouldn't let the girls do anything. One of the biggest problems we had at Westonbirt were the sticks coming down from the trees. You couldn't mow without picking them up and it all had to be done by hand. We had a great storm one time and a tremendous lot came down. I mentioned it to the bursar of the day. Next thing was, "I've got it all fixed," he said. "I'm going to have

all these girls picking up things." "Who is going to be in charge of them? I'm not!" You've never seen such a thing in all your life, fifty or sixty girls all walking round with one stick each. We had more to do clearing up after them. And you can't blame them – their dads weren't paying £3,000 a year for them to be lackeys, were they? I used to tell the girls to sit down and enjoy the view. They were very conscious of the gardens. But I used to make them clean up if they smoked, that was the only thing.

'I honestly can't think of any vandalism from the girls. There was litter sometimes, I used to tell Mrs O'Brien in the tuck shop that there were a lot of sweetie papers in the Italian Garden and she used to shut the shop till they had all been cleaned up. They used to decorate the Mercury statue sometimes. I used to come down of a morning and there he'd have a bra on, a hat and a boot on his foot, and lipstick. I used to leave it till they had taken their photographs.' For a while the junior girls had small gardens to work themselves, but this did not prove very satisfactory in the long run, and the area is now a flowery sun-trap designed by Bob.

Sports ground maintenance is very expensive, and particularly for a place such as a school, where the use is limited to specific term times. 'I've swept snow off the grass tennis courts so they could play.' The usual practice is for some of the courts to be rested, to allow the base lines to recover while the others are used, but in this case it could not be done, as all the girls played sports every afternoon. So the grounds had to take a lot of wear. Too much fertiliser makes the grounds too soft, so that was not a solution at Westonbirt. They did try renting out the sports facilities in the holidays, but then they couldn't control what happened. 'You may spend £7,000 doing your tennis courts, and people come in wearing all sorts of shoes, and when the surface of a court is broken, you can't really do anything about it.

UNUSUAL SPECIES

Amongst the more unusual trees they have on the estate is one of the oldest and largest metasequoias in Britain. They also had the largest sugar maple, although this has now gone; and an *Aesculus turbinata* grows on the lawn which is supposed to be the very one which A J Bean used for his drawing of the species in his well known book *Trees and Shrubs Hardy in the British Isles*. Bob used to grow some trees from seed and tried to keep the garden as it was, according to A Bruce Jackson's 1927 catalogue on Westonbirt. Sometimes Bob found it difficult to get the old varieties, which are now defunct; and the new and probably smaller varieties which have been developed are not always suitable for the size of Westonbirt. 'The house is so huge, it needs something to bring it down. We had the first *Gleditsia triacanthos*, the soap tree. The form you see a lot is *inermis*, or 'Sunburst.' There were two planted at the same time, one at Kew. The Westonbirt one just got better and better. It used to have fruit like laburnum. Apparently it was used years ago as soap in Japan. Lovely tree, very feathery.' Bob never burnt leaves in autumn. Instead he raked them up and put them in the covers, the irregular clumps of trees which are dotted around the lawns. There they rotted down and provided food for birds and wildlife.

'When I first went to Westonbirt, you wouldn't credit it, I used to watch fascinated, because to make the running track they had a couple of sixth form maths girls with a piece of string, the right length, stretching it out and round, and marking it with the tracks. Miss Scott-Smith asked me to make a new track, and we took over doing it then. We had Olympic jumping pits, can you imagine it!'

Bob always wanted to make sports pitches out at the front of the house, which had previously been rough fields for grazing farm animals and horses. When Miss Newton came as headmistress, she was all for it. 'I spent a long time getting water levels and digging holes to discover the drainage and so on.' The work wasn't actually done till much later. Trees had to be felled to make room, though the three cedars immediately in front of the house could not be removed as they had been planted by Queen Mary, Edward VII and Princess Alexandra. 'I think some of the governors made a bit of a hoo-hah about it. They always try to disguise the fact that Westonbirt is a school. They put the swimming pool miles away, nearly into Shoeburyness.' The land in front of the house is now elegantly smooth grass for playing fields.

There used to be herbaceous borders in the Italian Garden, and Bob tried for many years to get rid of the convolvulus. Eventually he suggested that they should put the borders down to grass — after several years of mowing it they would be able to see if the convolvulus was still growing there. If not, it could be restored to herbaceous beds as it was. 'I didn't do anything there, that could not be easily restored.'

Sir George Holford liked daisies in his lawn. However, they don't wear very well in bad weather, and in some weathers they will root from the leaves, and seed like fury. 'I got rid of them. If you weedkill a lawn it would save two mowings, which may not sound a lot, but it gave me time to have men on holiday. Exams made a difference to the mowing. What you don't want is movement — sound doesn't matter, but

movement catches a girl's eye. We used to have to turn the birds off! We had to mow at lunchtimes. You had one day of rain and couldn't mow, and then you were never catching up. We were a bit restricted.'

Bob and his men managed grass tennis courts, lacrosse and hockey pitches, the athletics and the golf, and of course the superb Grade 1 listed gardens. English Heritage, the Garden History Society and the National Trust, who came to visit Bob from time to time, were always surprised that he could run Westonbirt with so few staff. Now Bob has retired, and lives with his wife Joy in a cottage filled with his expert wood carvings, many of them carved from trees which Bob once tended at Westonbirt.

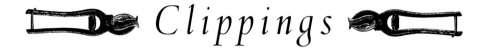

WARTIME GARDENERS

Allotments measured 90 x 30ft. In 1939 there were 815,000. By 1943 the Dig for Victory campaign got well on its way and there were 1,400,000 allotments. Gardens were formed all over blitzed cities in parks, on bomb sites, in back yards, on roofs, on top of Anderson shelters, and even in a bomb crater in a courtyard of Westminster Palace.

During World War II boxes of vegetable seed collections of seventeen assorted varieties were sent as gifts to the British people from their friends in America through the British War Relief Society Incorporated, New York.

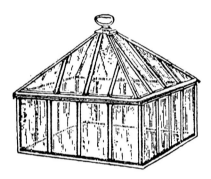

FLORA REMEMBERS
THE LAND ARMY

Florence Hutchinson was born near Whitby, Yorkshire, in 1907. She is a happy person with a gentle Yorkshire accent and even her voice seems to smile. She says she loved working in the open air and now she sits outside whenever the weather permits.

Flora, as she is now called, because of her love of flowers, was brought up on the family farm and became a Land Girl for Ilkley Council. It was wartime and she preferred to do this than to go into a factory or join the Forces, which were the alternative compulsory occupations for young ladies.

When war broke out in 1939, the nation relied on seventy per cent of its food and livestock feedstuff being imported, thus leaving itself dangerously open to blockade. The target was, therefore, soon set as self-sufficiency. The Women's Land Army came to the fore and by 1943, 87,000 girls were working in fields and gardens.

Flora volunteered early on, because she 'did not want

pushing anywhere'. Two million acres were reclaimed during the war in the nation's effort to become self-sufficient, and Flora did her bit. She planted potatoes for the war effort on patches of waste ground:

'One field, it was a grass field, they ploughed it out and we all, there were about four of us, planted potatoes, but we didn't plant them like they do all in rows. It was a bit, well, rather rough. We used to make holes with a dibber and just pop in a potato. Ooh! We had some fun! There was no-one showing us how to do it. There was a superintendent, but he didn't come round much.'

Some men did not give women much credit for their ability to work on the land, so perhaps this is why Flora and her team were left largely to their own devices. Flora and her chums also enjoyed helping in the nurseries growing vegetables and tomatoes. There was a greengrocer's shop in Ilkley that used to buy their produce. Petrol was rationed at this time, but this did not matter to the young ladies. The shop was only ten minutes away and they pushed the produce there on a trolley.

THE WOMEN'S LAND ARMY

The Women's Land Army was formed in 1917, disbanded in November 1919 and re-formed in June 1939. At the outbreak of war in 1939, 1,000 volunteers were available for duty and undertook all kinds of work on the land. By June 1944 there were 80,000 women in the Land Army and one third came from towns and cities. They earned less than £3 per week and had one week's holiday a year.

'She milks; she does general farmwork which includes ploughing, weeding, hoeing, dung-spreading, lifting and clamping potatoes and other root crops, brushing and laying hedges, cleaning ditches, haymaking, harvesting, threshing; in more specialised ways, she prunes and sprays fruit-trees, picks and packs the fruit, makes and lays thatch, makes silage, pulls flax, destroys rats, works as an excavator, reclaims bad land; works in commercial and private gardens, works in the forest felling timber, measuring timber, planting young trees ... It is quite an impressive list ...

Vita Sackville-West, 1944

USEFUL HINTS AND TIPS FOR LAND GIRLS

Remedy for Roughened Hands

Put 1 ounce of olive oil and 1 ounce chopped beeswax into a jar in the oven until melted. Cool and, when easy to handle, roll into a ball. Rub lightly into the hands after washing. A little oat flour will remove greasiness.

Making Shoes Waterproof

Cut up a little beeswax and put into a jar. Cover with a little castor oil or Neat's-foot oil. Stand in a warm place till wax is melted. Stir thoroughly. Allow to cool. If too thick add a little more oil. To use, warm a little, apply with stiff brush while quite soft. Let that coat harden, warm boots slightly, and apply another coat. Neat's-foot oil alone is quite good.

To Make Gum Boots Slip On and Off Easily

Sprinkle French chalk inside the gum boots from time to time.

from Land Girl, A Manual for Volunteers in the
Women's Land Army, 1940–46

TWO WARTIME RECIPES FOR SOAP

• Boil 125g of ivy leaves for five minutes in two litres of water, after which add six litres of water. When cold, wash the clothes in it. It is specially suitable for dark woollens or silk, but is better tepid for ordinary woollens.

• The solution is made by shredding six chestnuts upon which is poured four litres of soft water or rainwater. This is left uncovered for four hours. Then filter and warm up. This

lathers and cleans like good soapsuds, being specially suitable for stockings, blouses, and fine goods – also floors and kitchen furniture.

THE CHOICE

When skies are blue and days are bright
A kitchen garden's my delight,
Set round with rows of decent box
And blowsy girls of hollyhocks ...

Katherine Tynan, 1915

POTATOES

Who can have thought, says Roze, in his elaborate Histoire de la Pomme de Terre, that the Potato, having its home in Chile, naturalized in Peru, where it was cultivated from time immemorial, introduced into Europe in the sixteenth century, despised in the seventeenth, slightly esteemed in the eighteenth, would have taken so important a place in commerce and form a subject of abiding interest to almost all nations in the nineteenth century?

Gardeners' Chronicle, 1905

DANDELION LEAVES AS A VEGETABLE

Dandelion leaves are uncommon even as a salad, and still more uncommon when cooked. They should be washed well and left to soak for an hour. Then blanch them for a few minutes in boiling salted water, take them out and cook them in fresh boiling water. They should take about half an hour. Drain them well, pressing out as much moisture as possible, as with spinach, chop them up finely, and fry them with butter. Add a spoonful or two of cream before serving.

Ambrose Heath, 1941

THE OLD MOLE CATCHER

Old Albert had no qualms about catching those cannibalistic little creatures who could rapidly cover his lawns with hillocks of loose earth, providing attractive seedbeds for weeds and building sites for ants. He would skilfully seek out the run by finding a patch where the ground was hollow; this was usually near a molehill or perhaps between two. The run might be just under the surface or lower down '... according to the worm situation. In wet times the worms are at the top part of the ground. In dry weather you're not bothered with the moles so much because they've gone down deeper after the worms. They are still about, but deeper.'

After tracing the run Albert would cut out a piece of turf and put in a trap. Next, he would cover the trap with the turf so not a trace of light could penetrate. He would then wait until a mole came through. Albert set the traps in the evening and would inspect them every morning. Sometimes it could be a whole week before he caught a mole. The moles might also be cunning and fill a trap with earth. The secret was to catch them at the lawn's perimeter before they had a chance to invade the lawn itself, because it is very difficult to repair a lawn and it soon becomes uneven.

Albert once tried poisoning the moles, but he does not favour this method. 'You can use poison, but you've got to get a permit because it's strychnine. You collects the worms in a jar and then you feed them strychnine. Next morning you put the worms in the runs, but its only got to be the deep runs so when the moles have it, nothing else can get at it and pass it on.'

It takes from 300 to 350 moleskins to make a fur coat, and when Albert was a boy he used to collect their skins to make some pocket money. He would cure the skins himself by stretching them on a board, securing them with nails and allowing them to dry. However, Albert found 'It wasn't really worth it. The time they had graded them, you might only have two or three out the dozen that were top grades and you had the price according to the grade.' Nowadays Albert takes pleasure in occasionally helping out in a few local gardens.

ENEMIES

Mice... Breakback traps we set everywhere, and at first every day had its victim or victims, though later on the little creatures seem to have learned wisdom and avoided toasted cheese and smoked bacon. We found they did not touch bean seeds when they were sown with a little red lead, and for a time the smell of paraffin with which we rubbed the boxes of our frames kept them off, but when it grew fainter with time they came again. Finally we introduced a kitten into the garden, who began to make a havoc among the mice, but the fear of her being trapped in the midst of a gaming country such as ours, led us to feed her lest she should wander, and since then her life has been one of luxurious pauperism.

Helen Nussey and O. J. Cockerell,
A French Garden in England, 1909

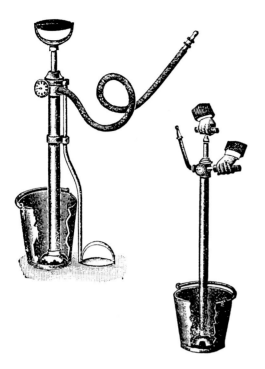

WEEDS

To the layman and the uninitiated in general, the study of weeds may seem a dull and unprofitable occupation; to them weeds are a nuisance and nothing more, but to the good gardener the study of weeds makes many appeals … The gardener recognises in weeds foemen worthy of his steel; enemies in the destruction of which all his skill and ingenuity are engaged. By dint of waging ceaseless war upon weeds, the gardener has learned many a useful lesson which in their absence might have remained unlearnt.

Gardeners' Chronicle, 1910

FLAGS

IF anyone having a few spare eaves to drop had dropped them near our garden fence on a certain day last week, they might have overheard me drawing the attention of Robinson to 'the German, or bearded, type'.

If from that day they had deduced that we were Fifth Columnists or deep in a discussion of racial physiognomy, they would have been wrong. To begin with, we weren't deep in any discussions, we were just beginning one. And we certainly weren't concerned with such things as Aryan whiskers. Our talk, at my neighbour's request, was of the Iris.

I had explained that there were many different species.

The bulbous rooted Spanish, Dutch and English Irises, which must be planted between August and October; the Japanese sorts, which thrive best in very damp places, such as the edges of ponds; the Cushion and Beardless varieties; and finally the Bearded Irises, comprising the popular May and June flowering plants known to most gardeners as Flags and to others as German Irises, Orrice Root or Fleur de Luce.

'I presume you're really interested in Flags?'

Raymond W. B. Keene, *Over the Garden Fence*, 1946

GARDEN GESTAPO – THE GREENFLY

DISTINGUISHABLE from the blue-bottle by its absence of steel helmet and stripes, this insect can be found in the garden clinging to lettuces, old bicycle tyres and empty tins. The most destructible of pests, a single greenfly has been known to eat a whole rockery and many of the wretched creatures made their way into Kew without paying for admission. It is an established fact that they breed in the spring mostly without going through the marriage ceremony. Codger says that the best way to deal with the greenfly is to ignore it, but an ounce of stale skate dissolved in drain water and applied to your marrows will teach it a lesson.

Peter Ender *Up the Garden Path*, 1944

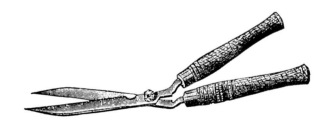

OLÉ

'TWO members of the Women's Land Army, Mable Sales and Joyce Newton, employed by Captain Pryce-Jones, of Frenchies Farm, Mark Cross, a few days ago pluckily drove off a bull which had attacked and gored their employer. Captain Pryce-Jones, who is well-known in the Tunbridge Wells district, was engaged in tying the animal up in its stall when it suddenly turned on him. It knocked him down and commenced to gore him. His shouts for assistance were heard by the girls, who ran into the stall and after driving the bull off, succeeded in rescuing their employer by dragging him to safety.'

The Argus, 1944

THE GARDENER'S LIFE WAS A HARD LIFE

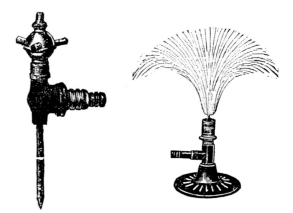

The garden has seen many changes and today, with the help of mechanical tools, only a few staff are necessary at one country house, Polesden Lacey, Surrey, compared with 38 before World War I, and 14 in 1938. Life for the staff is easier today in more ways than one: at one time there were notices forbidding them to walk upon the lawns; if caught, on the first occasion it cost the culprit a fine of half a crown, with worse to follow, for if disobedient a second time, apparently dismissal was the punishment.

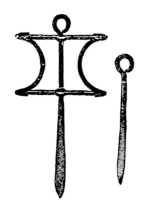

THE ROYALS VISIT THE ALLOTMENT

During World War II, Geoffrey Sleeman and his brother were billeted in the country to escape the bombing in London. 'During the evacuation, our school was kept separate from that of the country boys and girls, and we had a Nissen hut for our lessons; but we'd got no books or pencils, nothing, because there was a war on. They had to keep us amused somehow, and we'd go out on nature rambles identifying foxgloves and blackberries and so on. And collecting acorns for the farmer so that he could feed his pigs. Then they gave the school an allotment to use, and this became the be-all and end-all of everything.

'When we got to school one day, the headmaster called us all together and said, "We are going to have some very important visitors today. I can't tell you who, till they arrive, so I want you all to get your wellingtons on and get working down on the allotment." Who should arrive to see how London children were coping with evacuation, but the King and Queen! They did a tour of the allotment, speaking to some of us (not to me).

'After they had gone, the headmaster declared a half-holiday. My brother and I walked home (it was about a five-mile walk) chattering excitedly. Of course we were early, and that was the last thing the maids wanted. "What are you doing, playing truant?" "No, guess who's been to visit our school today – the King and Queen!" And they didn't believe us, and we were sent to bed without an evening meal for telling lies!'

SCENTS

To-day I think
Only with scents, – scents dead leaves yield,
And bracken, and wild carrot's seed,
And the square mustard field;

Odours that rise
When the spade wounds the root of tree,
Rose, currant, raspberry, or goutweed,
Rhubarb or celery;

The smoke's smell, too,
Flowing from where a bonfire burns
The dead, the waste, the dangerous,
And all to sweetness turns.

It is enough
To smell, to crumble the dark earth,
While the robin sings over again
Sad songs of Autumn mirth.

Edward Thomas, 1918

The Snare of
the Fowler

THE SNARE OF THE FOWLER

As ancient as the Dead Sea Scrolls, the net, snare, hingle or noose – there must be hundreds of local names – is a basic tool of the poacher's trade. Costing nothing and fashioned from horsehair, willow wands and ash poles he found around him, the evidence could easily be destroyed, while the confixation or loss of such gear was of no concern.

The net was another essential and the poacher evolved many ways of using it to advantage, be it for hanging from a gate for a hare, stretched out by the woodside for rabbits, for use with ferrets, for dragging over a stubble at night to catch a covey or for taking fish. No one could call himself a poacher until he had mastered the art of the netmaker.

Opposite: Waiting for the ferret to drive a rabbit from its burrow

LONG-NETTING

In Victorian times long-netting was the real money-earner; in those days when the rabbit was king and the market for them was eager, the rabbits caught long-netting commanded the best prices because they were clean and unshot. It was a job which called for no little skill and a good dog, and was the curse of the keepers because it entailed wholesale slaughter.

The best sort of night for this work was dark and blustery with a little light rain – not heavy and continuous, as then the rabbits would not feed or venture far from their buries. The net would be fixed at one end along a woodside or hedge at a time of night when the rabbits were feeding and unsuspicious, well out in the field and far from their homes. A second man would walk backwards unrolling the net as he went, until a great length of woodside was covered. Two companions would follow behind him sticking in the ground at fifteen yard intervals a hazel peg two-and-a-half feet in length, and fixing the top edge cord of the net to it.

kills it deftly with a single blow; he then returns swiftly to his position.

Best of all and most effective is the long-netters' dog when it has been trained and has a natural instinct for the work. The dog will scent rabbits that human beaters may have overlooked and start them for home, for there will always be a few rabbits which stay in the form and do not run straightaway. The dog will start the rabbit running and chase it for a distance, but always stop within a few yards of the net and not blunder into it. Such a dog is like gold dust to a long-netting gang.

Those without a dog could resort to other methods of starting the rabbits. The problem on some nights was not so much to drive them as to make them move at all. Without a lurcher to start them on their headlong dash for safety, the poacher needed to call on his ingenuity to find an acceptable second best. Sometimes he would catch a rabbit and take it to the furthest point on the beat and hold it firmly in his hands so that it squealed in alarm; this was often enough to start the other rabbits moving. Alternatively – but far more risky – he could strike a match from time to time; this would also have the desired effect, but was considered highly dangerous as any night watchers would see the sparks of light in a second and hasten to the spot.

Another way was for the beaters to take a long cord with lead weights attached to it at intervals. Holding one end each they would trail this through the grass or stubble and this would effectively disturb the rabbits. This system was less successful on ground studded with bushes or whins. Instead of lead weights, small sleigh bells could be used, or a handful of stones in a cocoa tin, in short anything which would alarm the squatting rabbits sufficiently to start them moving.

Hares were hardly ever caught in this method for the hare makes straight for open ground when disturbed; but sometimes a fox would rush forward and crash into the net causing some degree of upset and bad language as it would have to be set from scratch again.

The net mesh was made to exact dimensions – just large enough for a rabbit travelling at speed to force its head through, but difficult for it to remove it. As many as six nets would be set, each one a hundred yards in length, which will indicate the scale of such an operation, and the great amount of damage it could do to a rabbit population. One man would take up position at one end of the net with his fingers resting lightly on the top cord, instantly ready to react to the vibration of a rabbit hitting the trammels.

If the gang had no dog, the other men (and the operation called for at least three for it to be successful) would make a wide sweep round the field and beat it back to the waiting nets. The rabbits would be lying out feeding, and their first instinct would be to squat and trust to luck that they were not observed; but they feel insecure so far from their holes, and as the beaters approached they would break cover and make a headlong dash for safety, crashing into the net and getting their heads firmly caught in the meshes. The man at the net meanwhile feels the bump as a rabbit hits, slips quickly from his spot, removes it from the net and

PREVENTING LONG-NETTING

The keeper could sometimes set alarm guns, but these were not popular on fields where cattle were grazing or near the coverts where pheasants might be roosting. The observant keeper could tell if he was being long-netted simply by the sudden decrease in the number of rabbits in particular fields and by tell-tale signs on the grass. He might release a number of tame rabbits coloured black or piebald on vulnerable fields; their sudden and unexplained absence would tell him immediately that the long-netters had paid him a visit – the best poacher in the world could not distinguish between a common rabbit and a coloured one on a dark night.

It was rare for even the most careful gang to leave without forgetting at least one hazel peg – a sure giveaway. On dewy nights their tracks would be clear in the grass and in frosty weather their footprints were obvious, standing out stark and black against the pale background.

There was another ingenious measure which could be taken to prevent long-netting, but it was applicable only to those grass fields which lay along the covert side and where the landlord owned them; this was to buy a draft of rough hill bullocks of Welsh or Scottish strain. They should be fed late and their hay laid out in a long line by the woodside; they would spend the best part of the night eating it and then lie down nearby to sleep. On the arrival of the netting gang later on, the bullocks might think that here was more food on its way for them and rush up madly to the gang, giving it no peace but bellowing madly. The men might try to drive them off, but the general commotion would be more than enough to scare any rabbit which had not lost its sense of hearing.

If the poachers had a dog with them this would add to the chaos, for cattle will not leave a dog alone but will chase it hither and thither. If the nets happened to be down already the beasts would rush through them, entangling their legs and effectively wrecking the whole set-up. A crafty poacher would cut a truss of hay from a nearby stack, lead the bullocks to a far corner of the field and when they were quiet, resume business as before. However, not all poachers were so resourceful and there was not always a convenient rick for the purpose.

As in trail-netting, a bunch of scrubby thorns scattered along the probable line where a net would be set would cause great annoyance. However, unlike trail-netting, long-netting was a more careful and circumspect business, and an experienced team would send a spare man crawling in front of the net layer to feel and find the bushes with his hands, and throw them well away from its path. In counter ploy the keepers would sometimes peg the bushes securely to the ground; this would give the poachers more trouble, although it would not stop them entirely. Short, sharp thorns strewn liberally on the ground were as good a remedy as any, for they made the progress of the crawling man a matter of some discomfort.

The other drawback to bushing – which was, after all, only a moderate deterrent – was that the very presence of lines of cut scrub would indicate to all passers-by that this was a field full of rabbits, well worth a visit with the long-net.

Some estates discovered that bean straw was even better than thorns; it was easily obtainable and could be strewed thickly, and would cause great trouble in the net. Also when bone-dry and rotten it made a fearful racket when you walked on it, and thus would alarm every rabbit on the

field long before the net was in place.

An inbuilt drawback to long-netting was the fact that because of the rabbits' feeding habits, it had to take place within the same hour or two at night. The most likely period was shortly after chucking-out time at the local ale-house, or between then and dawn. Any keeper knew it was always possible for his estate to be the second in line for a raid, should the netters have bad luck at their first choice, so he could not be pin-point accurate in his estimations; but he could have a fair guess to within an hour or two.

Therefore at about 11 o'clock at night the keeper would go out with a brace of fast terriers and thoroughly beat the ground which he thought the poachers would tackle. The rabbits would be driven safely into their holes, and even if the netters arrived shortly after, they would not by then have ventured so far out again into the field. After a few nights of this regular disturbance the keeper would find that his rabbits would feed more often by day and would not go so far out into the fields. In this way the netters could be successfully thwarted.

BAGGING THE NETTERS

A netting gang usually numbered five people, and the keeper was advised not to tackle them himself but to wait until he could command a team to outnumber them by at least two, ie seven stout-hearted chaps. The idea was to come on the gang when they were all assembled, not when in the act of netting when they would be spread at their various posts about the field. The gang would certainly be armed with stout sticks, and stones were usually ready to hand, so a concerted attack at a single moment was believed to be the most effective.

The watchers should hide near a spot the netters were certain to visit and, each man leaving room for his neighbour to operate, leap out as one. If possible the net should be bagged, as such an item was expensive and the key to the whole operation; without it the gang was lost, and it would take some time and expense to make a replacement.

If the poachers were alarmed and given time to arrange their defence, things could grow ugly – they might form a hollow square like a military operation and hurl flints or stones. The advice in this situation was for each keeper to remove his coat and to wrap half of it around his arms allowing the tail to hang down, thus forming a shield which would take the venom out of the missiles. They should then organise a swift and concerted charge and hand out to the poachers the same sauce intended for them.

On the darkest of nights there was one more way which could be used to break up a poaching gang of netters. With a stout rope about forty yards long, two fast and powerful men would take an end each and run as fast as they could for the poachers, passing them one on each side. The rope should be tightly stretched and held at about knee height. In the dark the poachers were naturally concerned about the whereabouts of their assailants; trying to see where they were, they probably would not spot the rope racing towards them with deadly intent – with luck it would take them at the knee and throw them down in complete confusion. The rope runners should then return to their backup team and secure the gang. However, keepers at all times were advised to take care when tackling poachers who could be as desperate as rats when cornered, known sometimes to throw dust and handfuls of lime into the faces of their attackers.

Good advice was always to call on the men to surrender before wading in with the first blow, and only to attack if they refused and showed fight. However, most poachers would throw in the towel if they realised they were confronted by determined men who outnumbered them.

A surrender was far to be preferred to an uncertain affray in a moonlit woodland or stubble field.

PARTRIDGE NETTING

The partridge has never lent itself to poaching as, unlike the pheasant, it prefers open places and roosts away from cover in the safety of fields. However, it was vulnerable to a shot from a poacher's crazy open-bored muzzle-loader with its wide spread of shot and open pattern; and although pheasants with their proclivity to woods and enclosed places offered a better target, partridges were very common in those days and commanded a good price.

The way to come among them was by means of a trail- or trammel-net. This could be of any length depending on the number of men available to work it, but measured between twelve and fifteen feet in width with a bamboo pole at each narrow end. It was carried by two men who would hold the poles at an angle so that the net ran along at an angle to the ground, the leading edge at waist height and the trailing edge brushing the ground behind. The net was made of fine thread or preferably silk, and the trailing edge took the form of a fringe which brushed in the stubble.

A whole covey could be covered in this way, and when the net was dropped, one man would keep hold of his pole whilst his companions carefully knelt down and removed the birds from its meshes. The operation was silent and hard to detect, although tell-tale signs that netters had been out were scattered feathers and toe- and heel-marks on the scuffed ground – but even then it called for a sharp-eyed keeper to spot them.

A good trail-netter spent much time in observation. He would spend many days watching the stubbles to see where the birds 'jugged' for the night – the strident calling of an old cock bird would indicate where they were, and he would find the little piles of droppings which showed where a covey had settled overnight. The birds also gave away their whereabouts by arriving with a great clatter of wings, and would usually stay near to where they alighted. The poacher would bait the field with bird seed and dari, and this would draw the birds from great distances.

Partridges were especially fond of the last stand of corn left by the reapers. In those pre-combine days the harvest was a protracted affair, and many farms would have swathes of corn which remained uncut until well into autumn. This was a haven for game of all kinds, which came for food. When netting standing corn the poacher adapted his net to include a series of short cords on the trailing edge, each with a lead weight attached; this would help keep the net close to the ground in the tall crop. Even then it was not easy to drop the net firmly enough on a covey, for it could not be pressed down securely and birds would escape through the sides where the corn prevented the net from touching the earth.

Sheaves of corn were another draw and also a good place for snaring, while in cold weather the birds came to feed in stackyards and anywhere stock was kept. This gave the farm labourer a chance to have a quick shot with the crow-scaring gun, or to set snares in likely places. The poacher was a stranger to closed seasons, and even in the breeding season would snap up any trifles which came his way. For example, in the spring the cock partridge is very belligerent, calling loudly and proclaiming his territory and his new wife to all who can hear. A skilled man can imitate the call, and this would make the little cock come running like the wind to repel what he imagined to be an intruder. The poacher would wait in ambush until the bird came close, and shoot it on the ground, pocket it and make a swift departure from the scene. The keeper might hear the shot, but this was the time of year when the bird scarers were most busy and he would pay it little heed.

Another fruitful time for the opportunist was when the piles of muck were left in neat rows along the fallow fields before being ploughed in. These were full of all sorts of insects and hence very attractive to game, especially in hard weather when food was scarce. It was an easy matter to set traps or horsehair snares or 'sniggles' round the heaps, with a good chance of picking up a bird or two.

HIDING THE NETS

Only the most wealthy could afford the non-bulky, all-but-perfect nets made of silk, and the coarse and more commonly used variety were hard to conceal. Often they needed to be taken home for repair, or moved to another location, and the trick here was for a thin poacher to wind a hundred yards of string netting about his body and wear an overcoat on top. Thus as a moderately bulky poacher he could pass by all but those who knew him well. On arrival at the covert side he would lie on the ground and his pals would unroll him to retrieve their net and operations could begin.

BUSHES

The keeper had one simple and failsafe solution to the trail-netter; he could bush the fields. For this he would use a large clump of bramble, or bunches of blackthorn or whitethorn cut at the time when the prickles stand out at right angles to the stalk. The pieces need not be huge, and they should not be stuck into the ground because the poacher would feel the resistance immediately and remove the obstacle.

The trick was for the bushes to be loose and

unobtrusive so that the poachers would drag their net along to the headland ignorant of what they had picked up. The net would roll the prickles over and over, and at every turn they would become more lovingly entangled in the fine mesh until almost all the net was inextricably caught up. To remove such obstructions in the dark was all but impossible; even in full daylight it might take three patient men at least an hour's work and much bad language. This would put an end to operations for that night, and if the field had been generously bushed the poachers would deem it not worth their while to come to that place again.

In modern times the trail-net is still used, often in fields of short sugar-beet. A farmer could always tell when he had been 'done' because the beet was lying in neatly swept rows, alternately this way and that like a newly mown lawn. If the beet had many 'bolts' in it it was hard to net and usually safe, but if the farmer was worried he would bush the fields in the usual way. The traditional thorn bunches were safest; one farmer thought he would go one better and use iron stakes hammered into the ground at intervals – these would surely tear the net and make it unusable. Unfortunately he forgot where he had left his traps and the sugar-beet harvester picked up two of them, with disastrous consequences to the machinery.

HOW TO BEAT THE GATE-NETTER

Good advice from John Wilkins in the nineteenth century.
'To prevent gate-netting you should tar the lowest rail of the gate, so that when the hare goes underneath it she smears her back. She will then avoid the gate in future and find some other way in and out of the field, for whichever way a hare comes into a field at night, she will go out the same way if she possibly can. Now the hares thus driven to avoid the gate make through the hedges and the more runs there are through the hedges the more chances there are for the hares and the less for the poachers.'

THE LONG NET

From Alfred Curtis — a 'proper' poacher of the 1960s.

'We put up the old net fifteen yards from the hedge. Syd went out into the field to drive the rabbits with the aid of a tin can full of pebbles on a string dragged behind him.

And then striffing through the grass, the rabbits came. I heard the first one hit the net. I ran to it. Nothing there! Another came and another. I swore I could see them. There were more; they hit the net, I heard them strike it and hither and thither I ran and had never even the tail of a rabbit in my fingers. I was chasing phantoms of rabbits.

Alastair came running up with Syd. "What's the bag?" "Nothing! They've been here but I can't catch them." And with the coming of the grey dawn we saw: the net was punched full of holes where the rabbits had gone through. Our fine net that had looked so strong was completely rotten.

REVENGE!

'A clear ten days I gave those rabbits to forget then I set off again for Lady Eaton's with Syd to help me once more. There was no call for the string and can as I had brought Brinnie with me. We put up the new net and my fingers were glad at the sound strength of it. I whispered to Brinnie: "Go! find 'em boy!"

'He vanished in the vast shadow that was night over the field. We waited. A rabbit came thrumming on the ground. It came, it thudded into the net and Brinnie followed. We heard it squeal, and now there was no need for Brinnie to drive, for at the sound all the rabbits in the field bolted for home. The net was suddenly jerking, alive with leaping forms and not one rabbit went through.

'There was no time for orthodox killing; we ran up and down punching and slaughtering as fast as we could. Forty five rabbits in less than half an hour. How many poachers, I wonder, can say better than that? It took us several journeys working together till at last nets and rabbits were hidden safely in a little spinney. We made a little fire to keep alive the warmth we had acquired and brewed tea. It seemed scarcely half an hour before we saw the streaks of dawn in the sky and the sky paling through the trees: we should have to work fast.

'And fast we did work at gutting rabbits. We'd hang one up, split it from vent to chest with our knives that were as sharp as razors, grab it with forelegs and hind, throw it back over the left shoulder and cast — and out, of their own weight, came all the entrails into the bushes.

'We sold them for sixpence each — always provided we might have back the pelt, for rabbit skins were sometimes worth more than the meat in those days.'

From the Archives

To make a horse follow his master, and to find him out and challenge him amongst ever so many people.

Take a pound of oatmeal, to which put a quarter of a pound of honey, and half a pound of liquorice, make a little cake thereof, and put it into your bosom next to your naked skin, and then run and labour yourself till you sweat, and so rub all your sweat upon your cake; then keep the horse fasting a day and a night, and give it him to eat, which done, turn him loose, and he shall not only follow you, but also hunt and seek you out, when he has lost you, and when he comes to you, spit in his mouth, anoint his tongue with your spittle, and thus doing, he will never forsake you.

The Complete Horseman or Country Gentleman's Recreation, 1795

MOUNTING FOR LADIES

If she be very timid, she may practice mounting indoors, with her right hand on the top of an upright piano, and her left on a gentleman's shoulder…

Alice M. Hayes, *The Horsewoman*, 1903

ON TOOTHACHE

'…the horse rarely suffers from toothache; the nerve does not approach so near the crown of the tooth as in man.'

Lieut-General Sir F. Fitzwygram, Bart.,
Horses and Stables, 1911

ON GROOMING

… curry him well under his belly, near his fore-bowles, and in a word, all over very well, his legs under the knees and cambrels only excepted; and as you dress his left side, so must you the right also …

This currying is only to raise the dust, therefore, after the horse has been thus curried, take either an horse-tail nailed to a handle, or a clean dusting cloth of cotton, and with it strike off the loose dust that the curry comb has raised.

Then dress him all over with the French brush, both head, body, and legs, to the very fetlocks, observing always to cleanse the brush from the filth it gathers from the bottom of the hair, by rubbing it on the curry-comb; then dust the horse again the second time.

Then having wetted your hand in water, rub his body all over, and as near as you can, leave no loose hairs behind, and with your hands, wet, pick, and cleanse his eyes, ears and nostrils, sheath, cods, and tuel, and so rub him till he is as dry as at first.

Then take a hair patch and rub his body all over, but especially his fore-bowles, under his belly, his flank, and between his hinder thighs; and in the last place, wipe him over with a fine white linnen rubber.

When you have thus dressed him, take a large saddle cloth (made on purpose) that may reach down to the spuring-place, and lap it about his body: then clap on his saddle, and throw a cloth over him, that he may not catch cold…

The Complete Horseman or Country Gentleman's Recreation, 1795

RECIPE FOR HOOF OIL

Take 4 ounces of Venice turpentine, 3 ounces of the best rosin, of bees-wax 2 ounces, 1 pound of dog's grease and a half a pint of train oil; melt all these ingredients together, except the turpentine; then take them off the fire, and put in the turpentine, stirring it till it be well incorporated; then pour it out into an earthen gallipot, and keep it for use, but do not cover it till it is cold.

(Anoint his hoofs round from the coronet to the toe with this ointment. After this, stop his feet with cow-dung.)

The Complete Horseman or Country Gentleman's Recreation, 1795

THE NEGLECT OF CARRIAGES

A carriage requires as much care as a sofa, and is often treated like a wheelbarrow, thrust after use into a damp shed, to encourage the decay of the silk, velvet, or leather linings, and cause violent colds to the ladies who sit in it without the slightest precaution, when within doors they carefully dry and warm everything, from a pair of stockings to a pocket-handkerchief.

Samuel Sidney, *The Book of the Horse*, c.1880

COACHING ETIQUETTE

The usual hour for driving in the summer is from four o'clock to seven, and in the winter from three o'clock to five, or even a little earlier. Ladies driving themselves, in either a Victoria or a pony carriage, would drive in the morning or afternoon, according to choice, although the morning hours from twelve o'clock to two are the most fashionable hours. In town or at watering-places ladies would not drive unattended by a groom, neither would they ride in town unattended by a groom, unless accompanied by a male relative, when a groom's attendance might be dispensed with. A gentleman would always ride on the off or right-hand side of a lady. In the country, ladies frequently ride out alone when they are particularly good horsewomen, but ladies would not ride to hounds unaccompanied or unattended.

In driving in an open or close carriage no particular place is reserved for the owner of the carriage when accompanied by her friends. A guest or guests would always enter the carriage before the hostess; were there two guests present, and either of them were a young lady, she would naturally seat herself with her back to the horses, leaving the two married ladies to occupy the opposite seat; but this would be a matter of courtesy on her part, and not of etiquette.

A gentleman would sit with his back to the horses if a second lady were present; a gentleman also would be the first to descend from the carriage, with a view to assisting the ladies to alight, whether he purposed re-entering it or not. As a rule, the hostess would descend after her guest, and not before her, unless it were more convenient to do otherwise, when she could make some polite remark before alighting; but if a lady were merely calling on an acquaintance to take her for a drive, she would not descend from her carriage for the purpose of allowing her to enter it before her.

From *Manners and Tone of GOOD SOCIETY by
A Member of the Aristocracy*, c.1880

COACHING CHARACTERS

There were some quaint characters amongst the coachmen. Ned Mountain drove the Exeter Defiance. He left Basingstoke at ten at night, drove down till he met the up-coach, when the coachmen changed coaches, and he got back to Basingstoke at eight in the morning, driving from eighty to ninety miles every night. He was once unwell and sent for the doctor, who cross-examined him as to his habits. He said he always had a pipe and a glass at eight o'clock every morning, upon which the doctor expressed astonishment that he was alive after drinking in the morning. 'It may be morning to you,' said Ned, 'but it's my bedtime, and I can't leave it off.'

Saunders wore the most correct coaching costume; a low-crown flat-brimmed white hat, and spotted shawl round his neck, which he wore on the hottest day of summer, declaring that if he left it off 'he always got the chop-ache'. He also wore what some call overalls (otherwise knee-caps) of drab cloth that buttoned up from his ankles to the top of his thighs – generally over top-boots – in the hottest weather, declaring he got rheumatism if he did not. His top coat was the thick drab West of England cloth. It was necessary to make the sleeves very large on account of the stiffness and thickness of the cloth, and the consequence was that in wet weather the rain drove up them and wetted him. To obviate this he used to make Bill Emery get some clean straw out of the stables to fill them up, and to do this effectually Bill kept a short strong stick to ram the straw tight. One day whilst they were changing horses Bill purposely left the stick up his right-hand sleeve. They had not gone far when they came to a sharp hill. Wanting to hit his leaders with his whip, Saunders was perplexed and pained to find that he could not bend his arm, and was unable to use his whip, so he called to the guard to jump down and touch up the leaders, declaring that his arm was quite stiff from rheumatism. He did not discover the stick up his sleeve till he got to the next change…'

His Grace The Duke of Beaufort, *Driving*, 1890

GYPSIES

Gypsies have a fine faculty of evasion, catch them who can in the same place or story twice! Take them; teach them the comforts of civilisation; confine them in warm rooms, with thick carpets and down beds; and they will fly out of the window – like the bird, described by Chaucer, out of its golden cage.'

William Hazlitt

TO MAKE A HORSE LOOK YOUNG

Take a crooked iron, no bigger than a wheat corn, and having made it red hot, burn a little black hole in the tops of the two outermost teeth of each side of the nether chap before next to the tushes where the mark is worn out then pick it with an awl blade, and make the shell fine and thin; then with a sharp scraping-iron make all his teeth white and clean; this done, take a fine lancet, and about the hollows of the horse's eyes which are shrunk down, make a little hole only through the skin, and put in the quill of a raven or crow, and blow the skin full of wind; then take the quill out, lay your finger on the hole a little while, and the wind will stay in, and he will look as youthful as if he were but five years old.

The Complete Horseman or Country Gentleman's Recreation, 1795

WHEN TO MATE MARES

February is the best time to put the mare to the horse. If in hard condition she should have a dose of physic and cooling diet, and then if she shows no signs of being stinted, a few quarts of blood may be taken. But it is a much better plan to reduce the mare to a soft condition by degrees, with soft food and slow light work at drilling and harrowing, if she is not turned out to grass. *She should on no account be allowed to see the horse again under three weeks.* Many mares are rendered barren from allowing them to see the stallion frequently, to ascertain whether they are really stinted.

Samuel Sidney, *The Book of the Horse*, c.1880

A GOOD MAN

'Wanted a man to attend to horses of a Christian character.'

Advertisement quoted in 'A Lincolnshire Glossary' written by Jabez Good, the village barber at Burgh le Marsh, Lincolnshire, c.1900

TIDAL WAVE

On 9th September, 1899, a fissure opened up in the tow path at Dudley Port. A tidal wave of water from the canal gushed through the opening and into the marl pit of a nearby brickworks.

Two boatmen were caught in the rush of water. One saved himself, his boat and horse, by quickly securing his towrope round a telegraph pole. The other, not so lucky, lost his boat but by cutting the towrope, managed to save himself and the horse.

ROUGH JUSTICE

During the depression of the 1930s times were tough. Caggie Stevens, who features in the book, remembers how he and his father dealt with potential violence: 'There was only me and me father and as many as six big men would come along the towpath to raid our coal boat.'

But he used to prepare for such occasions. He looped a shortish piece of rope into a noose and got the boat horse to pull the noose up into a tight, hard knot. 'A blow on the back with that would fell a man.'

LAMPASS

Occasionally the gums or bars become congested, swell, and protrude beyond the wearing surface of the incisor teeth, rendering the mouth so tender the horse cannot eat. It is commonly owing to the teething process. This is called lampass; and the old race of farriers were in the habit of treating it with their favourite remedy – the application of a red hot iron – a brutal piece of ignorant folly. Gentle laxative and mash diet will generally reduce the congestion and relieve the animal. Sometimes it may be advisable to lance the gums, but in this affection it is seldom necessary.

Samuel Sidney, *The Book of the Horse*, c.1880

HUNTING BY RAIL

There is no more luxurious conveyance than a railway carriage. Hunting-season tickets have long been an established system…

The railway directors of the best hunting lines run specials, and put on drop carriages to express trains, for the accommodation of hunting-men. A party of from half a dozen to a dozen can engage a saloon carriage, provided with a dressing-room and even cooking arrangements. The finishing stroke has been put to the luxuries of hunting by the addition of American sleeping cars – dressing-rooms by day, bed-rooms by night – so that you may breakfast going down, dine, or take tea, and sleep or play whist returning. The Midland and London and North-Western Companies have found it worth while to make direct extensions for the accommodation of hunting-men; and all over the kingdom the locomotive has become a hunting machine.

Samuel Sidney, *The Book of the Horse*, c.1880

OF HUNTING HORSES

You may furnish yourself with a horse for hunting at some of our fairs, which should as near as can be, the following shapes.

A head lean, large, and long; a chaul thin and open, ears small, and pricked, or, if they be somewhat long, provided they stand upright, like those of a fox, it is usually a sign of mettle and toughness.

His forehead long and broad, not flat, and as it is usually termed hard-faced, rising in the midst, like that of a hare, the feather being placed above the top of his eye; the contrary being thought by some to be a token of blindness.

His eyes full, large, and bright; his nostrils wide and red within, for an open nostril is a sign of good wind.

His mouth large, deep in the wikes, and hairy; his thropple, weasand or wind-pipe-bag, loose and straight, when he is reined in with the bridle; for if when he bridles, it

bends like a bow, (which is called cock-throppled) it very much hinders the free passage of his wind…

…and some do not scruple to affirm, that wherever you meet with a horse that has no white about him, especially in his forehead, though he be otherwise of the best reputed colours, as bay, black, sorrel, he is of a dogged and sullen disposition, especially if he have a small pink eye, and a narrow face, with a nose bending like a hawk's bill.

The Complete Horseman or Country Gentleman's Recreation, 1795

OF STABLES

As to the situation of a stable, it should be in a good air, and upon hard, firm, and dry ground, that in the winter the horse may come and go clean in and out; and if it may be, it will be best if it be situated upon an ascent, that the urine, foul water, or any wet, may be conveyed away by trenches or sinks cut out for that purpose.

By no means let there be any hen-roosts, hog-sties, or houses of easement, or any other filthy smells near it, for hen-dung or feathers swallowed, oftentimes prove mortal and the ill air of a jakes sometimes causes blindness; and the smell of swine is apt to breed the farcin; and there is no animal that delights more in cleanliness, nor is more offended at unwholesome favours than a horse.

The Complete Horseman or Country Gentleman's Recreation, 1795

THE 'BLUES AND BUFFS'

Scarlet is the uniform of very established fox-hunting club in the kingdom, except one – the Badminton – an hereditary pack in the family of the Duke of Beaufort through four generations, since, in the time of the fifth duke, a pack of fine staghounds was converted into foxhounds. Curiously enough, although the Somersets were among the stoutest friends of the first Charles and the last James, and have since the Georgian era been distinguished for the stiffness of their Tory politics, the uniform of their hunt has always been the blue and buff of Charles James Fox, of his Whig followers, and of their organ, the Edinburgh Review. The best thing that can be said about it is that, made double-breasted, it is a very becoming riding-habit when worn by the ladies of the hunt.

Samuel Sidney, *The Book of the Horse,* c.1880

Longtails

LONGTAILS

The pheasant – a foolish, strutting bird, popular with the well-to-do who value its sporting powers and strong flight, epitome of gourmet fare on the table, imported from China by the Romans who knew a good thing when they saw it – has been responsible for more expenditure, sorrow, injury and death than any other bird in the kingdom.

Opposite:
The poultry shop
on Christmas Eve,
1938

The sportsman who fills his woods with pheasants and sets a man to protect them is an object of interest to the poacher who likes a spot of pheasant on his plate and knows of others who would gladly buy such a bird from him, so over the years he has devised ways many and artful to come to terms with it. He risked transportation or shooting or prison, and would fight like a tiger to avoid such fates, but surely such a noble bird was well worth the sacrifice.

THE LONE SHOOTER

Perhaps the hardest of all to deal with was, and is, the poacher who shoots at night on his own. Such a one can prove an expensive adversary, unless dropped on by pure good luck as he rounds a bend and walks into the arms of the keeper. His tactic is to shoot and move, never staying in one spot long enough for the watchers to pinpoint him and come to the place. He enters the coverts at night and, keeping near a path, makes a note of every roosting pheasant as he goes. When farthest from home, he retraces his steps taking the birds he has marked earlier, avoiding those near tangled undergrowth, shooting and running to the next place until, with as many as he can carry, he leaves the wood at the point he entered it.

The keeper hears the first shot and rushes to the place, but too late; there is no-one there. Then he hears another and again runs forward, then a third shot rings out, until in the end the firing ceases and he has lost his man. The best advice for a keeper is to lie in wait at a spot nearest the wood exit, for there is a chance that the poacher will come home by that route. At least by staying in one place he has more chance of an arrest than by blundering about chasing will o' the wisps. Sometimes such a poacher would lie low for a good half-hour waiting for the coast to clear. A waiting keeper should be equally patient and not give up his vigil until certain that the intruder has gone.

SNARING AT ROOST

In coverts where the trees are not of any great height, some poachers will snare roosting pheasants with a wire slip-noose on the end of a pole. This is best done with young and foolish pheasants in October in the days before they have

learned sense; though even then it is a very uncertain game.

The pole is constructed along the lines of a fishing rod so that its length can easily be increased or diminished to suit the height of the tree. The noose is fastened to the end, the other end of the string running down to the hands of the poacher. A young pheasant is not easily disturbed when it has gone up to roost and the poacher is helped by the bird's instinct to poke out its neck to see better what the commotion below is about. Assuming that there are not too many twigs in the way and all things being favourable, the poacher may slip his nooses round the neck of the bird and snatch it down to him. This is a silent method and therefore hard to detect and while a poacher will have many failures, the man who wants only a bird or two for himself will find the method a good one.

The only signs that snaring has been carried out are sprays of feathers and dislodged earth on the ground for the bird flails its wings mightily as it is being drawn down. Some poachers use a spring-clip instead of a noose which grasps the bird and holds it securely.

WOODEN PHEASANTS

A common dodge was for the keeper to carve a number of pheasants from wood, inserting the tail feathers of a real bird to aid realism. These he would set on likely branches near paths and rides, though not where members of the public could see them. The poacher would see one silhouetted against the night sky and fire a shot. He might be surprised that the bird did not fall, but not that it did not fly away, for roosting pheasants can take a great deal of disturbing. He takes careful aim and fires his second shot, but with the same effect.

With luck he would go from dummy to dummy, growing more puzzled by the minute. Many such wooden pheasants were found to be plastered with shot fired at them by unsuspecting poachers. The wise keeper would move the birds from time to time as pheasants do not roost every night on the same twig, and the poacher would grow suspicious unless their locations were regularly shifted.

Cruder models have also proved successful: chicken wire roughly shaped and covered with sacking, tin cutouts, straw dolly pheasants, and even whole sugar-beet with a crudely fashioned head attached – all had their day and doubtless saved many a real bird from premature death. In each case the model would have the tail feathers of a real pheasant inserted.

A good idea once is a good idea always, and this very day I see the 'Pheasifoil' has hit the market place. This is our old friend the model pheasant designed to be fixed in a tree to fool poachers. There is little new under the sun. The Pheasifoil makes used of modern technology, for it contains an inflated balloon and when this is punctured by a shot or a stone from a catapult and the air released a trigger is activated and a 100-decibel alarm sounds, more than enough to wake the dead and certainly to bring a sleepy keeper from his bed and provide the poacher with a shock from which it will take him some days to recover.

Made of a synthetic material and machine-produced, this is a most realistic bird, especially when painted in pheasant colours, though the addition of real pheasant tail feathers is recommended, even to this hi-tech device.

FIRE AND BRIMSTONE

A popular myth and one of the oldest of old wives' tales concerns the legendary method of stupefying a roosting pheasant with the fumes from a blend of oily rags and sulpher; these were put in an old tin, lighted, and puffed until they smoked mightily. The smoke was to be conducted by means of a long pipe up to the head of the pheasant roosting above until overcome by the fumes, it came crashing down.

We have tried this method ourselves (strictly in the line of research) with palpable lack of success, and no-one can be found who admits to having tried it successfully. Until such a person may be found, this wonderful theory must continue to be regarded as a fabulous myth.

WOOD BLINDNESS

Alfred Curtis worked hard to feed his family: 'for minutes on end, for half an hour, an hour, I peered into the lacing of the boughs, seeing nothing but the grey of the sky behind and the interweaving branches and blobs that were pheasants. I made the cross on the tree, seeing it

still interlaced with the tracery of boughs. I went to the next tree and peering up saw the same boughs I had seen before and before that and all evening. I was blind with wood blindness known only to poachers and keepers.

I crouched where I was, there on the earth and buried head in hands waiting for sight to return and Bill waited beside me, gun resting lightly in his arm, ears alert for the first warning sound. At last the blindness passed away and the trees came back to their own form. There we might rest until day was near for the pheasants would wait…

MARKING THE TREES

'We needed only a .410 gun, a pocketful of cartridges and a lump of whitening, the sort that was used by everybody to whiten the hearth, a penny a lump. We peered into the boughs till we made out the dark blob of a pheasant and then on that tree we made a large cross with out whitening, facing so that we should see it on our return.'

ONE FOR THE POT

There were many ways by which a man could by ingenuity take a few birds for himself and stand a good chance of escaping detection. Grain soaked in brandy was a favourite; the birds became stupefied by the liquor and could be picked up before they recovered. Raisins on fish hooks were also worth a try, but these were best used on a springing bough so that the bird could not get a direct pull on the line and break it.

Trailing the birds away by feeding them was harder to bring about. Favourite foods like black oats and buckwheat which were hard to see on the ground, and old favourites such as raisins and acorns, could be used to lead the birds from home. Much value was placed in the dari seed which is said to be a special favourite, drawing birds great distances. On one farm it was thought that every covey of partridges on the place had gathered on the one field where dari seed had been spread.

On one occasion a keeper stood idly watching the shepherd busying himself round his sheepfold. He noticed that the man had a bag of corn on his back; nothing odd in that, until he noticed the shepherd set off in the direction of the nearest covert which was a hundred yards or so away. Looking round to make sure he was not observed the shepherd pulled a plug of straw from the bottom of his bag and walked slowly back, allowing a trickle of corn to leak from the

bag onto the ground behind him. Thus he returned to the sheepfold.

The keeper was about to rush out in indignation and accuse the man, but then reflected that proof was hard to supply and the man would certainly deny that he had done any wrong. He waited, watched and bided his time until one morning he found a pheasant in a snare in the sheepfold. The shepherd's task was made easier because pheasants often frequent places where there are animals, going there for spilled food; so that shepherd had little trouble in attracting the odd bird to his traps.

COCK FIGHTING

From The Amateur Poacher *by Richard Jefferies.* When cock fighting was common, the bellicose inclinations of the cock pheasant were sometimes excited even to its own destruction. A game cock was first armed with the sharp spur made of the best razors and then put down near where a cock pheasant had been observed to crow. The pheasant cock is thoroughly game and will not allow any rival crowing in his locality; the two therefore quickly met in battle. Like a keen poniard, the game-cock's spur either slew the pheasant outright or got fixed in the pheasant's feathers when he was captured.

VARIOUS TRICKS

The partridges were sometimes driven into the nets by a dog. The partridges that appear on the first of September are said to be netted, though probably by those who have a right to do so. These birds by nature lend themselves to such tricks, being so timid. It is said that if continually driven to and fro they will, at the last, just cower in one spot, and can be taken by hand or knocked over with a stick.

The sight of a paper kite in the air makes them motionless till forced to rise; and there was an old dodge of ringing a bell at night, which so alarmed the covey that they remained still till the net was ready, when a sudden flash of light drove them into it. Imagine a poacher ringing a bell!

The partridges then were peculiarly liable to be taken; now, perhaps, they escape better than any other kind of game. Except with a gun the poacher can hardly touch them, and after the coveys have broken up it is not worth his while to risk a shot very often. If only their eggs could be protected there should be little difficulty in maintaining partridge numbers.

SNARING PHEASANTS

This was a far more successful and often-used system, and it operated in much the same way as snaring rabbits. Pheasants always prefer to run rather than fly, and this habit makes them vulnerable to the snarer. His ideal site would be a narrow belt of trees or scrub connecting one wood with another, and half-way down this he would make a secure little fence of small bushes and various brush collected from round about. This fence would be stout, but not easily noticed by a passing keeper; a good man could make such a fence and it would escape detection for a season, even though the keeper might be often in the wood.

At every yard interval the poacher would leave a gap large enough for a pheasant to run through, and across it would bend a bowed stick with each end stuck in the ground, and would hang a snare made of a single strand of wire from the exact centre of each one. Starting back at the end of the wood the poacher would beat the covert, walking in a zigzag manner to cover all the ground, driving the birds before him. If caught in the act he is an innocent man out for a few blackberries or to cut a stick – search him and there is nothing incriminating on his person.

When the pheasants arrive at the newly made fence they head straight for the openings, their heads are caught in the nooses and they are soon choked by their struggles. The poacher comes up, removes the birds, goes to the other end of the belt and repeats the process. The fence may be left in place for a future visit.

INSTANT HEDGE FOR PHEASANTS

Alfred Curtis has a successful night.

'As I cut and the pile of little stakes grew, he set to work on the hedge, criss-crossing the twigs, putting back the grasses and vegetation so that nothing showed, and so he worked his way twenty yards or so through the wood. Every two or three feet where a branch hung conveniently overhead Lammie left a gap big enough for a pheasant to go through.

'We went along the fence and in each gap Lammie placed some food, pheasant food, a few raisins, a sprinkle of corn and some blackberries. There was more food each side of the gap so that from whichever way the pheasant came there was something to lead him into the gap and through. We passed another night in the woods and in the morning the food had all gone. Again we fed the gaps and it was the third day. Lammie said, "Alf, you get some more blackberries and the last of the food; I'm going to feed again tonight and the next night we shall take the lot."

'At every gap a branch hung down held lightly under a notch on another twig pushed into the ground and to each branch was tied a wire noose and every noose was held by a twig ready for a pheasant to run into.

'We awoke at first light but did not go straight to our fence. We went to the outside of the wood and took a good look around then worked back through the wood from opposite ends, a zigzagging and making plenty of noise and a fine time we had of it after all those hours of enforced silence.

'When we came to our fence there were pheasant red and gold above our heads and among them a rabbit or two still limp and warm. We set to cutting them down and destroyed the fence, hiding the sticks in thickets and throwing the rest in the stream.

'We washed in the stream, our first wash for days, made ourselves presentable and went home with empty hands. There we shaved and put on what good clothes we might have and set forth again each carrying a carpet bag for tools with a

tool or two showing for all to see. Back at the haystack we filled those bags with all they could carry and set off home again like respectable artisans with not a breath of suspicion about us.

'I went with Lammie again after to different woods and many a pheasant has walked home in that carpetbag and so to the tables of those who know good food when they see it.'

A PLOUGHBOY'S TRICK

James Wentworth Day was one of the great writers about field sports, the Fenlands and the countryside generally. In his fine book Sporting Adventure, *he explains ingenious ways of taking pheasants.*

I think I prefer the ploughboy trick of making a dozen cones of thick brown paper, like ice cream cones, smearing the insides with bird lime, filling the bottoms with maize and then sticking them in the newly ploughed furrows just outside the covertside.

The pheasants were bound to come sneak-

ing out for worms and grubs and equally bound to stick their beaks into the cones. And then the cones stuck and half a dozen old cocks and hens would be tumbling wildly about with April Fool's caps stuck over their eyes, too blinded and too bewildered to fly.

You can, of course, take your pheasants by salting their feeding grounds with maize soaked in gin – they provide a perfect 'morning after' police court parade – or choke them with peas through which are threaded horse hairs, but that is a cad's trick.

The crude method of shooting them at roost is not to be recommended. In the first place, if the keeper has a sense of humour he will plaster the trees nearest the rides with wooden dummies. In the second place, the orthodox method of carrying a short-barrelled gun down the leg of one's trousers and trying to look like a wooden-legged sailor has its drawbacks. I know a man who tried it. The gun when off. He has a wooden leg now.

DROPPED A BRACE

Gil Gaylor, the Gatcombe Park poacher recalls a lucky escape.

'I had not time to collect my thoughts as I pelted across the fields to reach the stream. The immediate necessity was to put enough distance between me and the young gamekeeper and his dogs. Eventually I slowed down and with the sleeping fields all around me I sat down in a dry ditch under a hedge feeling breathless.

'I was a good two miles from forbidden territory and I reflected on the night's events. I thought with some satisfaction of the young keeper and how I had managed to fool him yet again – by my jumping the stream his dogs would lose the scent. Luckily they had barked when some way off and this had given me time to make my escape. Half-an-hour before I had shot three brace of pheasants with the catapult.

'Then it was that suddenly I realised that somewhere in my flight I had dropped a brace, and I cursed my carelessness. The keeper would surely find the birds on the rideway, examine them and find they had been shot with a catapult. Knowing me and my reputation his thoughts would turn my way and he would nail the crime to me. But I chuckled to myself as I sat smoking a roll-up. I had evaded capture yet again.'

OWEN THE WHIP

Ian Niall tells of an unusual pheasant-catching technique.

'Owen poached only once in his life by the strangest method one is likely ever to hear. He drove a van for a country butcher in the days before motor vans buzzed round the farms and

villages. He was sitting up behind his horse, letting the tired creature take its time on a long hill when he saw before him three pheasants feeding on a bank above the road. There was plenty of time to think. Owen looked for a weapon. There were no loose stones by the roadside, he had no gun, but his eye caught his whip.

'At a distance of a few yards from the feeding birds he drew up the horse and stepped quietly down onto the grass verge. Somehow the movement of the horse or even a man on foot on a road does not excite a feeding bird or animal. Own crawled up the bank without a sound. The hen pheasant nearest him jerked up her head in alarm and in that instant the whip cracked out and coiled itself about her neck and she scrambled and fluttered on the grass. The cock and the other hens burst into flight as Own threw himself on top of the bank and grabbed the hen before she could become disentangled and take flight. The practised hand of the butcher's man quickly wrung her neck and, when the horse began its journey again and Owen leant forward on his seat to replace his whip, the pheasant lay behind him under the canvas.'

DUBIOUS EVIDENCE

The late Richard (Dick) Walker was internationally acclaimed as a famous angler, long-standing record-holder for the best common carp, writer of some classic fishing books and trail-blazer for many of the angling styles now in common usage. His widow Pat Walker kindly sent Dick's own account of a poaching exploit carried out by him in times of wartime shortages.

'Some of my colleagues and I did succeed in supplementing our rations by shooting a variety of wildlife, including grey squirrels, rabbits, hares and pheasants. On one occasion my driver Vic Page and I stopped twice on our way through Norfolk to Bircham Newton. We were equipped with a .45 revolver for which Page had a proper firearms certificate, and a .22 Remington rifle with a telescopic sight – with which I shot two pheasants.

'After shooting the second one we had gone no further than a couple of hundred yards, when out of the ditch covered with camouflage vines sprang one PC George Mortar, who stopped us and said, "You will be charged with killing game," and so on. Having examined our two pheasants he said (and I quote) "Gor bugger boy, you don't miss much, do you?"

He asked to search the van, but we pointed the Webley revolver at him and said "No, you mustn't , it's filled with secret equipment" - which was true. He had the good sense not to press the point, but he did report us and we were charged with killing game without a licence. In due course we appeared at the Magistrates' Court at the Petty Sessional Division of Smithton and Brothercross in the county of Norfolk; we pleaded guilty.

'The constable gave evidence in the most formal "out-of-the-notebook" way. The Chairman of the Magistrates asked "Have you anything to say?" to which I replied "No, Sir, except the evidence that the constable gave was not quite exact." The Chairman said "In what respect was it incorrect?" and I replied "Well, he didn't say: 'I have reason to believe that you have just shot a pheasant.' What he did say was 'Gor bugger boy, you don't miss much, do you?'" There followed what the press usually describe as laughter in court, which went on for a long time and involved the entire bench of Magistrates as well as members of the public and press. Then the Chairman said "Constable Mortar, is what the Defendant says true?" The constable stood up and said "Yes, Sir" and sat down again. The Chairman conferred with his colleagues and said "You will be fined £1 each – that is our usual price for pheasant-poaching – and you will remain at the back of the court until the Court rises."

'When the Court rose this gentleman, who was a retired colonel, strode up to us and said "Now, you young devils, if you want to shoot my pheasants in future do me the courtesy of asking my permission first, and you may come and shoot two or three whenever you want." We became friends with him, and never abused his hospitality; we never shot more than we were allowed, and it did supplement our meagre meat ration for the rest of the war.

It was an interesting episode, and I have laughed about it ever since. It is the only time I ever got caught poaching, and I should have been more careful! It's not as if I haven't done much poaching: I am not ashamed to admit that from schooldays, through university and right through the war, I did plenty. It transpired that we fell into a trap laid by the Norfolk police to catch some Canadians who had been shooting at anything that moved with everything that they had, including Sten guns and even Very pistols. It was them, and not us, that the police were trying to catch.'

WILKINS' WOODEN PHEASANTS

John Wilkins used wooden pheasants with great success. Monk and his two comrades shot six times at my false wooden pheasants which I used to nail up in the trees in place where poachers would be likely to see them. They fired three double shots at one bird and then climbed up the tree to see if old Satan was there, for they had shot it full in the breast, then in the right side and then in the left and still the bird kept sitting serenely on. Then they have in, having fired off six barrels and getting nothing for their pains but loss of time and waste of powder and shot. Monk got something, however, in the shape of six months in Chelmsford gaol.

In Good Service

Margaret Jackson : Buckinghamshire

IN GOOD SERVICE

In pre-war days of relatively cheap labour virtually every 'big house' in every village had a generous complement of staff. Among the most indispensable were the innumerable housemaids, girls from mostly humble backgrounds who generally expected very little out of life and who knew their place in the pecking order. Some were cruelly maligned as 'mere skivvies', yet the stalwart domestics of those days generally had considerably more social standing than their modern counterparts. Their pay may have been abysmal, but in a good house they were virtually part of their employer's family and inevitably displayed great loyalty and took much pride in their work.

Opposite:
Mr R Payne
auctioning produce
at the Wavendon
Flower Show which
was held in the
Parish Hall and
enthusiastically
supported by young
and old alike

Other, newer forms of employment may have tempted with higher wages, but they could not offer dignity, as Miss Margaret Jackson recalls: 'There were new factories in our area, but on no account would Mother let me go to them as that was considered degrading. Mother had always been in good service herself; you could tell that by the way she spoke and conducted herself.'

Thus it was no surprise that, at the age of sixteen, Margaret followed the family example. Her three older sisters were already in service and her younger sister would soon follow suit, but

Margaret was luckier than most in securing a local position. With her sisters working and living away (they only returned for holidays), pressure on the family purse and space at home had already been reduced, but Margaret was still required to live with her employer. Remarkably, she was destined to remain in her native village all her life.

Edith Margaret Jackson was one of seven children, and always known to her close family as Meg. She was born on 13 July 1913 at the Buckinghamshire village of Wavendon, 'within

Wavendon
Oddfellows group
(including
Margaret's father)
in the late
nineteenth century

Happy in her work – a maid in service in the 1920s

the sound of the anvil' as her cousin was a black-smith there. Sadly she never really knew her father, a timber worker and general labourer who helped build houses in the village: he suffered from consumption (tuberculosis) for years and died when Margaret was only three. Fortunately, she had a 'wonderful' mother to care for her, and she remembers her early years with great nostalgia.

'People helped each other much more then, and we were supported by the love of our neighbours when Father died. Also, they made up for much of what we missed out on financially, people often bringing us things such as fruit and eggs.

'My earliest recollection is of a very simple gesture: picking a strawberry and showing it to Mother. The garden had everything in it in those days: a really lovely Blenheim, a greengage tree, plums, lots of gooseberries, and that lovely maiden's blush round the door – roses don't smell like that now.'

Margaret's grandfather also died young, in his forties. He once kept the village post office, but was better known as PC Collyer, the last resident policeman for Wavendon. However, he had not looked forward to being posted there because the place was notorious for 'the rough element'. The area was once known as Hogsty End, combining most of Woburn Sands with Wavendon.

Wavendon is unusual in having had only three clergymen in over 150 years, and the strength of the church there had a great influence on Margaret from an early age.

'For a start we were blessed with a Church of England school. Every year we had an exam for the Bishop's prize, and once I was runner-up. The dear old rector always used to go up to London and choose the prizes himself. I suppose you could say I was clever at school, and I was certainly very happy there. The only lesson most of us hated was learning to sing with the modulator. We always started school with assembly, with a hymn and prayer, and the last lesson of the day was from the scriptures. That school served the village well then, with about seventy pupils within walking distance; now, however, it would have closed long ago if it weren't for people dropping children off in cars. It's all very different from when every pony and trap used to come along with candles in their lamps, and those of us on foot often had to go across the fields by full moon or lantern light.'

Some seventy years later, Margaret still treasures a few of her school books, not least her prize volumes and one containing her painstakingly prepared sewing patterns. She also cherishes thoughts of 'the many poems we used to learn by heart, all about Mary Queen of Scots and brave Horatius. The standard was very high.' But of course not everyone was academically inclined, including Margaret's brother Hugh.

'Opposite the school was the slaughterhouse where the pigs were taken, and if "it" happened in the afternoon all the boys would go out to watch. They used to stand on the forms at the back of the class with their eyes out the windows. One day the teacher said to Hugh: "What's more interesting out there?" "Harry Gurney comin' up the road with a load of muck, sir," he replied. Hugh was only ever interested in farming and couldn't leave school quick enough. He and the other boys used to make the ink every week, using a powder, and us girls often got splattered.

'Mind you, the teachers weren't all perfect then. If our schoolmaster knew the Whaddon Chase hunt was meeting anywhere near he'd get off after them on his ol' bike, a lady's model. So the boys thought they'd go too. But Mr Buxton always knew who was missing and was heavy with the cane. Then one day he went berserk and the boys had him on the floor. Everybody was wringing their hands and didn't know what to do – but next morning nothing at all was said.'

The Jacksons lived in a simple cottage, one of fifty-three homes which have disappeared from the parish since Margaret was a girl. They encountered considerable hardship, although Margaret also remembers the many happy days during her childhood, just after the Great War.

and all singing "A hunting we will go….". The scout group had a band in which my brothers Fred and Hugh played the kettle drums. When they marched through the village with flags flying we sisters ran alongside trying to keep up. Now that hut and the school have gone.

'As we paid under £5 a year rent we received "the parish coal": one ton a year dumped at your gate free of charge, courtesy of the Duke of

'In 1921 the village purchased a disused Canadian army hut, and as the first scout group had just been formed it became known as the BP (Baden Powell) Hut. The day it opened was a red letter day for us. I can see it now, and all the fun times we had in it. Mothers, fathers and children were all so delighted to join in the festivities, playing musical chairs and tripping up the long room with Charlie the postman on the piano

Bedford's estate. We had lovely great lumps then and the boys barrowed it into the barn. And if you had more than a dustpanful of dust to sweep up after, you'd complain. Today there aren't the number of people applying for free coal, and if you get two hundredweight you're lucky.

'On Sundays Mum stayed home to cook while us children went to Sunday school and church. When we came home we had lovely beefsteak

A typical scout group band outside the local saddler

pudding and vegetables, and this would fill us up so we didn't want so much roast beef afterwards, making it a cheaper meal. That was the general trend for all the working people then, and it was the only time of the week a family would sit down together. There was no electricity, and everything was cooked on a coal-fire range. We never had a sweet after Sunday lunch, but Mother would have made a pie or tart on the Saturday and we'd have that with cold vegetables and other things after church on Sunday evening.

'Mr Neale, the baker, used to go round the houses, and on a Saturday he'd bake your cake for you. We used to love going in the bakery to hear the crickets.

'In the week there was always jam roll or spotted dick on the menu. And in the winter when we came home from school we would open the door and smell dripping toast for tea – that was a lovely thing to greet hungry children. And darling Mum was always there to welcome us.

'We lived very close to the school and always envied the "dinner" kids – those who lived more than one and a half miles from school. They always brought the first spring flowers, the crab blossom, and if snow was coming or a thunderstorm was threatening they'd be sent home early.

'No matter how poor we were we never wore on Sunday what we wore on Saturday. We always had pretty little cotton dresses and pinafores, a lot

GOOD VALUE RABBIT

'When the milkman came, by pony and trap from a local farm, he often had a rabbit for a shilling, and that would do us two meals done in a brown earthenware jar in the oven. Then Tommy Allen, the rag-and-bone man who came round with a donkey, would give us sixpence for the rabbit skin, so the rabbit really cost us only sixpence.'

made at home by my sisters, and nice little warm coats in winter. We had long plaits, but our hair was loose on Sundays, with a bow.

'During 1920 terrible diphtheria swept through the village; we all had it and the school was closed. Afterwards the whole school was disinfected, and that smell was in every pen, pencil and book for years. Darling Mother nursed we, her three young children, alone for fifteen weeks; and then, on a lovely day in February, a dear young cousin called Rosy brought the first snowdrops. She put them on a broom and lifted them up and I opened the bedroom window and took them in. It was so wonderful to smell those flowers and the fresh air after being indoors for so long. I can smell them now.

'One of my hobbies was recording the weather and I used to measure the winter solstice with the almshouse roof, in the yard nearby. We had some real winters then. We always had a slide in the road, and one lady used to come out to peel her potatoes on the ice to make it melt. We also had our whipping tops – known as "window breakers" – and hoops, and we used to go all the way to Walton. The "snob" (Collins the cobbler) used to put the peg in the top for us, and

when we sang "Uncle Tom Cobley and All" we used to end up with "Snob and all".

'In the autumn we used to go acorning for Mr Gurney's pigs, and if there was a gale the children always went "sticking" for fuel. In those days I don't think anyone complained when children were missing from classes because the schools were so crowded. I still can't pass a bit of rotten wood.'

Despite the hardships, there were several annual treats to look forward to. For the Jacksons, the highlight of the summer holiday was a trip to Bedford, 'a lovely little town then', where two of Margaret's sisters were in service. 'We'd go into Woolworth's there and nothing was above sixpence. I still use the little birthday book I bought then.'

But for some thirty children of all ages the highlight of the whole year was the choir treat and Margaret remembers it well.

'Margate was the favourite destination. The train left Woburn Sands station at 5.30 am, so we always used to wake everybody up with all the noise we made, and we would reach the coast at about 9.30. The first thing we did was hire a

Musical chairs at Wavendon Church Sunday School New Year Party, with the Reverend C L Elliott on the fiddle

CHRISTMAS MEMORIES

'The choir always went round carol singing on Christmas Eve: first we went up to the Rectory, then Tower House, and ended up at Wavendon House about 10pm, where there'd be a lovely supper laid on for us.

'The bellringers always started getting ready for Christmas on 5 November. At first they practised only once a week, but it ended up being daily. Nowadays they're not allowed to ring on Christmas Eve for fear of disturbing people, but us children used to love lying in bed listening to them: it was part of Christmas.

'We never had much in the way of Christmas presents. At first we just had a sugar mouse, an apple and orange, and perhaps a few pennies, all in the toe of a stocking. But later there might be a book by Angela Brazil or a jack-in-the-box, and if we were very lucky a flaxen-haired doll peeped out the top.

'But getting ready for Christmas was half the fun, with all that fruit to be washed and puddings and cakes to be made. There were three shops in Wavendon then and one was run by a dear old spinster, Miss Stradling. People used to say: 'Have you seen her window? She's decked it out for Christmas.' And what a lovely job she made of it. In the middle was an old oil lamp and we children used to gaze in at all the wonders carefully placed around it, looking at what we hoped to get for Christmas: dolls, toy pianos, skipping ropes, tops, dulcimers and nets of sweets. And when Miss Stradling put the light out in the darkness of the evening it was a sign for us all to go home. We used to buy our wooden hoops there, too. There was everything in that shop – even a chair to sit down on if you were tired.

deckchair, and I always ended up sunburnt. Then there was a lovely lunch and a fish-and-chip tea, and we always bought presents for those left at home. We generally returned about midnight. Dear old Reverend Phillpotts paid for it all – he even gave us our spending money. That went on right up to 1939.

'Then there was Percer's shop, where they had a great many ramshackle old bikes – you could hire one for a halfpenny for half-an-hour to learn to ride. If we were lucky we had a penny pocket money on a Saturday, and what you could buy for a penny then was nobody's business.

'The other big treat was the Sunday school party, usually on about 1 January in the school. We only had plain bread and butter, plain rice cake and fruit cake, but it was lovely because we sat down with the lady from Wavendon House, with her fine china and silver teapot. Wavendon House was the squire's house and Mrs Bond who lived there was like the Queen Mother to us.

'After the meal the seats were rearranged, out came the harmonium and we sang carols while we waited for the parents to come for the marionettes show; everybody was invited and it used to be packed out. If we had anything in the village today hardly anybody would turn up, but in the old days everybody went to everything.

'When the puppets were over we had the presentation and prizes for the marks we had gained in Sunday school. And we always finished with the national anthem, and three cheers for the rector. And when we went outside all the children were given an orange and a bun. We'd sing the national anthem on any occasion then, and on Empire Day we'd salute the flag, too.'

Like so many clever children of her generation, Margaret was denied the opportunity to go on to higher education because her family just could not afford to keep her. As a result, she left school at the customary age of fourteen 'in floods of tears'. But there was no full-time job for her to go to at first, and she was sixteen before she went to work as a housemaid for widow Waudby at The Old Rectory. Margaret describes those early days in service:

'I was a general help to everybody, but especially the cook and senior maid. There was also a chauffeur, a gardener and a garden boy. Mrs Waudby was a marvellous artist who had exhibited at the Royal Academy, and she had over seventy paintings in the drawing room alone. There were others all over the house and they took us ages to dust.

Empire Day dancers at Wavendon endowed school, 24 May 1923. Margaret is in the middle row, sixth from the left

'My wages were about ten shillings a week, and I slept right at the top of the house. In 1939–40 it was so cold the water tanks were frozen solid, and at night, Edith the maid and I would be covered in ice where we'd breathed. So we had to go down and sleep in the guest chambers. In 1940 three lovely young men from the RAF were billeted with us, but they didn't mind the cold so much.

'The main reason why housework was much harder then was that there was no electricity, and no such thing as vacuum cleaners; it was all lamps and candles, dustpans and brushes. But we still managed to have fun.

'Edith always called Mrs Waudby at 7.30am and took her hot milk. She also took up hot water for washing, in lovely brass cans which we had to clean every day along with the silver candlesticks. Mrs Waudby took breakfast in her room at 9am and she'd be down by 10am, going straight into the Oak Room in winter. Her great creed was: "You never got a cold through being cold" and as a result there were only ever four

fires lit in that great house, including the kitchen range. But at least the house was lovely and cool in summer.

'Poor old Mr Paxton the coachman/chauffeur (a descendant of Sir Joseph Paxton) used to be perished when he got down off the carriage – but Mrs Waudby was always nice and warm inside with a lovely sable rug. Even so, he hated it when he was given a car. There was also a brougham and a two-seated, two-wheeled dog cart. Mr Paxton had special livery for summer and winter as well as Sunday. The brougham was very handy in the war for one of the young RAF men billeted with us: he had a tendency to stay out late with the girls, but Mr Paxton had told him that the house doors would be locked at a certain time, and that was that. So if he was too late to get in, the young man used to sleep in the brougham and come creeping in when he saw Mr Paxton light the fires first thing in the morning.

'As well as general cleaning I made the beds and did mending and sewing. And when the fruit came in ripe I had these great big trugs of gooseberries and other berries to top and tail. But for much of the time it was quite easy work, really, and we didn't reckon to be working all the time; for example I was generally up about 7am but there wasn't much to do in the afternoon when the lady went calling. We had much more work when visitors came, however, and I'd have to look after Mrs Waudby if Edith and Mrs Paxton were out for the day. In the morning I wore a blue check cotton dress and in the afternoon I was smarter, with a black dress and white apron to receive people. We always knew when Mrs Waudby was coming back because one of her dogs – a Kerry Blue terrier – always barked when her carriage was on its way.

'There was this wonderfully scented magnolia tree, and Mrs Waudby would cut one of its flowers and put it in a wicker basket to take to a friend when visiting. I think the tree must have been there since the house was built, in about 1850; but sadly it died in the frost of 1940.

'One of the worst upheavals was spring-cleaning, especially with all those pictures and clutter about, and after the sweep had been in to clear the birds' nests from the bedroom chimneys. It used to take two of us a whole week just to spring-clean the drawing room – we needed a day just to empty it. The carpet had to be taken out onto the lawn where the garden boy beat it; but he couldn't help bringing bits of lawn back in with it. When we did the spring-cleaning Mrs Waudby would go away with Mrs Paxton to a hotel for a week or so.

'The curtains were taken down and changed and cleaned several times a year. In spring and summer they'd be white lace tied with green bows, and the gardener would bring in white arum lilies; when autumn came they were changed to a thick, dark red material and the gardener brought in those lovely chrysanths.

'Mrs Waudby would never take a chair near the fire, and would often sit alone with just one lamp light in that enormous sitting room. Even in the dining room there was just one silver oil lamp in the middle of this huge table,

and I often heard the gentlemen cursing because they couldn't see to carve the game or joint.

'We kept some things in the cellar because that was the coolest place in the house, but sometimes it flooded and had to be pumped out. One day I went down to fetch the cream jug and there was a great big toad in it; I had to tell Mrs Waudby, but she just smiled.

'Mrs Waudby never, ever went to the kitchen; I suppose she just trusted us. The only exception was at Christmas when she came in to see the wonderful staff decorations, as she had none of her own. You should have seen the holly among the gleaming copper pans!

'Mrs Waudby's old wireless had earphones, and all the wires ran under the carpet. There were three sets of earphones and whoever was there of a Sunday was allowed to listen to the service as long as they didn't make a noise; though it was difficult not to when taking the earphones out of the box.'

When the war started, Margaret joined the ARP first aid and went to lectures at Woburn Sands. Mr Paxton joined the Home Guard, which Margaret regarded as 'the biggest joke of all: he

Opposite:
In common with
many other women
Margaret spent
time working in a
factory during the
war. Here a
volunteer is tinning
conductors at a
BET transformer
factory in the
south of England

always said he was glad he joined because the only way he kept warm was through wearing their overcoat. When the water tanks froze we had to let the kitchen range go out and it was perishing.'

It was during the war that Margaret took her 'nicest holidays ever', when her brother-in-law Bill was stationed at Banff, on the Scottish coast. She went there three times on the 'puffing Billy' (steam train), 'which changed its tune when it got to the top of the hill and went down again. It took twenty-four hours to get there and you couldn't move in the carriages for khaki.' That was quite an adventure for Margaret, because before that her annual fortnight's holiday was usually spent not far away, visiting an aunt at sedate Leamington Spa.

Things were 'a bit on the tough side' during the war, when 'thousands of Wrens were stationed in the area', as Margaret recalls:

'We had to eke out most things because of the rationing, but we got by. Most people took on allotments and many shared out their produce. But clothing was very difficult, and you could easily get rid of your allowance in no time at all.

'One of my worst memories is seeing that terrible red glow in the sky when they blitzed London in 1941. And there was that awful night they bombed Coventry, when the houses shook with all the bombers going over. One old lady I knew said: "They've been going over all night. They've shook the firmament and I haven't got a dry thread left in my body." But at least we didn't get any bomb damage at Wavendon.'

After some twelve years at The Old Rectory, Margaret spent about a year working at another local house, where her wages increased three-fold

and the hours were only 8am to 3pm; she found it 'a piece of cake', particularly as it was equipped with more up-to-date appliances. But then she had to go to help with the war effort, and work at a factory on the outskirts of the village, making transistors for the Navy. However, she had liked the new house so much that she still called in there each day on the way to the factory.

When the war ended Margaret went to The Tower to work as housemaid for the Marler family. 'They were very agreeable people, estate agents, and I was happy there for eleven years, until the family moved away. The only hard work I had to do was endlessly washing pairs of breeches because Major Marler and his elder son used to go out hunting with the North Bucks Beagles so much, often two or three times a week.' Like so many others, Margaret regarded the end of the war as a major turning point in the British way of life.

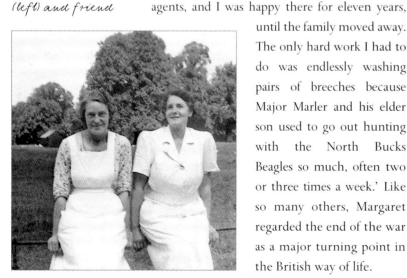

Happy in domestic service – Margaret (left) and friend

'Once it was over, everything we held dear disappeared: the women didn't want to stay at home any more, and that was the beginning of the home life breaking up; and the large staffs went from the big houses.'

Gone were the days when people were content to 'get round the lamplight in winter to play ludo or snakes and ladders': a new spirit of independence was prevalent. People generally became financially better off, they were more mobile, and they wanted to venture further afield; and with so many folk looking at life beyond their native haunts it was not surprising that village life and community spirit gradually deteriorated. Margaret's home patch suffered more than most because it was engulfed by new town development: her observations are tinged with considerable sadness:

'When the Marlers moved away, that lovely house, The Tower, went to Milton Keynes Corporation for their headquarters, and there they planned the destruction of thirteen of our beautiful villages, including Milton Keynes itself. It's criminal that the new town should have taken the name of that delightful little place –

there'd been a wonderful Bible with a chain through it in the village since Cromwell's day. The town should have had a new name. Later The Tower went to an American firm. You have no idea the lovely buildings that have gone, that used to be round that old house.

'In Wavendon there used to be four pubs: The Red House, The Plough, The Wheatsheaf and also The Leathern Bottle, just over the road where the Ancient Order of Oddfellows used to have a Whit Monday feast in the room attached. The carthorses used to be shod at The Red House, and it was wonderful watching the children help blow the bellows and seeing the sparks fly. We used to love singing that song: "Busy blacksmith, what are you doing at your smithy all day long . . ." I expect you know it – Handel wrote the tune. Now two of them are private houses. All the old chaps used to have their own special places and seats in the pubs. There was much more drunkenness then – it was quite usual to see men staggering about the village, but people used to respect the policeman, and there was never much trouble.

'But there are not the characters around now, people like Charlie the postman, who wouldn't finish till gone three on Christmas afternoon and often called whether he had letters or not. He used to see you in the window and shout up things like "You've got a postcard, but you won't like it!" Nothing was sacred then.

'Another great character was the old verger, who held office for many years. She tolled the bell and tended the lamps, as there was no electricity in the church; if one started to burn low she'd stand on a pew, pull the lamp down and fill it. She often left an oily mess and smell on the pews, so you had to watch where you sat. Also, if anyone misbehaved in church she would tell them to leave. The rector called her "Boss". He never charged to marry people in church, but would say: "Give Boss half a crown".

'There used to be a great many vagrants, mostly begging for hot water for a cup of tea. One old couple used to come round regularly and Mum gave them slices of bread and dripping. How they survived just sleeping in the hedgerows I'll never know, especially as we used to have such cold winters. The worst I can remember was 1947, when the snow was ever so deep. You couldn't cross the fields, though the scenery was magnificent. I'd love to see another one like that: it would do everyone good.

'Tommy Dodd used to sweep the roads on a Saturday and everything was always tidy. Then there was one man from Northampton who used to open his van and there were all these shoes hanging up in rows – talk about a sight!

The men used to buy all their heavy boots off him. And right up to the second war a tallyman came round from Stewkley on his bike and sold Mother articles such as tea towels. Another man went round with a van and sold buckets and things. It was always easier to buy at the door when you didn't have a car or the time to spare.

'I never drove, but I wished I did. When I left The Tower I went back to the factory where I worked in the war, but things were very different then and you were in good company. It was convenient for me as Mother died in 1959 and I was on my own; also our cottage was deteriorating in condition so I went into a bungalow. Later I

During the 1930s a great range of goods were sold door-to-door, either from horse-drawn carts, or by motorised transport

The British Legion marching through Wavendon; at one time it was strongly supported and contributed a great deal to the solidarity of the village

nity spirit. She even still rides a bike, 'but not too far', despite an accident when she was in her thirties in which she broke her hip. She has been closely involved with the church all her life, and after she retired from the factory, aged sixty, she was able to devote even more time to it.

'It's a full-time job, really. I was a member of the parochial church council for many years, and now I'm the verger, cleaner and sacristan, which means I look after the altar and sacred vessels. St Mary's Church dates back to the twelfth century, and we're very proud of the Grinling Gibbons pulpit, which is said to have been rescued from the Great Fire of London. We only have the one service now: Holy Communion on Sunday. It's just a matter of form, really – I don't like these new services – and then only thirty or forty people come. Anyone can take a service here now. In the old days we had 8am Communion, 11am Matins and 6pm Evensong.

'They never sing those lovely hymns now – the only chance you get to hear them is on TV. I was in the choir for thirty-five years, from 1925 until 1960, and I've nearly forgotten how to sing the Te Deum. I sang the solos when I was young, and we used to sing for funerals, too.

'There was a time when you wouldn't get a seat at harvest festival evensong if you weren't there by 5pm. Now it's all different, but I've always stuck to the rule that Sunday should be separate. When we were young even shoes had to be cleaned on Saturday.

'We also used to have a great many lovely events outside the church; for example there was terrific fun with the village concerts and socials. What with "Wings Week" and "Soldiers' Week" to raise money for the troops, whist drives, parades and so on, there was something happening almost every night. And the children's nativity plays were beautiful, too. The British Legion was strong here once, but most of the people who ran it have become too old or have died.'

However, not all has been doom and gloom in Wavendon since the war, and the spark of community hope long nurtured by Margaret

moved into this modern block, owned by Milton Keynes – and so I've come back onto my former stamping ground because this is where our house used to be. I still love the place and have some good friends – but life can be lonely in a flat, even with people so close; it's not so social. There's something very special about living in a cottage; on a nice day you can open the door and sit and watch the world go by. But you can't do that up all these steps. And you do miss the garden. In the old days you thought nothing of someone coming round with a bushel of peas.'

Although Margaret has many regrets regarding the demise of traditional village life, she has never been one to sit idly by and be overwhelmed by so-called progress. On the contrary, she remains very active in promoting commu-

Jackson has occasionally been coaxed into flame by celebrities who have adopted the village. John Betjeman came to read poems, famous actors and actresses visited, and The Old Rectory has become one of the homes of the internationally acclaimed musician and composer Johnny Dankworth and his celebrated jazz-singing wife, Cleo Laine. In the very house where Margaret once heard nothing livelier than the 'awful crackle' of those first wireless sets, the air became vibrant with innovation and creativity. The Dankworths turned the old stables into a theatre, and when this was extended Princess Margaret and the actress Joyce Grenfell were among the guests at the opening. For that very special occasion Margaret was invited to help out, and was delighted to wear her old maid's frock and apron again, 'just for a bit of fun'. But she did find it strange to wait at table in a dining room which she had known as a kitchen for so long, and she did have to laugh when Princess Margaret's detective asked if she was local.

When Miss Margaret Jackson talks to local schoolchildren about how village life used to be, she also enthuses about the occasion that Johnny wrote the mass and Cleo sang in church. She is proud to be such an important link between very different generations.

Overleaf: Children bringing produce to the Harvest Festival service

The fiercely competitive world of the village whist drive!

Man of Iron

George Ranger : Surrey

MAN OF IRON

It seems odd that a man who has spent over fifty years shoeing horses has never ridden one, but it is no more surprising than the fact that for much of that time he has successfully operated from his home on a town council estate. Of course, the days have long gone when the clip-clopping of horses was an everyday sound about our streets, so George James Alfred Ranger became one of those great survivors who ply their trade from the boot of a car. And on his wide journeying afield, from Godalming in Surrey, he has acquired a knowledge of animals that is second to none.

Opposite:
A travelling
blacksmith in the
early 1950s

Born at Newhaven on 30 November 1924, George was the son of a chauffeur-gardener and the grandson of a farm labourer. The family moved to Godalming in 1927, when the old Surrey town was a great centre of rusticity far removed from the commuter stop fast-train travellers know today. Nonetheless, the surrounding countryside remains sufficiently unspoilt to provide George with enough work for the reminder of his days, and shoeing horses is what he plans to do until the day he drops.

In the late 1940s
George had to
endure great heat
in the old-
fashioned forge

With 'big brother' Guildford nearby, even in the 1920s communications were relatively good in the area, so when the Ranger family went walking, as they often did then, it was easy to get a bus back. They never kept horses – 'just a dog and a few chickens.'

While still at Busbridge School, George and his brother collected sacks full of leaves and sold them to keen gardeners for a penny a barrow. But at that time he had no special aspirations and certainly never imagined that he would become a farrier.

'In those days jobs was few and far between so it was a question of get what you could.' So, like so many of his contemporaries, when he left school at 14 George took a position as a garden boy. 'There were three of us in Sir Fred and Lady Radcliffe's garden, and for working from 7am till 5pm Monday to Friday, but 12 on Saturday, I had five shillings a week. Mother took half.

'For the next two years I was expected to do everything – especially weeding and hoeing. One of the head gardener's favourite tricks was to get me weeding the crazy paving on a cold February morning; then my fingers were nearly dropping off.'

At the age of 16, George learned about a job at a local forge through his brother. When George told Sir Fred that he was leaving his employment, his boss offered to increase his wages to ten

shillings a week. However, he wanted a job with more of a future, so joined 66-year-old Frank Brown at the Shackstead Lane forge, even though his starting wage was only five shillings a week.

George did not undertake a formal apprenticeship with indentures, but in Frank Brown he had an excellent teacher, the old master having practised at the forge since 1915, following an apprenticeship with local firm James Luck. Brown truly loved his work and had been shoeing a horse only a few days before he died at the age of 82.

Fortunately for George, he was not called up when war broke out.

Besides the fact that he was deaf in one ear, farriers were in demand for shoeing the Army mules. In fact, his was a relatively peaceful war; the closest he came to seeing action was when he watched a German bomber crew – 'I could see their faces' – who flew low over Godalming to drop their load. 'But only a few windows were broken.'

It was during the war, on a visit to his sister at Newhaven, that George met and married Lily.

When George started at the forge in 1941, the tractor revolution was not underway, so there were many farm horses to shoe. But horses were also used for road transport – fourteen for Stovold's Dairy, three for the Co-op and one for the bakery. 'I particularly liked the baker bringing his old horse up because he used to bring me fresh cream buns and lardy cakes so greasy you haven't been able to get the likes of 'em for years.' The dairy ponies were the first horses George ever handled.

Most villages had a farrier then, including nearby Milford, Compton, Farncombe and Eashing. Godalming still had two farriers, but the town had five up until the early 1920s.

But George's work was never entirely devoted to horses. At the old forge they did general blacksmithing, including ornamental ironwork such as gates. George was a very good wheelwright and they made entire wheels, not just the metal 'tyres'. Another popular line was wheelbarrows, which were completely hand-made from wood and iron for just seventy shillings.

The old brick forge had been converted from two cottages. One half contained the main forge and workbench and the bottom half was devoted to shoeing.

'By golly, it was hot in there, especially when we had a big wood fire going for the tyres. Those cartwheel tyres needed a huge blaze. It was very heavy work and needed several of us working quickly together. Smaller tyres were made whole and knocked firmly onto the wood before cooling and shrinking, when they were nailed into place.

'But the bigger tyres had to be made in sections and were nailed separately to the wheel. The biggest we ever made were ten feet high and went on a timber cart at Busbridge Hall. It was used for hauling great trunks out of the forest. The wheel stocks were elm, and the spokes and felloes (circular bits) ash. We last made wheels in the 1950s.

'In the very dry weather tyres sometimes had to be taken off and a piece of metal taken out

Fitting metal 'tyres' to cartwheels in 1950. After the hot tyre is knocked into place, it is cooled quickly and shrinks, to secure a tight fit. George Ranger is pictured centre wearing his beloved beret

because they had shrunk and become loose. To avoid this some old boys used to wrap wet sacks around the wheels when they were not in use.'

In those early days, when local communities had to be more independent and every hard-earned penny had to be accounted for, farriers such as George were called upon to be horse doctors. For example, if a septic spot was encountered while shoeing a horse it made sense to cut it out there and then. In the vast majority of cases this was straightforward, the customer was happy because more often than not he was not charged anything for the extra service, and George gained a little goodwill for his business. But inevitably, with the development of animal welfare and jealous guarding of veterinary practice, such work is now a thing of the past. Since the Farriers

Registration Act 1975–7 you even have to be a registered shoeing smith to shoe your own horse.

Putting the shoes on is only part of the work. Trimming the feet, which like fingernails grow continuously, is necessary too, for goats, cows and bulls as well as horses. 'And trimming an ol' bull is no joke either, as their owners know. I always remember General Molyneux at Loseley Farm getting me out there under false pretences to do a horse, but I coped with his bull all right. These great big animals are a bit different from the mini donkeys at Crystal Palace and Battersea Park children's zoos, where I have been going for some years.'

When it was still common to see work horses on the road, many animals were brought to the forge for attention, but even in the early 1940s

George had to go out to some on the farms. 'And this was no mean feat on a push-bike, laden down with two sets of cart horse shoes weighing sixteen pounds, not to mention all my tools, including hammer, pincers, rasp, tongs and buffer. This was all cold shoeing, of course, the animals having already been seen and their shoes shaped pretty accurately back at the forge.' So it was a marvellous day when George first acquired a car.

In 1941 a set of shoes cost about 7/6d, but nowadays George charges from £30, his prices being very competitive – 'one cowboy charges £69 for a simple set.' Overcharging is even less excusable today when the bulk of shoes come ready made, supplied by specialist factories. All the farrier has to do is order the closest size, heat the shoe up and knock into precise shape. Special shoes are usually made in consultation with a vet.

'Even bars of shoe iron come ready-grooved now, whereas we used to start with 12–16feet lengths of straight iron and had to put the groove in ourselves. Racers, of course, generally have aluminium plates. As the old trainers used to say, "an ounce on the foot is worth a pound on the back."

'On average, a horse wants shoeing every six weeks, even if the shoes aren't worn, because the feet need trimming. But there are individuals among horses just as there are among humans, some nails growing quicker than others and some shoes wearing quicker. One of Stovold's old dairy horses needed new shoes every four days, but then the trouble was there were so many nail holes it was a job to find space for new ones. And it is important that the nails only go up the wall of the hoof, as the centre part over the sensitive area is surprisingly thin.

'At the other extreme, one pony I used to do only needed shoes every two years. And when the feet are trimmed it is perfectly all right to put the same shoes back on if they are not worn.'

Although farriery suffered a major setback with the widespread use of tractors after the war, the great upsurge of interest in leisure riding more than compensated. Previously, it was

generally only the wealthy who rode for pleasure, but now, with an ever-widening network of pony clubs and riding stables, there is a good future for farriery, as long as adequate training is provided. Furthermore, George has had steady work with polo and show ponies in summer and hunters in winter.

But even with the advent of mechanisation, a surprisingly large number of work horses lingered on. Some villagers still used a horse and cart to empty toilet buckets for many years after the war, and a few very traditional farmers clung to their plough horses up the early 1970s. For example, 'old Mr Secret kept his on because he believed that the tractors hardened the soil too much deep down'.

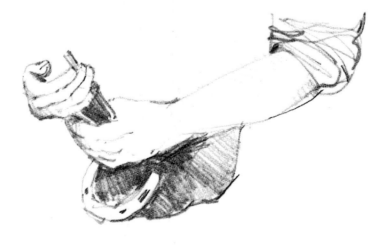

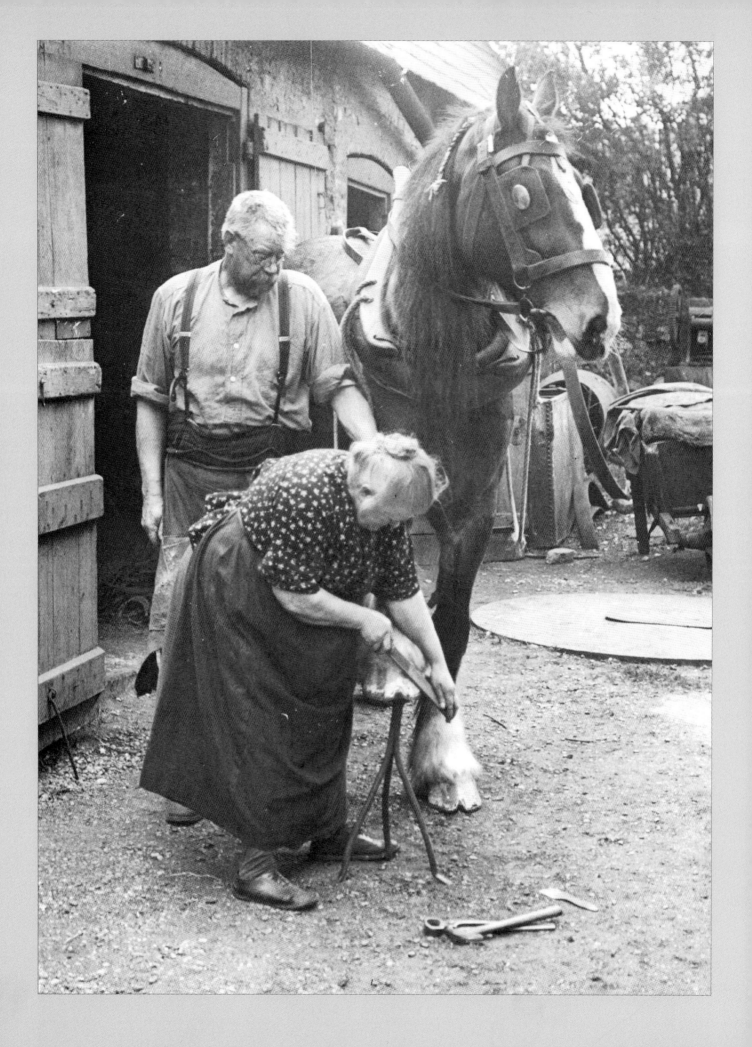

There was a wonderful partnership between the ploughman and his horses; he knew that to get the best from them they had to be treated with kindness and understanding. Consequently, they would be worked in teams and they all had a couple of months off each year, on a rota. It was George's job to take their shoes off before they were turned out in the fields.

George did not start with an innate love of horses, but he acquired great respect for them. And, as Lily Ranger emphasises, 'he's got an awful lot of patience'. He is convinced that they have a fair degree of intelligence, too. 'One little Shetland I used to shoe would often pull my braces as far as he could and then let them go with an almighty thwack just for the fun of it.' And there is no denying the fun they have given George: 'I used to wear a beret which became so nibbled it looked like a colander'.

However, George has had his fair share of accidents, too, having been burnt, bitten and kicked on many occasions. His worst burn happened when he slipped and the welding torch seared the back of his hand. The scar on his upper arm is a reminder of the day when he was bitten by a mare with a foal, whose feet he was trimming while it was held by its lady owner.

Some ten years ago he was knocked unconscious by a kick on the side of his head. 'I have no idea what happened, but when I woke up there was a lady standing over me with a wet towel and a glass of whisky. She took me to the house, where I had two more Scotches before driving home. Apart from a headache, all I suffered was a black eye.'

According to George, the way to avoid being kicked is to work 'as close to the animals as possible'. But there are bound to be times when the unexpected happens, for example when 'one old shire had both feet over my shoulders – a very lucky escape for me'. Then there was the time when he was tapping a shoe-nail in, the horse flinched and the nail went into his arm.

George had always used coal for his forge – 'you can get a much greater heat than with gas. Also, gas does not produce a big enough hot area for larger items such as the S-shaped wall retainers.'

Opposite: When this photograph was taken in 1938, 70-year-old Mrs Elizabeth Arnold, was thought to be England's only woman blacksmith. She is seen at the forge in Walmer, Kent

The boot of George's car is just big enough to take his mobile forge, anvil, block and tools, but only if they are packed in precise order, which he does without thinking, having done it a thousand times before. But there was at least one occasion when his generally meticulous routine ailed. After a shoeing, the powdery coal must be extinguished with water so that the forge can be put back into the car. But one day George did not put it out properly and as he motored along black smoke suddenly started to billow from the boot. Fortunately, the customer he had just left was one of many who constantly supply him with flasks of coffee and on this occasion the beverage was sufficient to douse the unwanted fire.

But it is not just coffee that George has been given by grateful customers, some of whom he has been visiting almost since the day he started. In 1991 friends and clients put on a surprise party for him in recognition of his fifty years in the business. And what a variety of clients he has had, ranging from a 95-year-old with two active hunters to a little girl who said: 'Why aren't you miserable like all the other blacksmiths?', from nobility and high-ranking officers with strings of polo ponies to celebrities such as Tubby Turner of television's Emmerdale Farm.

Yet George would never pretend that his clientele is one big happy family. Indeed, there have been many thoughtless or selfish people in his life, especially those who ring up late in the evening and expect a pony to be shod for a show the next morning. In fact, George often attends shows as duty farrier, ready to replace shoes which, for example, have been kicked off in horseboxes on the way to the events.

George has certainly not made a fortune from farriery and neither has it left him fighting fit. On the contrary, he now walks with a

The travelling blacksmith – a rather grander affair than George's pushbike! This mobile smithy is attached to the side-car of a motorcycle

*Opposite:
A Champion
ploughman with
his winning team.
Part of George's job
was to remove the
shoes of plough horses
before they were
turned out into the
fields for a rest*

*Below: A photograph
of George with his
mobile forge taken
in 1990*

pronounced stoop after all those back-breaking years. 'But I'm lucky because I'm not very tall; a lot of taller ones end up with serious back trouble.' He also emphasises that great strength is not a prerequisite for farriery: 'It's your way with animals that counts.'

Apart from working closely with animals, George has found wrought-iron work most rewarding, and now many of his pieces adorn the houses of friends and relatives, including that of his daughter. She, too, has a keen interest in horses, and this in turn has rubbed off on George's grandson whom he would like to see follow him at the forge. But he will have a long wait because George insists that 'I won't give up horses until they give me up.'

Lucky Jim

John Penfold : Gloucestershire

LUCKY JIM

A blue haze of flax fills the fields, magically disappearing for part of the day and then returning to surprise you with its wash of colour. Scarlet poppy swathes sweep through the cornfields here and there, and the uncut road verges are rampant with other wildflowers in soft mauves and bright yellows. The landscape is one of gentle hills and broad vales, dotted with mellow golden stone villages and farms. This is the English jewel: summer in the Cotswolds.

Opposite:
The town square of Stow-on-the-Wold. The photograph, made in 1957, was taken from the church tower

It is dawn, between four and five in the morning. Foxes slide across the lanes ignoring lone humans at an hour that belongs to the wildlife. Flocks of pigeons and a few crows peck in the grit of the road, taking advantage of this empty time before the vehicles claim it as their own. Down in the vales the cows are calling each other up for milking, in voices that carry far in the stillness of the morning. The sun rises slowly, tingeing the horizon clouds with colour, and the views towards sunrise are wide and full of promise of the new day.

Around the town of Stow-on-the-Wold, the lanes spread out towards local hamlets and become increasingly narrow and apparently aimless. It is an area that is notably short of signposts, a place for locals who know where they are and do not need guidance. No doubt many a new country vet has been lost in these lanes, searching for unnamed farms hidden in the folds of the hills.

Fortunately the route has been carefully described. The approach to Hunters Spinney is by a long drive, its entrance marked by a luxuriant display of flowering plants. The extensive gardens are immaculately kept and beautifully stocked, drawing the eye to a wholly rural view across the fields to a distant, tiny stone village. The house is spacious and pleasant, with the feel of a beamed barn in the book-lined living-room with its big, comfortable chairs.

John Penfold opens the door to greet me. He is a faintly Celtic man with thick, short black eyebrows, a stiff limp, and a vague air of suppressed anger. He has reason to be angry. His career as a veterinary surgeon was cut short far too early when in November 1991 his car was smashed into by a continental bus whose driver had forgotten he was on the English side of the Channel, and was driving on the wrong side of the road. As a result, John ended up with a foot injury so bad that the doctors told him he would never walk on that foot again. By determination and courage and with a great deal of support from family and friends, he proved them wrong, after a year in plaster, but he has not been agile enough since the accident to practise again, and is fighting for adequate compensation for the loss of his livelihood and way of life.

He has recently trained to work as a veterinary arbitrator, and continues his involvement with several veterinary societies devoted to unusual species such as deer and llamas. He is also in demand as a speaker for local organisations such as the WI, and has joined a Speakers Club. He seems to have a natural flair for telling good stories.

John was born in 1942 in Hertfordshire, although his father, a cabinet-maker, was originally a Sussex man. When the boy was about thirteen or fourteen, his father introduced him to a long-standing family friend, Bill Widdicombe, a dairy farmer with a large herd of Ayrshires at

Bill Widdicombe

Ditchling, beneath and on the Sussex downs. 'He wants to be a vet,' father told Widdicombe. 'Would you confirm or refute his feeling and take it from there?' And so John began to spend his holidays on the farm, taking the train to Sussex on the day school broke up.

'Widdicombe taught me really how to conduct myself. He didn't pay me, but I was fed and educated and entertained. If he was showing, I went to the show; I was introduced to young farmers, I entered the Ayrshire Club judging competitions – oh, he taught me a tremendous amount. He taught me not only what I already knew, which was that I wanted to be a vet, but also – much more valuable to me – he taught me things from a farmer's angle. I could see life in general and its problems from a farmer's angle as well as from a vet's.'

The farm was quite large: they were milking two hundred Ayrshires and had a pedigree Wessex Saddleback herd of pigs as well. Much of the land was up on Ditchling Beacon, most of it down to barley. It had originally been scrubland,

but it had been fenced and a few Wessex sows at a time were put on the Beacon to farrow and run with their litters. The pigs soon cleaned up the land, fetching out the bracken and gradually working their way through the gorse until the land could be cultivated for barley. 'We must have had three to four hundred acres on the Beacon, mostly down to barley by then, and we would bring the harvested corn all the way down the hill to Court Gardens Farm, in the days when tractors had no brakes.

'My job in those days was to bucket-feed the calves at five in the morning, and to give the young stock their concentrates and forage in the winters. After breakfast it was mucking out the pigs. I didn't do a lot of milking to start with as I wasn't strong enough. They had a very modern abreast parlour with twelve standings and it took three hours to milk the herd. It didn't change much in my time there: when I left, there were still two chaps milking, and all the milk went into churns which had to be individually cooled with rotating inserts and then

Mrs Widdicombe with an Ayrshire calf

Jim would often accompany Bill Widdicombe to agricultural shows where he too became involved in judging his favourite Ayrshires. This fine example, Copt Hall Ideal Lady, was selected as champion dairy cow at the Bedford Agricultural Show in 1954

transferred to the loading platform by the dairy for collection by lorry.

'In the harvest field my job in the first few years was to ride the home-made sledge. This thing comprised two heavy great sheets of corrugated iron, with a bar joining the two across the front, leaving a two-inch gap down the middle. I would stand on the front, building piles of bales on the two sheets: the first two bales across the sledge, the next two at right angles and so on to a stack four or five high. When I had enough bales in the pile, I would grab a crowbar and stick it between the two iron sheets, stabbing it into the ground to stop the bales moving, and jump off while the sledge carried on ahead. Then I had to yank out the bar and run after the thing to jump again while it was still moving and catch the next lot of bales as they left the baler. It was very stony up on the Beacon, great big flints that frequently tipped the sledge over. And of course the tractor driver sometimes had a bit of fun with me by accelerating – you can imagine…'

John loved his working holidays on the farm but realised there was no hope of becoming a farmer himself: that would need capital. But he was more than content to follow his original dream of becoming a veterinary surgeon and he entered college in London, qualifying in 1965. In the meantime, like all veterinary students, he saw practice in different parts of the country during his three final years; he also organised himself a six-week summer job at a mental hospital as a relief ambulance driver. The patients at that time were mainly war victims, especially those suffering from shell-shock, and he rapidly learned a great deal about human psychology.

'Those sort of institutions were fairly self-sufficient: they had a farm, greenhouses and so on, and a builder's yard for maintenance of the houses, and they used the inmates as labour – it was also occupational therapy for them.'

During his second or third year at London he attended his grandmother's funeral in Chepstow, Monmouthshire, and chatted to a local vet, Ken Morgan, who suggested that he should come and see practice with him. 'Ken was a marvellous man; I saw practice with him for about three years. He had his own herd of cows

and I would milk them on the herdsman's day off, and I would dehorn the calves for him. He had qualified just before the war and ran a practice single-handed in Southampton in the days when the place was full of draught horses working for the breweries and the docks. There was a theory that the beer was essential for troops' morale and so Ken was excluded from military service in order to keep the horses fit. There weren't so many lorries about at that stage – they'd all been taken abroad for the war – and so people pulled old carts out of sheds and got the horses working again.

'Ken was slightly built and his hair was already turning grey in my days with him. He wore horn-rimmed glasses and had a trim moustache that he would absent-mindedly preen with finger and thumb when he was thinking. He was a stickler for personal hygiene and was always tidily dressed: he wore a thornproof jacket with a red-and-white spotted handkerchief sticking out of its pocket. And he had this very cultured voice if he was talking to the aristocracy or to old ladies, but he could cuss and swear with the best of them when necessary. He drove a Land-Rover and always had a wire-haired fox terrier on the seat beside him. Fantastic man. He was a strong supporter of the Rotary, and he was also official veterinary surgeon at Chepstow races.

'Morgan had an Irish assistant, Chris Jolley, as broad Irish as they come, and a larger-than-life character with an enormous chest and thin little legs, a mouthful of teeth smiling from a brightly shaven face, and smiling eyes under a very large double forehead. He greeted everybody with "Hey, be Jesus, good to see you. Let's have a jar!" – except little old ladies: to these he would offer "tea", and they all loved him.'

Like Morgan, Chris would be impeccably dressed, and his brown brogues always shone brilliantly. He rarely got himself into messy situations in his work, but if he did, he would go straight home for a shower and a change of clothes. He was usually careful to ensure that the messier jobs were handled by John, but John so enjoyed his company that he didn't mind it all. 'Chris taught me more about how to handle people than anyone else could ever have done. He taught me how to talk to people and to make them feel at ease, how to understand their problems and convey that understanding to them.' And they shared some interesting experiences, too.

'One very hot summer's day we had to do a TT test for Jack Williams at Treleck Grange. Jack was blind, but he farmed a dairy herd with the help of his two sons – who took every advantage of his blindness (much to Chris's disgust). Anyway, come lunchtime and we were nowhere near finished with the job. Jack invited us in for bread and cheese and pickled onions, all washed down with pint glasses of an amber liquid; this went down well, and we happily consumed a second pint. Then we rose from the table to continue our work – but Jack was the only one whose legs did what they were supposed to do. We had to abandon the test until the following day, during which Jack showed us the source of the amber liquid. He had a cider press in the yard, covered in dead flies and a dead rat and…well!'

From college John went to Hugh Frost's practice in Lincolnshire for a year. Then John and his wife Kathy, a midwife, moved to Cranleigh in Surrey for a couple of years, where a caretaker and his wife lived over the surgery. 'He was as thin as a knife, she like two plump saltshakers one on top of the other.' John remembers being called out to Cranleigh School to attend to a swan that had flown into some

wires and broken its wing. He brought it back to the surgery and the caretaker's wife took one look at it. 'Humph,' she said, 'I know what to do with that!' She went into the yard, found a broomstick, put it across the swan's outstretched neck on the ground, stood her substantial weight on either end of the stick and pulled. It was a quick, clean death for a bird beyond saving. 'And it seemed a pity to waste it, so she plucked it and roasted it. Very dark meat, but very good.'

One day the fire brigade called the surgery, requesting veterinary assistance for a pony in a bog. There was a field with a huge old shell-hole in it from the war, where the farmer had habitually dumped his slurry until the pit was full; he had then left it to green over and form a little glade, solid at the edges. A young girl on a pony had been unaware of the hazard and had ridden across it. The pony began to sink, the girl managed to scramble off and escape but the pony was floundering deeper and deeper into the treacherous muck. With the help of the fire brigade, John laid a tarpaulin over the surface and put a ladder over it, then crawled flat on his belly to distribute his weight, just as if he were crossing

Overleaf:
A farm labourer squelches his way through thick mud and melting snow as he carries hay to cattle on a farm near Tewkesbury, Gloucestershire. Taken in 1956, the photograph shows the fields flooded by the River Avon

Workers in the exquisitely named Happyland, near Ashton Keynes, Wiltshire using a primitive iron cider hand press with horsehair mats to filter the juice

thin ice. His task was to give the animal a tran-quilliser to calm its floundering so that the fire-men could winch it out.

John and Kathy were happy living in Cranleigh, but the practice itself was somewhat old-fashioned and unwilling to change. So they began to look for more of a challenge elsewhere, and finally came to the Cotswolds to join a prac-tice in Stow-on-the-Wold with Peter Harrison, Alec 'Robbie' Roberts and David Stewart. In 1970, after twelve months with the practice, John became a partner. When Harrison died two years later at the early age of fifty-two, John found himself in charge of the practice's financial administration – a challenge he readily accepted, though it entailed a great deal of work.

One of his many clients has been Joe Henson, joint proprietor of the Cotswold Farm Park, one of the earliest and most famous centres for rare breeds of farm livestock in England.

'I first met Joe on a cold morning in November; his farm is an exposed one, and it was wet and windy up there. He had a lot of calves in buildings round a yard beside the house and they were scouring like fury – it sounded like sal monella. When I arrived the whole place was in turmoil but someone showed me where the calves were and I did my assessment, took swabs and decided what needed to be done; then I was ushered into the kitchen to meet Joe. There were folks in top hats and tails and women in hats everywhere: it was his brother's wedding day. Someone came up and said, "I'm Joe." I observed that it was evidently not the best moment to talk about scouring calves, and he agreed, so I came back on the Monday. There are no airs and graces about Joe, no pretensions at all, and he is a great showman.

'I knew nothing about rare breeds then, and at that time he had only a few, in the early days. But he has gradually added more over the years, and every time I went to test the herds there'd be something different to see. I had known that things like Longhorns and Highlands existed,

and I had seen Dexters, but I'd never heard of White Park cattle, for instance, and frankly my attitude was that they were becoming extinct because they were useless, so why bother? But the Longhorns, for example, have begun to prove their worth, so perhaps I was wrong.

'I remember a few Longhorn crosses arriving somewhat by mistake when somebody's fences were not what they might have been: a Longhorn bull on Limousin cows, and they were magnificent. You know, the real beauty of some of those old breeds with a long history is that they were bred by canny Scotsmen and Yorkshiremen because they could convert feed-stuffs that nothing else could use into something useful like good meat.'

John has another story about the Cotswold Farm Park. 'One day I had to caesar his Gloucester, this small young heifer trying to calve, with no hope at all of managing on her own, in a loosebox in the yard. So we did a caesar and it all went perfectly; we got a super live calf, everything was as it should be, and I disappeared on my rounds, feeling well pleased. When I got back to the surgery, Joe had been on the phone: the cow had split her stitches and her guts were hanging out.

'It seems that the lad who had been helping us with the operation had thought the cow would like some fresh air after her ordeal and he'd opened the top half of the stable door. And the heifer had thought, yippee! And tried to jump out. She had landed smack on top of the half-door and everything had burst. Her guts landed on the floor and she had trampled on them…well, we managed to hose it all off and push it all back in and stitch it up again, and she never looked back!'

'There used to be so many problems with birds, especially the use of anaesthetics – more of them died because of inappropriate use of anaes-thetics than they did of the original problem. But vets know a lot more about it now.'

They also know a lot more about unusual species, such as deer and llamas – two favourites of John's. He remembers one particular drama

THE PARROT SKETCH

Every vet has a parrot story, and the slow practice was no exception.' This parrot arrived in the surgery accompanied by a very well spoken, well groomed lady in a very well cut tweed suit; she had an appointment with our senior partner, David Stewart, the Scotsman. He examined the parrot, and it looked like a pregnant duck: it had a huge abdominal tumour. He and the client agreed on investigative surgery to see what should be done about the lump, and so she left the bird with him. He anaesthetised it, plucked the operation area, took out a tumour the size of a golf ball, sewed everything together again and laid it on the floor of its cage, covering the cage with a cloth until it came round properly. He checked it at intervals: gradually it regained consciousness, realised where it was, and eventually climbed on its perch; it seemed stable, so they left it on the perch but still under the cover to keep it calm.

'David carried on with whatever he was doing, asking for it to be checked every ten minutes. Suddenly there was an almighty shout; David raced over and found that when the parrot had woken up fully, it had realised there was something different about its belly and carefully undone it, stitch by stitch – its guts had landed on the floor of the cage and it had shrieked! David, in his broad Scots accent, called the bird every name you could think of, put everything together again and stitched it up once more, but this time giving the bird a little collar to stop it pecking at the stitches.

'Well, it was discharged the following morning; the woman in tweeds came in and went off proudly with the bird. She returned with it a week later for a check-up and for its stitches to be removed, and in reply to David's inquiries assured him that its behaviour was almost normal. 'But there is one thing. It's talking. It has never said anything in all its life before, until this last week. And now it's saying all sorts of things, in a strong Scottish accent…'!'

when a llama jumped over a wall on a hillside and landed in a small tree on the other side, completely wedging itself in the branches and scraping all the skin off its inner thigh. But, as with so many animals, they soon patched it up. Then there was a farmed deer in difficulty with her calving: the youngster's nose and one foreleg had emerged, but then it had stuck. The deer were in paddocks, but these were huge, so it was impossible to corner her. They went to a local zoo and asked for their expert to dart her with a tranquiliser so that they could help the calving. It happened that the man had only ever used his weapon in enclosed areas and it took three goes before he managed to land a dart in his target. But the calving was then successfully assisted.

PATCH UP A PENGUIN

Then there was the penguin. It had dived into its pool when the pool was empty, and had smashed its beak on the concrete base. So the practice resorted to a tube of UHU, glued it together again and gave it a fibreglass cover.

The penguin owner would import penguin eggs and hatch them to increase his stock. He used to feed the hatchlings with a human enema syringe. 'They are always incredibly hungry. One chick was so strong and so hungry that it grabbed the nozzle of the tube in its beak, pulled it off the end of the pump and swallowed it. You could feel this five-inch-long piece of stiff rubber stuck in its gut. But we managed to open it up and remove it and it was fine!'

It may seem strange that a man who has devoted his working life to saving animals' lives has also relished the sport of deer-stalking, but John did indeed enjoy a day out on the Scottish hills – out in glorious scenery, spending hours flat on his stomach peering through binoculars as much as through the sights of his rifle. He has come to know a great deal about the veterinary care of deer, and the art of handling these essentially wild animals without causing undue distress. The typescript of a Veterinary Deer Society publication lies on his table awaiting his editing; his involvement continues, even though he is no longer physically capable of undertaking the rigours of handling large animals.

'Vetting has been a fantastic profession. It has given me so much, and it's far from easy coming to terms with having to cease practice. I have no wish to divorce myself from it all; I have made wonderful friends within the profession, I have so many happy memories, and I still have many contacts within it and within the community through it. It has been excellent to me, very rewarding in every way. Yes, it could be miserable on occasions: you see everything. You have to deal with every kind of person, whether you like them or not (and on the whole, I do like people). If you are rude to those you don't like, you jeopardise your income, so you learn to bite your tongue and swallow your pride. And often at the end of the day you find that your first judgement of them was not a hundred per cent accurate anyway.

'The job is fairly hectic, the stress can be huge and the suicide rate seems to be very high within the profession. The pressures do get to people: the phone is always ringing, one client wants this, another client wants that, your interests and their requirements are often in conflict, there is never enough time. If I hadn't had support – if Kathy hadn't been the sort of wife that she is, I would never have got through some thirty years of it since 1965; I couldn't have coped. There's a lot of behind-the-scenes activity that people don't really appreciate. The administrative side of running a practice today is just bedlam.

'And the job really is an abuse of your own body! It's not like being, say, a milkman, loading the van every morning and then discharging the bottles one by one in a consistent routine. One minute you will be struggling to pick up animals' feet, or heaving a calf out of a cow, doing something incredibly strenuous in one direction that needs a lot of strength; the next you are carrying out a delicate operation on a small animal in the surgery, or breaking the bad news to a client that their pet will have to be put down.

'I wonder if that part of it is something women handle better? The colleges now are half full with girls, and this is a major change. London takes in seventy or seventy-five students in a year, and nowadays forty of those will be women. There were only four girls out of sixty students altogether in my year, and they were all super. One married a vet and became an animal nurse instead – full of personality, she was. Another I remember as being a diminutive girl in glasses who did nothing, said nothing, never joined in any social functions – and she is now top dog in the Blue Cross. Yet another married even before she took her finals; she passed her final exams but was already pregnant by then, and has never practised. The fourth, a very good-looking girl, qualified and immediately went to America, where she married a well-known neurosurgeon; she has never worked in earnest. But she does have a most successful hobby in which her veterinary training happened to help: she makes beautiful bronze sculptures of horses, and the anatomy is perfect!

Just as every vet had a parrot story, so too do they all have a story about women: 'I must tell you about Sister Mater Die at the convent. They had a herd of cows there and a message came to me on a cold winter's night that a cow was in trouble calving; could I help? So I went over, and

JOHN'S FAVOURITE TALE

'I was called out to a remote farm cottage about an injured cat. When I found the place, I knocked at the door and nobody came, so I kept banging – it seemed to be dark inside. Eventually a man came to the door, ingrained with grime and dressed only in filthy Yfronts. He let me in, gruffly. It was a very basic cottage indeed, no carpets, no furniture, no knick-knacks or anything. 'Where's the cat?' I said. 'What cat?' he grumbled. 'Oh, it's in here, in the bedroom.' He ushered me into this dim room with a bed in it – and on top of the bed there was a large mound. It moved: it was a huge woman, as grimy as he was and totally naked. 'Where's the cat?' I asked nervously. She pointed down to the floor and then ignored me, rolling over in a leisurely fashion on to her stomach. All I remember is this mountainous pair of buttocks. I took the cat and departed hastily.'

the place was in darkness, nobody around. I checked various buildings and eventually saw a dim light in one of them. In I went, and there was sister Mater Die, stripped to the waist and with her arm up the cow's backside dealing with the stuck calf. She'd completely forgotten they'd asked me for help and she was simply getting on with the job. She wasn't the least embarrassed – but I was!'

*Opposite:
A hop yard
worker laden with
strings used for
attaching hop
bines to the wires,
April 1937*

INDEX

THE CONTRIBUTORS

LOUISE BRODIE lived abroad for many years before returning to England to bring up her children. After completing an Open University degree she worked for the Museum of London, where one of her responsibilities was to conduct over two hundred interviews with people who worked on the River Thames and in Docklands. She has also worked on a television series on this subject.

EUAN CORRIE was brought up in southern Manchester, and on leaving school worked for a ship's agent, dealing mostly with Soviet cargo ships. He was then skipper of a pair of hotel narrowboats on the canals, before joining the editorial staff of the leading inland waterway magazine *Waterways World* in 1986. Since 1997 he has been Books & Guides Editor for Waterways World Ltd, also contributing a wide variety of articles to *Waterways World*, particularly of a historical and photographic nature. Euan bought his own narrowboat in 1979 and has travelled the English inland waterway system widely.

JENNIFER DAVIES' father was a Herefordshire farmer of the old kind, who used horses until tractors became prevalent. She has worked as a television researcher and associate producer, and has written a series of books concerning the Victorian garden and kitchen. She has also written books on Gypsies and the progress of the flower shop in Britain. She lives near Ledbury and combines writing with looking after poultry, old hayfields, bees and trees.

JOHN HUMPHREYS was born and brought up in a Fenland village where the land was worked by Shire horse power and the people were close to the land. The eldest son of a parson, early exposure to the countryside and its pastimes were to shape his life. He has written the popular 'country Gun' column in *Shooting Times* for many years, and twenty books on fieldsports and country ways, including *Poachers' Tales* for David & Charles. He trains gun dogs, runs a lowlands shoot, chases grouse in Yorkshire and geese in Scotland, and fishes for trout and carp on his own little reserve in Cambridgeshire, Hunter's Fen, which won a Laurent-Perrier conservation award in 1991.

BRIAN P. MARTIN has written numerous books on country life and natural history, including seven in David & Charles 'Tales from the Countryside' series, as well as the award-winning *Sporting Birds of Britain and Ireland*. After many years as a commissioning editor for *Shooting Times* and *Country Magazine*, he has been a full-time author since 1991. He has contributed to many magazines and newspapers, and is well-known for his 'Rusticus' column in both *Shooting Times* and *The Countrymen*. When not writing, he may be found propping up the bar in his local village pub, the Dog & Pheasant, where he has been a regular for over twenty years.

TOM QUINN has worked on everything from *The Times* to *Trout and Salmon* magazine and is a former editor of *The Countryman*. He has written three books for David & Charles in the 'Tales of the Countryside' series and has also written books about sporting art, World War One, antique collecting, and a biography of the artist and writer Denys Watkins Pitchford.

VALERIE PORTER lives in a Sussex cottage next door to a vet. She edits numerous agricultural veterinary and biology books, as well as writing her own books about wildlife, livestock, pets and rural life in general, three of which have been published by David & Charles. She is also the author of the highly successful title, *Yesterday's Countryside*, also published by David & Charles.

JEAN STONE is an historic garden consultant and garden designer who has lectured for horticultural societies, garden schools and the Architectural Association. Once winner of the *Sunday Times* 'Design a Period Garden' competition, her entry a 'Victorian Rustic Garden', was built at the RHS Chelsea Flower Show, where it won a silver medal. This was followed by her book, *The Rustic Garden*. Another of her books, *Voices from the Waterways*, is an invaluable record of an almost vanished way of life as once lived on British Waterways.

PHOTOGRAPHS were supplied by the following:
Pages 1, 4, 7, 46, 52, 56, 60, 67, 68, 83, 84, 95, 96, 99, 113, 114, 115, 116, 125 128, 134, 136138, 144, 146, 149, 150, 156, 160, 162, 165, 170, 175, 176, 183, 188, 190, 197, 202, 204, 210, 225, 226, 229, 239, 242, 244, 247, 257, 258, 271, 275, 276, 278, 281, 286, 288, 291, 292, 295, 297, 299, 300, 307, 312, endpapers: Hulton Archive; 11, 13, 16, 17: The Waterways Trust/British Waterways Archive; 12: Nottingham Historical Film Unit/Alan Faulkner Coll: 14: Derbyshire Libraries; 15: Euan Corrie; 19: Leslie Hales; 20–1, 23, 25, 26, 29, 36: Derek Croucher; 22, 28, 35, 37: Jennifer Davies; 34: Stanley Bywater; 40, 42, 49, 51, 54, 55, 86, 88, 89, 91, 93, 101, 105, 107, 109, 112, 121, 132, 133, 152 (top), 169, 173, 178, 182, 186, 219 260, 261, 265, 267, 272, 274, 280, 296, 298: family collections; 59: Valerie Porter; 63, 64: Astolat Fencing Company; 71, 72: National Railway Museum; 74: Milepost; 77: Derby Museums & Art Gallery Industrial Museum; 78, 80, 81, 119: Tom Quinn; 100, 102, 104, 106, 111: Museum of English Rural Life, University of Reading; 140, 141, 142, 143, 283, 290: Brian Martin; 152, 161, 187: Berta Gillatt; 172: NFC; 193, 198, 200: Birmingham Post and Mail Ltd; 214, 216, 217: Westonbirt School; 262, 263, 273: The Beaford Archive.

ARTWORKS: pages 10, 228-237, 246–255, 268: John Paley; 14: Richard Dean; 18: Edward Paget-Tomlinson; 103: Graeme Puckett; 194-215: Avis Murray; all others by Philip Murphy.
Pages 24, 30, 32, 33 reproduced by kind permission of the Duke of Beaufort.